Societies Under Siege

Societies Under Siege

Exploring How International Economic Sanctions (Do Not) Work

Lee Jones

OXFORD
UNIVERSITY PRESS

OXFORD
UNIVERSITY PRESS

Great Clarendon Street, Oxford, OX2 6DP,
United Kingdom

Oxford University Press is a department of the University of Oxford.
It furthers the University's objective of excellence in research, scholarship,
and education by publishing worldwide. Oxford is a registered trade mark of
Oxford University Press in the UK and in certain other countries

© Lee Jones 2015

The moral rights of the author have been asserted

First Edition published in 2015

Impression: 2

Published in the United States of America by Oxford University Press
198 Madison Avenue, New York, NY 10016, United States of America

British Library Cataloguing in Publication Data
Data available

Library of Congress Control Number: 2015936180

ISBN 978-0-19-874932-5

Printed and bound by
Clays Ltd, St Ives plc

Acknowledgements

The research for this book was funded by a major grant from the UK's Economic and Social Research Council (RES-061-25-0500), enabling the lengthy and costly periods of fieldwork and archival research involved. I am deeply grateful for this support. Britain's funding councils face unprecedented pressures from mindless fiscal austerity and an incessant emphasis on non-academic 'impact'. Sadly, these external threats to academic freedom have their internal counterparts, in the form of disciplinary gate-keeping. One review of my ESRC grant application, for instance, stated that while I would (presumably) wish to use 'quantitative indicators' to explain how sanctions worked, since 'no such methodology exists', I would be unable to proceed. Thankfully the ESRC ignored this narrow-minded counsel. Long may it continue to do so!

My research benefited from extensive intellectual input from others. My research assistants, Kelly Gerard, Sahar Rad, Zaw Nay Aung, Kyaw Thu Mya Han, and Aula Hariri, provided invaluable support. Dozens of interviewees kindly gave their time (and often considerable hospitality) to help improve my understanding of their countries. Kyaw Thu's assistance in Myanmar was particularly important in accessing local informants and providing translations. I am also grateful to Clara Portal for her collaboration on sanctions research; Merle Lipton for her extensive and wise counsel about South Africa; Indré Balčaitè, for stimulating my thinking on Buddhism in Myanmar; Martin Smith, Kevin Woods, and Patrick Meehan for illuminating conversations about, and their superlative work on, Myanmar; Matthew Sheader and Khin Maung Nyo for their help in Yangon; and Christopher Alkhoury for his assistance at the Conflict Records Research Centre of the National Defense University in Washington, D.C. Feedback from Toby Dodge and Elin Hellquist on earlier drafts was extremely helpful, as was input from three Oxford University Press reviewers. I am also very grateful to OUP's Olivia Wells, Sarah Parker, and especially Dominic Byatt for their efficiency and encouragement.

I am also indebted to my wonderful colleagues in the School of Politics and International Relations at Queen Mary, University of London. In Britain's increasingly instrumentalist university sector, it is rare to encounter such a warm, collegial, and intellectually engaged group of scholars in one place.

Acknowledgements

I am particularly grateful to James Dunkerley, Adam Fagan, Ray Kiely, Rick Saull, and David Williams for their advice during the project. The school also generously funded a workshop on the political economy of security in January 2013, and a policy development workshop at the Foreign and Commonwealth Office in April 2014. My thanks also to Lady Margaret Hall, University of Oxford, where this project initially germinated during my stint as Rose Research Fellow in International Relations.

Special thanks must go to my friend and intellectual collaborator Shahar Hameiri. In 2011, I had the dubious fortune of simultaneously receiving two large-scale research grants—the aforementioned ESRC award, and an Australian Research Council grant for a project with Shahar on non-traditional security. Despite the enormous workload thereby generated, it has been a real joy to work with Shahar, who has provided constant intellectual stimulation and comradeship, plus feedback on this manuscript and earlier papers. Shahar's colleagues at Murdoch University's Asia Research Centre—Richard Robison, Garry Rodan, and Kevin Hewison—have also been consistently supportive, as well as intellectual inspirations.

Finally, I want to thank my family and friends, who helped me through two periods of severe personal difficulty during this project. My parents and sister provided boundless love and support. For their true friendship—and intellectual stimulation—I am also deeply grateful to Alastair Fraser, Philip Cunliffe, Mubin Haq, Vidya Kumar, Emily Paddon, Darren Parker, Allan Patience, Seb Perry, and Rosanna Philpott.

I dedicate this book to my treasured grandparents, Cyril and Lily. My grandma succumbed to severe dementia while I was writing this book, and passed away while I was preparing the proofs. The process has been heartbreaking. But perhaps there is some comfort in the fact that, having raised a large family and instilled in them deep commitments to compassion and justice, her influence continues to echo through the generations. I hope this book is worthy of all that she tried to teach me.

Lee Jones

London
June 2015

Contents

Contents

List of Figures

List of Tables

List of Abbreviations

AFPFL	Anti-Fascist People's Freedom League
ANC	African National Congress
ASEAN	Association of Southeast Asian Nations
ASSOCOM	Association of Chambers of Commerce
BDS	Boycott, Disinvestment, and Sanctions
BSPP	Burmese Socialist Programme Party
CBM	Consultative Business Movement
CEC	Central Executive Committee
CIA	Central Intelligence Agency
CODESA	Convention for a Democratic South Africa
COSATU	Congress of South African Trade Unions
FCCI	Federated Chambers of Commerce and Industry
FCI	Federated Chambers of Industry
HSE	Hufbauer, Schott, and Elliott
ICP	Iraqi Communist Party
IIS	Iraqi Intelligence Service
IMF	International Monetary Fund
INA	Iraqi National Accord
INC	Iraqi National Congress
IR	International Relations
ISG	Iraq Survey Group
ISI	Import-Substituting Industrialization
KDP	Kurdish Democratic Party
KIO	Kachin Independence Organization
MK	Umkhonto we Sizwe
MTMA	Myanmar Timber Merchants Association
NC	National Convention
NLD	National League for Democracy

List of Abbreviations

NMD	National Monitoring Directorate
NP	National Party
OAU	Organization for African Unity
OFFP	Oil For Food Programme
PAC	Pan-African Congress
PCT	Public Choice Theory
PFP	Progressive Federal Party
PUK	Patriotic Union of Kurdistan
RCC	Revolutionary Command Council
RG	Republican Guard
SACP	South African Communist Party
SADF	South African Defence Forces
SAIRI	Supreme Assembly of the Islamic Revolution in Iraq
SCA	Social Conflict Analysis
SLORC	State Law and Order Restoration Council
SPDC	State Peace and Development Council
SSC	State Security Council
UDF	United Democratic Front
UK	United Kingdom
UN	United Nations
UNSC	United Nations Security Council
UNSCOM	United Nations Special Commission
UNSCR	United Nations Security Council Resolution
US	United States
USDA	Union Solidarity and Development Association
WMD	Weapons of Mass Destruction

Introduction

The Sanctions Debate

Over the last two decades, international economic sanctions have become a central instrument in global governance. Typically, sanctions involve states or international organizations attempting to coerce target governments into making political changes by restricting economic interactions with their territories, including trade, investment, finance, and travel. In the mid-twentieth century, only five countries were so targeted; by 2000, nearly fifty countries were (Hufbauer et al., 2007: 17). The terrible suffering thereby inflicted on civilian populations during the 1990s, particularly in Iraq, spurred a retreat from the multilateral use of comprehensive embargoes, but not from sanctions in general. 'Smart' or targeted sanctions have taken their place, and today virtually every crisis—from Israeli war crimes, to the alleged pursuit of nuclear weapons in Iran, to Russian intervention in Ukraine—elicits demands for the imposition of (more) sanctions. The disastrous US-led military interventions in Iraq and Afghanistan have only reinforced the case for coercive measures that avoid warfare. Indeed, targeted sanctions advocates argue that the Iraq war might have been avoided altogether had their advice been heeded (Cortright and Lopez, 2004). Sanctions thus occupy a central place in the post-Cold War order, which is unlikely to change any time soon.

This centrality, and scholars' desire to be seen as 'policy relevant', spawned an academic cottage industry on sanctions in the 1990s. Hundreds of articles and books have been produced, establishing a major subfield in International Relations (IR). Yet, this book argues, extremely important questions have been largely overlooked. While scholars have exhaustively debated whether sanctions 'work', they have virtually ignored the mechanisms by which they are supposed to operate. The general logic underpinning sanctions is that economic pain will (somehow) produce political gain: 'material deprivation...will translate into political compliance' (Doxey, 1999: 12).

Yet, despite nearly fifty years of sanctions research, we have very little idea of how this 'translation' is supposed to occur. While many scholars have acknowledged the importance of finding out, only a handful have actually attempted to do so (Kirshner, 1997; Rowe, 2001; Blanchard and Ripsman, 2008; Solingen, 2012b).

This book advances this alternative research agenda, deepening our understanding of what actually happens to societies and states targeted by sanctions. Without this understanding, we can only guess haphazardly whether sanctions might succeed in a given setting, or merely inflict pointless suffering. Drawing on Gramscian state theory, the book advances a Social Conflict Analysis (SCA) of sanctions episodes, applying it to three case studies: South Africa, Myanmar, and Iraq. The SCA begins by identifying the specific social conflicts and political economy relations within target states. It then explores how the material impact of economic sanctions conditions the power, resources, and strategies of the socio-political coalitions contesting state power. Finally, it traces out the political ramifications, whether they are those sought by the 'senders' of sanctions or not. The book argues that sanctions 'work' insofar as they strengthen those socio-political forces most closely aligned with the senders' goals and facilitate the realization of these forces' strategies for obtaining state power. Thus, sanctions episodes are highly context-specific, making the question of whether they 'work' in general an unhelpful distraction.

This introductory chapter situates the book within the wider literature. It critically discusses the scholarly and policy debates, highlighting the importance of considering the mechanisms through which sanctions operate, and provides an overview of the chapters that follow.

The Mainstream Sanctions Debate

Sanctions scholarship was sparse and pessimistic until the late 1980s, but became increasingly optimistic as political interest in sanctions grew. Researchers increasingly and explicitly sought to respond to policymakers' presumed need to know *whether* sanctions 'worked' to achieve their goals. This section surveys this mainstream debate within its political context in order to contrast it later with the central concerns of this book.

Renewed scholarly interest in sanctions in the late 1980s reflected geopolitical changes. With the end of the Cold War, the ascendancy of United States (US) 'unipolarity', and widespread liberal triumphalism, there was apparently a historical opportunity for what President George H. W. Bush dubbed a 'new world order', in which the United Nations Security Council (UNSC) would be harnessed to a new, liberal-interventionist agenda of democracy promotion, human rights protection, conflict resolution, and statebuilding. This agenda involved the use of force in several cases, such as Iraq, Somalia, and Haiti, and the mobilization of large-scale, multilateral statebuilding missions through the United Nations (UN) in many more. It also involved a vast expansion in the use of international economic sanctions.

This expansion, and the concomitant growth of sanctions scholarship, was inherently bound up with the US-led promotion of global economic and political liberalization. Sanctions were a central means to establish dividing lines within the 'new world order', a mechanism to identify, isolate, and rally support against new international pariahs. These 'backlash states'—subsequently rebranded as 'rogue states' and the 'axis of evil'—were condemned for attempting to 'thwart or quarantine themselves from a global trend to which they seem incapable of adapting' (Lake, 1994: 45). Sanctions appealed to governments and activists seeking to promote liberalization and democratization without incurring the costs and risks associated with military action. Accordingly, the proportion of multilateral sanctions regimes used to promote regime change increased from one quarter during the Cold War to one half during the 1990s (Hufbauer et al., 2007: 131). From 1990 to 2005, 70 per cent of sanctions regimes were directed at changing the internal governance of target states (Staibano, 2005: 35).

Growing political enthusiasm for sanctions rekindled scholarly optimism over their potential utility. During the Cold War, high-profile embargoes directed at Rhodesia, South Africa, and the Soviet Union attracted some academic interest, but the general consensus was that sanctions generally failed (Galtung, 1967; Doxey, 1980; Wallensteen, 1983). However, in the mid-1980s, amid growing agitation for stronger Western sanctions against South Africa, some scholars began revising this pessimistic judgement. In a study explicitly billed as a 'handbook for princes', Baldwin (1985) argued that sanctions were useful insofar as they were more effective than alternative policies. Shortly thereafter, Hufbauer, Schott, and Elliott (HSE) produced the first large-scale quantitative study of sanctions, arguing that they had succeeded in about a third of cases since 1915, a ratio reiterated in subsequent editions of their book (Hufbauer et al., 1985, 1990, 2007). These authors personally lobbied for sanctions to counter the Iraqi invasion of Kuwait in 1990, illustrating how scholarship and policymaking in this field became swiftly intertwined (Elliott and Uimonen, 1993).

The 'one-third' success ratio is now entrenched as the subfield's orthodox position. Despite considerable problems with HSE's dataset and methods (see Dashti-Gibson et al., 1997; Drury, 1998), the absence of alternative data sets, and the growing dominance of quantitative methods, particularly in the US, consolidated this position (Drezner, 2000: 221–3). Robert Pape launched a major attack on HSE's data set in the late 1990s, arguing that most of their

3

'successes' had actually been caused by other factors like the threat or use of military force. A thorough recoding suggested a success rate below 5 per cent (Pape, 1997; Elliott, 1998; Pape, 1998; Baldwin and Pape, 1998). HSE seemed unable to rebut this critique but, by ignoring it in their later editions, they simply restated the one-third ratio. Their position was reinforced by qualitative case studies showing a similar success rate (Cortright and Lopez, 2000). Despite mounting criticism from business lobbies and policy think tanks that sanctions were uniformly ineffective (e.g. Preeg, 1999), the mainstream consensus established by HSE prevailed.

This new optimism was also indirectly supported by emerging Comparative Politics research on the destabilizing consequences of economic 'shocks' for non-democratic regimes. Observing the 'third wave' of democratization following the 1980s third-world debt crisis, theorists noted that economic downturns seemed to destabilize all sorts of regimes (Remmer, 1995: 112–13; Geddes, 1999: 117–19). While strong economic performance apparently correlated with the longevity of authoritarian systems (Geddes, 2004: 22), downturns were thought to be very destabilizing, given these regimes' weaker popular legitimacy, more fickle supporters, and reliance on repression or cooptation that could be rendered unaffordable (Remmer, 1995: 113; Gleditsch and Choung, 2004: 16; Escribà-Folch, 2012; Escribà-Folch and Wright, 2010). Similarly, research on the so-called 'new wars' of the 1990s, which were frequently (and controversially) said to be motivated by 'greed', supported the notion that economic deprivation caused political unrest (Collier and Hoeffler, 2004; Blattman and Miguel, 2010). All of these insights supported the intuition that states' internal politics might be manipulated by economic sanctions.

A secondary strand in mainstream sanctions research took a slightly more critical view, pointing out that a one-third success rate still implied failure in two thirds of cases, begging the question as to why policymakers continued using such an unreliable policy instrument. The main argument was that sanctions were imposed not to achieve changes in target states, but to assuage domestic pressure groups, including activists and rent-seeking business interests (Preeg, 1999; Dorussen and Mo, 2001; Lindsay, 1986; Kaempfner and Lowenberg, 1988; Askari et al., 2003: 76, 94–7; Hovi et al., 2005: 492–4; Drezner, 2000: 213; Haas, 1997: 75–6; Drury, 2000). Others suggested that sanctions were largely symbolic and were not seriously intended to effect changes overseas (Nossal, 1989; Davidson and Shambaugh, 2000).

The implications of these arguments for sanctions' purported success rate were never properly drawn out. Sanctions advocates merely dismissed criticism of their one-third success rate, arguing that sanctions were still useful insofar as they were better than alternative policies (Baldwin, 1999–2000). However, as earlier scholars had highlighted, the goals of sanctions relate not only to target states, but also domestic politics and the wider international system (Lindsay, 1986; Barber, 1979). If the real goal of a sanctions regime is, say, to appease domestic constituents, they are successful insofar as they achieve this, not insofar as they affect the ostensible target. Accordingly, sanctions may be far more 'successful' than commonly suggested—though this raises vital ethical and political questions about inflicting harm on foreign peoples to pursue potentially unrelated domestic or international objectives (Jones and Portela, 2014). This book focuses on how sanctions change target states' political dynamics, since this is important to understand regardless of sanctions' 'real' goals. However, the conclusion revisits the multiplicity of senders' goals, and their normative implications.

By the mid-1990s, there was increasing concern outside US policy circles about the harm that comprehensive economic embargoes were inflicting on target societies, notably Iraq. Opposition surfaced in the UNSC, which imposed no new comprehensive sanctions after 1994. This spurred some scholars to start asking whether 'political gain' was worth 'civilian pain' (Weiss et al., 1997b). However, rather than abandoning their support for sanctions, leading researchers instead pioneered the technical design and implementation of 'smart' or 'targeted' sanctions, aimed at governments and elites rather than wider populations (Cortright and Lopez, 2002b; Wallensteen et al., 2003; Wallensteen and Staibano, 2005). Targeted sanctions have subsequently replaced comprehensive embargoes in multilateral settings.[1] By the mid-2000s, they were regularly being imposed, despite zero evidence as to their efficacy (Elliott, 2005: 11). Subsequent research yet again asked *whether* they worked. While pessimists rejected smart sanctions as 'irrelevant or malevolent' (Tierney, 2005; see Drezner, 2012: 159–62), optimists again identified a success rate of around one third (CCDP, 2011).[2] Other scholars tried to identify *when* sanctions worked, to generate more refined advice for policymakers (e.g. Blanchard and Ripsman, 1999; Drezner, 1999).

Clearly, mainstream sanctions research has tacked very closely to political developments, focusing on policymakers' presumed interest in sanctions' 'utility'. This leaves other, arguably more important, questions unanswered. What is supposed to happen when sanctions are imposed on a target? *How* is economic deprivation and 'civilian pain' supposed to translate into 'political gain'? What are the social and political mechanisms through which sanctions actually operate?

---

[1] However, in practice, 'targeted' sanctions, particularly when directed at strategic sectors, can approximate the effects of comprehensive embargoes, e.g. oil sanctions in Iran.

[2] Unilateral sanctions are regarded as far less effective. Elliott (1997) argues that only 13 per cent of unilateral US sanctions since 1970 have succeeded, at an annual cost of US$15–19 billion.

Shifting the Debate: Towards 'Mechanisms'

The logic of sanctions expressed by most policymakers and analysts is 'deceptively simple': imposing economic costs either directly prompts the target state to revise its cost-benefit analysis of its current policies or, indirectly, causes domestic discontent and pressure on the government, leading to a change in its behaviour (Askari et al., 2003: 69). However, despite extensive sanctions scholarship, the question of *how* we get from the imposition of economic sanctions to a potential change in policy has been left virtually unexplored. The overwhelming focus on *whether* sanctions work has marginalized the analytically prior question of *how* they are supposed to work, and what they actually do in practice. As this section argues, this is a serious shortcoming, acknowledged by many authors, which this book seeks to remedy.

The question of how sanctions are meant to operate is not new. Johan Galtung raised it in 1967 in a discussion of Rhodesia. Policymakers, Galtung argued, apparently worked with an implicit 'naïve theory' of sanctions, whereby inflicting economic suffering on a society would automatically generate political unrest and government concessions. Rhodesia clearly disproved this: key societal groups instead supported the Smith regime more vociferously. Consequently, Galtung (1967) urged scholars to analyse the socio-political 'transmission belt' through which sanctions must inevitably travel to affect target governments. Subsequently, many authors have endorsed this call. Margaret Doxey (1980: 120–1) emphasized that, since sanctions' causal logic was that they would 'encourage internal opposition to the government...and bring about a change in policy', analysing target states' domestic political dynamics was essential. Seventeen years later, Weiss et al. (1997a: 241) concurred that

> a more sophisticated understanding is needed of the ways in which...[sanctions] influence the decision-making of leaders in target states...research needs to be conducted on precisely how sanctions affect the various political forces and dynamics within a target nation, especially the status of, or potential for, democratic opposition movements.

Chesterman and Pouligny (2003: 511) likewise urged scholars to develop a 'micro sociology of local actors, of their interests and strategies...to understand their different reactions when sanctions are imposed'. Yet, nearly four decades after Galtung's appeal, another leading author rightly observed that 'the mechanisms for translating "economic pain into political gain" are still not well understood' (Elliott, 2005: 3).

One reason for this is scholars' overwhelming focus on the perceived need of policymakers to know *whether* sanctions work. Leading researchers' involvement in designing 'smart' sanctions regimes has exacerbated this focus by incentivizing them to defend the use of sanctions and channelling their energies towards improving them.

A second, related reason for the neglect of the 'how' question is the reliance on economistic models and research methods. Since the 1970s, many IR theorists have conceptualized states as unitary, rational, utility-maximizing actors, modelling international politics using neoclassical economics and game theory. Their focus narrowed to explaining solely interstate interactions, losing their interest in, and theoretical apparatuses to explain, how international dynamics might transform domestic politics (Halliday, 1994). Sanctions scholarship was particularly affected by this tendency, because 'variables' like economic losses and the duration of sanctions episodes can readily be measured quantitatively, offering apparently endless opportunities for game-theoretical modelling and statistical analyses. HSE, for example, are a team of economists, and many recent articles asking when sanctions work use game theory. This approach generally lacks a sense of the domestic dynamics animating state policies, focusing instead on whether or when one can inflict 'costs' sufficient to outweigh the 'benefits' of pursuing an 'objectionable' policy and thereby induce targets to rationally alter their behaviour (e.g. Baldwin, 1985; Drezner, 1999; Shambaugh, 1999; Hufbauer et al., 2007; Cortright and Lopez, 2000: 223).

A third reason for sanctions scholars' insufficient theorization of domestic dynamics mirrors the second: Comparative Politics' relative neglect of international dynamics. As late as the 1990s, international factors were branded the 'forgotten dimension' in models of domestic political change (Pridham, 1991: 18). Even comparativists incorporating international changes into their explanations often produce overwhelmingly descriptive accounts (e.g. Stoner and McFaul, 2013). As Barbara Geddes (2009: 291), a leading democratization theorist, observes:

> What has been lacking in most of the efforts to link international causes to regime transition are theoretical arguments about the interaction between international factors and the behaviour of domestic political actors. Empirical tests of the effects of international factors have treated domestic politics as a black box that might be shoved this way or that by neighbours, sanctions, or whatever.

The consequent lack of suitable models in Comparative Politics has probably deterred IR scholars from moving in this direction.

The consequences for the political and scholarly contributions of sanctions research have been very serious. First and foremost, neglecting to theorize the domestic impacts of sanctions fails to challenge irresponsible political behaviour. As Weber (1946: 120) argued, an ethic of responsibility requires that political leaders provide an account of the foreseeable effects of their actions.

But most scholars can provide no guidance on how sanctions might affect target societies. Accordingly, they are simply imposed—with sometimes colossal costs for those targeted—in the vague hope that they will, somehow, yield the desired outcome.

The narrow focus of research also undermines its policy relevance. As Rowe (2001: vii) remarks:

> In the rush to provide policy-relevant advice, these studies seek to infer 'lessons' from past uses of sanctions and neglect the much more important tasks of developing rigorous causal theories to explain how and why economic sanctions influence the behaviour of targeted actors. This is a serious shortcoming. Sound causal theories are fundamental to sound policy advice. For policymakers to use sanctions wisely, they must be able to accurately predict the consequences of their actions. Yet it is precisely this causal knowledge that scholars have by and large failed to generate.

Similarly, Kirshner (2002: 166) insists that the mainstream debate on 'whether economic sanctions work' is 'apolitical and largely irrelevant' to policymakers, since a target's likelihood of complying can be ascertained only by analysing its domestic situation and how it might be influenced by sanctions. Thus, 'security specialists need to know not "if they work", but rather "how they function"' (Kirshner 1997: 32).

Furthermore, neglecting how sanctions work actually leaves scholars unable to determine whether they work. Without a detailed sense of how economic deprivation causes political outcomes, how can we reliably claim that a given outcome was produced by their policies, or something else? This was precisely the nub of the Pape–HSE controversy. While HSE assign a 'score' to sanctions' contribution to an outcome, without methodological agreement on understanding *how* sanctions are mediated into political outcomes, others can always dismiss such assessments as subjective. Accordingly, establishing how sanctions work—or do not work—is *analytically prior* to understanding how often they work.

Finally, the narrow focus on utility produces crude explanations of outcomes that stunt our understanding of how regimes targeted by foreign intervention survive and evolve. Without a theorization of target states' domestic politics, explanations of 'success' or 'failure' dissolve into ad hoc lists of factors. Reflecting the field's quantitative bias, these mostly involve readily measurable factors like the quantity of economic losses, the timing of sanctions, and the degree of international cooperation. Explanations relating to domestic politics are often remarkably crude, most frequently positing a 'rally-around-the-flag' effect, whereby nationalism induces a population to support a targeted regime (Pape, 1997: 107–8; Hufbauer et al., 2007: 101, 159–60). This is unlikely ever to capture the complex dynamics of domestic reactions. As Kirshner (1997: 42) emphasizes, 'states are not unitary economic actors...sanctions affect groups in society differentially'. Some domestic groups may suffer greatly while others can actually benefit (Cortright and Lopez, 2000; Weiss et al., 1997b; Rowe, 2001). Coupled with the diverse interests and ideologies motivating different social forces, this means that entire populations *never* 'rally around the flag'. Transcending such crude explanations is essential for understanding how targeted regimes survive sanctions episodes, but also how they may, nonetheless, be substantially *transformed*. These questions—impossible to capture in binary measures of success/failure—are the focus of this book.

Mainstream scholars have recognized that parsimonious models of interstate interactions cannot adequately explain sanctions outcomes, but have not yet found a satisfactory way forward. As Weiss et al. (1997a: 241) remark when urging greater attention to domestic 'political forces and dynamics', 'rational-actor theories and unitary decision-making models undoubtedly only have limited utility'. Cortright and Lopez (2000: 20-1) also rightly criticize the 'minimal' exploration of 'how sanctions alter internal political dynamics within the targeted state'. However, despite promising to correct this problem, in reality, they focus on the *humanitarian* rather than the *political* consequences of sanctions. While assessing humanitarian suffering is undoubtedly important, it is not the same as analysing how the burden of suffering is distributed, how this affects power relations between domestic groups, and the political implications of this. The focus on humanitarian suffering was merely part of the late-1990s attempt to salvage sanctions by advocating more 'targeted' measures. Since the *political* analysis of sanctions impacts were neglected, 'smart' sanctions are now also being imposed without any real guidance as to what their likely political effects will be. As Andreas (2005: 338) observes, 'the larger tendency in much of the literature [is still] to gloss over the political economy of how targeted states strategically cope and adapt to sanctions...it pays inadequate attention to the mechanisms by which sanctions change behaviour in the targeted country'.

In this crucial respect, then, mainstream scholarship has barely advanced since Galtung's criticism of 'naïve theory' nearly fifty years ago. This book remedies this shortcoming. It is inspired and informed by the small amount of scholarship that bucks the aforementioned trends, elaborating what Blanchard and Ripsman (2008) call a 'political theory of economic statecraft'. Its central focus is not whether or even when sanctions may 'work', in the sense of 'succeeding' in delivering senders' objectives—though it arguably provides better guidance for approaching these questions. Rather, it considers sanctions from the target's point of view. It is concerned with exploring the ways in which sanctions affect the interests, resources, and strategies of domestic groups and their interrelations, and how this contributes to political change—whether or not this is the change sought by the senders. It is thus concerned with *how* sanctions work to transform the politics and regimes of targeted states.

Outline of the Book

Chapter 1 develops the theoretical framework used to explore the impact of sanctions in selected target societies. The basic argument is that, to understand how sanctions work, or do not work, we must begin with a coherent analysis of the societies and states they seek to influence. What is required, therefore, is a theory of state power—a model of domestic political contestation into which sanctions intervene and through which they are mediated. The chapter teases out and critically assesses the state theories that are explicit or (mostly) implicit in existing sanctions literature, classified as liberal, public choice, institutionalist, and neo-Weberian approaches. The chapter then presents an alternative approach, drawing on Gramscian state theory, as developed by Poulantzas (1976) and Jessop (1990, 2008). This approach views state power as a relationship between socio-political forces struggling for power and control over resources. Political regimes are understood as being underpinned by coalitions of social forces and secured by a combination of coercion, material concessions, and ideological projects. This perspective directs our analysis to the impact of sanctions on the interests, strategies, resources, and power of socio-political groups and their alliances, how this conditions their struggle for state power, and how this ultimately transforms political regimes (or fails to do so). Chapter 1 also describes the method used in the empirical chapters, and explains the case selection.

Chapter 2 presents the first case study: South Africa. The claim that sanctions 'worked' here, and so will do so elsewhere, assumes that the transformative power of sanctions inheres in the restrictive economic measures themselves, such that they can simply be deployed elsewhere with similar effects. The South African case actually demonstrates that sanctions' effects are primarily determined by domestic social conflict in the target state, and thus are never straightforwardly replicable. In the early period of sanctions, during an era of Keynesian, state-led development, arms and oil embargoes actually played into the ruling coalition's strategy, enabling it to develop new industrial capacities and co-opt rising social forces. It was only amidst growing societal resistance and structural economic crisis in the 1980s that sanctions could make a (modest) progressive contribution. By then, business groups were outgrowing state patronage and, as sanctions bit, they found it more in their interests to negotiate an end to South Africa's racial strife. Sanctions could now help fragment the ruling bloc and assist the opposition's transition strategy.

Chapter 3 presents the second case study: Myanmar. Much of the over-wrought enthusiasm and optimism generated by the South African embar-goes, and even many anti-apartheid campaigners, transferred onto Myanmar in the early 1990s. After twenty years of direct military rule ended with Myanmar's 2011 elections, many Western campaigners congratulate them-selves on their achievement. In reality, sanctions did not generate this out-come, because the balance of social forces here differed starkly to that in South Africa. Myanmar's entrenched military regime was primarily concerned with the threat of ethnic separatism and was determined to curtail this prior to relinquishing power. The ethnic minorities, and the pro-democracy forces led by Aung San Suu Kyi, were relatively weak and fragmented. Moreover, the state's historically more central role in economic development had failed to generate the social forces that proved so critical in South Africa—an independ-ent big bourgeoisie and a large, organized working class. Sanctions actually exacerbated this problem, retarding the emergence of potential opposition groups. Despite the extensive use of targeted sanctions, the burden fell mostly on non-state-linked groups. Accordingly, the ruling bloc strengthened while the opposition was progressively weakened. While sanctions perhaps kept the opposition on life support, they also perpetuated a losing strategy based on moralistic opposition and political boycotts. Insofar as they had any political effect, they arguably delayed Myanmar's liberalization.

Chapter 4 presents the final case study: Iraq. Like South Africa, Iraq is a seminal case because it attracted huge public controversy and precipitated the shift towards targeted sanctions. The usual view is that comprehensive sanc-tions did not 'work': Saddam Hussein's regime was only proven to be dis-armed, and overthrown, through the 2003 US-led invasion. Closer inspection, however, shows that the embargo had dramatic political effects. It seriously damaged the ruling coalition, forcing it to abandon swathes of supporters and forge alliances with newly empowered mercantile and agricultural groups. As state capacities withered, societal rebellions and intra-regime divisions escalated to crisis point by the mid-1990s. This generated a wide range of concessions to Western states. However, even amidst this crippling economic damage the regime survived; again, this was due to the fragmented, weak nature of opposition forces, crucial parts of which were actually forced by sanctions into a de facto alliance with Saddam. Thus, the balance of social forces and their struggles again determined the outcome.

The conclusion compares findings across the three cases, identifying some general propositions about the mechanisms through which sanctions operate and the limitations of their coercive and transformational power. It considers the effects of sanctions on ruling coalitions and opposition forces, concluding that sanctions are unlikely to effect change in contexts were opposition is already weak, and highlights changes in the global political economy that are making it harder for progressive coalitions to organize. The utility of targeted sanctions is also critically assessed, with their intrinsic logical and practical contradictions highlighted. The conclusion then returns to the multiple goals pursued through sanctions, suggesting that target populations are frequently instrumentalized for reasons unrelated to the target state's policies. The normative connotations of this are evaluated, followed by a final set of recommendations for policymakers and campaigners.

1

A Political Theory of Sanctions

The basic logic behind all international economic sanctions, and economic statecraft in general, is that altering the welfare of people in the targeted society—whether many with comprehensive sanctions, or few with targeted measures—will somehow generate political changes desired by the 'senders'. Yet, as the Introduction showed, currently 'we have little knowledge about how economic distress...might be translated into political support for or against sender policy preferences' (Askari et al., 2003: 74–5). Policymakers and scholars rarely specify the mechanisms linking economic pain to political gain, and few theoretical frameworks have been developed to help us analyse this issue. This chapter critically surveys the existing treatments and elaborates the framework used in this book.

There are various ways one might analyse the mechanisms through which sanctions operate. One is simply to list them. In a pioneering survey, Crawford and Klotz (1999a) collate the dynamics suggested or implied by the existing literature into a typology of four mechanisms. The first, 'compellance', involves imposing costs to shift elite decision-makers' cost-benefit analyses, leading to a rational change of policy. The second, 'normative communication', is where decision-makers are 'persuaded' by the moral disapproval expressed via sanctions. In the third, 'resource denial', the target state is deprived of resources needed to sustain its objectionable behaviour. The fourth, 'political fracture', involves stimulating a legitimation crisis, which generates political dissent or revolution, prompting a change of government. Thus, sanctions can operate via several channels and sites, including decision-makers, government structures, the economy, and civil society.

While helpful, this framework is problematic because it places sanctions, rather than target societies, at the centre of the analysis. Crawford and Klotz are primarily concerned to identify how different *types* of sanctions 'work'. For instance, cultural boycotts supposedly 'work' through 'normative persuasion', while arms embargoes 'work' via 'resource denial'. This wrongly implies that the effects of sanctions are inherent to the particular measures selected.

In reality, an arms embargo in one context could involve resource denial; in another, it could stimulate import-substituting production that actually creates resources; in another, it may have no effect, with the targeted state simply sourcing its weapons elsewhere. Thus, the effects of sanctions are not determined by the type of measure, but how they interact with the local context.

Because Crawford and Klotz's framework centres on sanctions, it neglects to theorize adequately the political dynamics of target states. For example, it is only through 'political fracture' that the impact of sanctions is understood to be mediated through the target's society and polity. The rest supposedly work directly against decision-makers or 'government structures', for which we apparently require no knowledge of the broader socio-political context. However, this claim rests on an implicit assumption that decision-makers or government structures are autonomous from their societies. The wider population plays no role in their acceptance or rejection of senders' demands, and their views can be safely ignored by decision-makers (and scholars). For now, whether this assumption is accurate is unimportant. The crucial point is that any understanding of how sanctions operate is always based on some conception—again, usually only implicit—of state–society relations. If this conception is flawed, then the mechanisms relying upon it will also fail to operate. For instance, if governments are *not* autonomous from powerful supporters, they may maintain their policies regardless of how much 'compellance' they personally endure.

Accordingly, our theoretical discussion here centres on understanding the nature of target states. Since this is the basic context into which sanctions intervene, this is necessarily the baseline for analysing how they subsequently work, or do not work, and how they transform target societies and regimes. The chapter thus begins by teasing out and critically evaluating the explicit and implicit state theories used in existing treatments of sanctions, classified as liberal, public choice, institutionalist, and neo-Weberian.

The liberal view often approximates Galtung's 'naïve theory' of sanctions. It proposes that economic pain will translate fairly automatically into desired political outcomes, since those suffering discomfort will pressure their government for change. Following the debunking of this assumption in the 1990s, this perspective was totally inverted. Liberals now assume that whole populations are incapable of political action: they are instead victims of tiny ruling elites, who are also responsible for the policies to which senders object. The latter, therefore, should be singled out through 'targeted' sanctions. This view is no less 'naïve' than its predecessor, however, because it neglects the social constitution of state power and political regimes. Targeting sanctions at small groups of individuals overlooks the socio-political dynamics shaping leaders' choices, wrongly assuming that they can be manipulated merely by tweaking their personal wealth or status. A third strand of liberal scholarship focuses on the distributional impact of sanctions on domestic coalitions. This approach is more promising, but theorizes coalitions too crudely.

Public choice theory (PCT), which also sees sanctions as operating through domestic interest group politics, has several shortcomings. By adopting a pluralist understanding of states as neutral brokers between interest groups, PCT neglects the strategic selectivity of state institutions, which offer different social groups variable access. They also neglect state-based interest groups such as bureaucracies and militaries, and their interpenetration with other social forces, thereby overlooking many ways through which societal groups influence state power and policies. PCT also involves a reductionist, unpersuasive account of political motivations, reflecting their arid conceptualization of politics as a marketplace.

The institutionalist, 'regime type' approach explains sanctions outcomes by reference to the kind of regime operating in the target state. Developed largely to account for *when* sanctions work, not how, it proposes that authoritarian regime types are typically more resilient than democracies due to their narrower popular bases. Unlike inverted liberalism and PCT, this approach usefully recognizes that even non-democratic regimes require some popular support, and takes institutions seriously. However, close scrutiny suggests that 'regime type' is an unpersuasive explanatory variable.

The neo-Weberian perspective is the most sophisticated approach yet developed—again, to explain when, not how, sanctions work. Neo-Weberians argue that a target's 'stateness', particularly state institutions' 'structural autonomy' from society, determines its capacity to resist external influence attempts. This rightly recognizes that state autonomy varies, avoiding the misguided assumptions of Crawford and Klotz and PCT, and offers a promising, relatively parsimonious basis for research, but it remains limited by its foundational assumptions. Like liberals and PCT, neo-Weberians expect sanctions to stimulate societal pressure for political change; they differ only insofar as they identify a variable capacity to resist this pressure: 'stateness'. Consequently, they associate low stateness with 'success'. These assumptions do not hold in practice. Moreover, 'stateness' is not simply an institutional attribute, as neo-Weberians suggest. Rather, because state power is socially constituted, the state's capacity to adapt to sanctions and resist external demands derives from its cooperation with powerful domestic groups, not simply its insulation from them. Hence, a more society-centred approach is required.

Consequently, I advance an alternative perspective: Social Conflict Analysis (SCA). Drawing on Gramscian state theory, states and regimes are analysed as expressions of social power relations that unevenly distribute power and resources. Consequently, they are neither neutral arbiters among nor evenly autonomous from social groups. They exhibit strategic selectivity, granting access to some forces pursuing certain strategies while excluding others.

Exploring how sanctions affect political regimes and their policies therefore involves identifying how they condition the interests, resources, power, and strategies of socio-political forces in their struggles over state power. Having elaborated the SCA, the chapter then describes how it will be deployed in our three case studies.

Liberal Theories of Sanctions

This section discusses three liberal approaches to sanctions. The foundational assumptions of *classical liberalism* are implicit in most of the policy and scholarly discussion of sanctions. Its view of human beings as rational, utility-maximizing individuals fundamentally underpins sanctions' central logic: that imposing costs upon a target population that outweigh the benefits of an objectionable policy will lead them to change their behaviour. However, classical liberal assumptions—particularly the privileging of economic incentives and the assumption that those harmed by sanctions can and will effect political change—have been repeatedly vitiated by historical experience. Consequently, *inverted liberalism* has emerged, reversing many classical assumptions, particularly on the political capacity of target states' citizens. Authoritarian states are now understood to be dominated by tiny elite groups, with the wider population merely passive victims—justifying a shift from comprehensive to targeted sanctions. However, this is an equally naïve view of such states. *Coalitional liberalism* is far more promising, emphasizing the domestic alliances underpinning target regimes and the distributional consequences of sanctions upon them. Yet this approach remains too underdeveloped to be fully embraced.

Sanctions have always been closely associated with liberalism. As Mayall observes, 'it follows from [liberals'] view of war as essentially irrational that a rational alternative must be found . . . within the rational, commercial world'. The liberal view of humans as utility-maximizing *homo economicus* 'meant that every state had its price, just as every man had his'. Consequently, 'the denial of benefits of free commerce to any state which threatened the peace would quickly force it to comply' (Mayall, 1984: 634). This basic emphasis on changing targets' cost-benefit calculations has influenced all modern discussions of sanctions, including the rival approaches discussed below, and sanctions have been central to liberal statecraft since US President Woodrow Wilson first proposed them as a general alternative to war in 1917.

The *classical liberal* view of sanctions rests on three core assumptions relating to three of Crawford and Klotz's channels of influence. The first two assumptions underpin the 'compellance' mechanism implicit in many liberal accounts. The first is that target states' policymakers make decisions on the basis of cost-benefit analyses and are highly responsive to economic incentives, such that economic pain will induce them to abandon objectionable policies. This is underpinned by the second, related assumption: that a state's function is to promote their population's general welfare through economic growth and free trade. However, the expectation that 'economic stimuli should regularly overwhelm political preferences ... is too strong and contradicted by key events' (Blanchard and Ripsman, 2008: 376). For instance, massive Soviet aid to Egypt did not prevent its defection to the Western bloc in the 1970s, while sanctions against Iraq in the 1990s generated crippling economic pain but little political change. Obviously, not all states share liberal regimes' emphasis on free markets and commerce. Some are willing to endure significant deprivation to defend illiberal social structures, as South African resistance to anti-apartheid sanctions illustrated.

The third and most important classical liberal assumption, which relates more to the 'political fracture' mechanism, is that those targeted by sanctions enjoy the capacity to effect the political change desired by the senders. If the targeted government does not respond immediately through a revised cost-benefit analysis, classical liberals expect the resultant welfare loss to stimulate public pressure on the government to capitulate (Galtung, 1967). The assumption that the public can do this is rarely stated explicitly, but it would be perverse to inflict sanctions on people incapable of responding as desired.[1] It flows from the liberal view of individuals as rational, autonomous actors able to influence their governments—which are only legitimate insofar as they are responsive to their citizens. The Kantian logic of the liberal/democratic peace, for instance, is that individuals facing high economic costs from war, caused by trade disruptions, higher taxes, and military service, will mobilize against it, thereby restraining their governments (Chan, 1997: 74–7). While one might think that this logic could be limited to liberal democratic states, liberals like President Wilson initially applied it universally, arguing that the public opinion stirred up by sanctions 'brings a pressure upon the [targeted] nation which, in my judgement, no modern nation could resist' (Hufbauer et al., 2007: 1, n. 1).

However, it subsequently transpired that those most harmed by sanctions were often those least able to compel their governments to capitulate. In Iraq, Dodge (2010: 84) observes, sanctions were premised on classic liberal logic: if they caused 'enough suffering within the society, then popular discontent [would] eventually force the ruling elite to change their policy'. Yet massive suffering was inflicted without apparently stirring popular unrest. The

---

[1] This would reduce sanctions merely to punishment (see Nossal 1989). Sanctions scholars and policymakers generally reject this, insisting that sanctions are a means, not an end (cf. this volume's Conclusion).

estimated 500,000 Iraqi children who died had no opportunity to change the regime's policies. The classical liberal assumption that this pain would still, somehow, generate political gain nonetheless survived for many years, despite undermining the liberal presentation of sanctions as a civilized alternative to war. As US Secretary of State Madeleine Albright infamously remarked, Washington deemed 'the price' of 500,000 children to be 'worth it' (CBS, 1996). Weiss et al. (1997a: 227) report that, in response to calls for 'smarter' sanctions, one UN ambassador 'dismissed all suggestions of changes in the practice of sanctions as inimical to their basic purpose: to cause civilian suffering. To reform sanctions, he said, would be to weaken them.'

Eventually, however, liberals reacted to this humanitarian suffering by upturning their earlier assumptions, creating *inverted liberalism*. Reflecting on the 'sanctions decade', leading scholars Cortright and Lopez (2000: 20) conceded:

> There is no assurance that a sanctioned population will redirect the pain of external coercion onto political leaders and force a change in policy, especially with the authoritarian or dictatorial regimes that are the usual targets of sanctions. When civilian populations are terrorised and lack basic democratic rights, they have few means of influencing government policy. On the contrary, they are more likely to be victimised by sanctions, as the leadership of a targeted regime redirects external pressure onto isolated or repressed social groups while insulating and protecting itself.

Implicit in this typical assessment is a complete inversion of classical liberalism. Target states' citizens are no longer regarded as active, capable political agents who can therefore serve as conduits for external economic pressure. They are now viewed as 'vulnerable' (Cortright and Lopez, 2002a: 2), abject 'victims' of the regime—and potentially of sanctions, too—with little or no agency to exercise. Sweeping statements like this now abound. UN officials Mack and Kahn (2000: 281) insist: 'those who bear the brunt of sanctions *have no power* to influence policy; those in power tend to be relatively unaffected' (my emphasis). Allen (2005: 118) flatly states that in 'autocracies...popular accountability and fear of removal are minimal'. Similarly, Thinan Myo Nyun (2008: 454, 490–1, 495) argues that in 'autocratic' states the populace simply 'does not have the capacity to rise up' and governmental accountability is merely 'wishful thinking'. In Myanmar, he argues, 'the military controls every aspect of...political life'; the 'docile' people never 'express their political will', being 'conditioned...to plod through their lives and adapt to any new economic challenges', their lacklustre performance 'shaped in part by religion, culture, and fear'.

This new perspective on state–society relations reflects broader trends in post-Cold War liberal thought. Classical liberal attitudes, which emphasized autonomy and rationality as universal human characteristics, have been replaced in much liberal-interventionist discourse by an image of postcolonial subjects as little more than suffering victims awaiting Western rescue (Badiou, 2001). Simultaneously, Western governments' belief in their own capacity to liberate these victims has diminished. After the Cold War, they initially imagined that 'ethical' interventions could topple autocratic governments, enabling their citizens to establish flourishing liberal democracies. The failure of subsequent humanitarian and statebuilding interventions to establish stable democracies, coupled with post-9/11 security dynamics, made Western governments, and many scholars, far more pessimistic. Postcolonial populations are now often depicted as incapable of supporting liberal democratic institutions due to political, social, and cultural shortcomings, explaining away the West's inability to effect serious political transformation (Hameiri, 2010: ch. 3; Chandler, 2010: ch. 2).

The new practice of targeted sanctions is underpinned by this more pessimistic, 'inverted' liberalism. If target states' citizens are passive and incapable of effecting political change, it is profoundly unethical to harm them using economic statecraft. Instead, sanctions should 'target the decisionmakers responsible for wrongdoing and deny the assets and resources that are most valuable to the[m] . . . [hurting] the specific groups and individuals responsible for objectionable policies' (Cortright and Lopez, 2000: 223–4, 240). The mechanisms by which sanctions are supposed to work are thus radically transformed, signalling a retreat to 'compellance'. Sanctions no longer seek to provoke popular unrest, but instead try to tweak the incentives and 'personal perceptions' of individual policymakers and their personal associates (Eriksson, 2011: 3). Travel bans, for example, are considered 'attractive because they focus pressure on specific decisionmakers . . . while minimising adverse humanitarian impacts on vulnerable populations'. They are intended as a 'psychological tool for isolating and denying legitimacy to targeted individuals and groups' (Cortright and Lopez, 2000: 244). Accordingly, multilateral sanctions regimes now focus not on inflicting maximum economic damage but identifying a few dozen to a few hundred elites—typically state officials, state-linked business operators, and their relatives—and seizing their assets and imposing travel bans or other restrictions upon them.

However well-intentioned this shift may have been, it is based on a fundamentally flawed political theory. By substituting a moral calculus of suffering for political analysis of target states, inverted liberalism introduces highly dubious assumptions about how political outcomes are derived. The key assumption is that, in countries of perhaps tens of millions of people, a tiny group of 'decisionmakers' are entirely 'responsible' for a particular 'policy'. Thus, in Iraq, for instance, Graham-Brown (1999: 192) suggests that Saddam Hussein's regime relied on only 700 supporters, while Post and Baram (2002) cited just one, claiming that 'Saddam is Iraq: Iraq is Saddam' and therefore providing extensive psychological analysis of the dictator. Similarly, in Myanmar, Washington's top diplomat claimed that 'fifty people...decide the future of fifty-five million' (US Embassy, 2006a). Thus, despite being vastly outnumbered, a few dozen or a few hundred people are supposedly able to rule over everyone else, apparently entirely by force and terror, and solely for their personal benefit, such that curtailing those benefits could generate a complete policy reversal, or even regime change.

This perspective combines undue pessimism about the possibility of popular resistance with a naïve, asocial view of how state power is constituted and an exaggerated faith in 'targeted' governance. Authoritarian regimes may not be 'representative' or 'accountable' in a narrow, liberal sense, e.g. through regular elections or parliamentary scrutiny. However, political opposition can nonetheless be expressed through extra-parliamentary measures, including passive resistance, strikes, guerrilla warfare, and mass insurrection. Indeed, it is often precisely such methods that establish democratic institutions in the first place (Rueschemeyer et al., 1992; Eley, 2002). At the very least, such actions make a regime's strategy of rule more costly; at best, it can render a country ungovernable and compel fundamental political change, even in highly authoritarian states. The supposedly 'docile' Burmese people toppled a military-dominated regime in 1988; other examples include Ghana and Nicaragua in 1979, the Philippines in 1986, Romania in 1989, Thailand in 1991, Nepal in 2006, and Tunisia and Egypt in 2011. The Arab Spring, whatever its subsequent trajectory, was merely the latest rebuttal to inverted liberalism (Tripp, 2013).

Moreover, while some regimes do retain power via coercion and terror, none do so exclusively or indefinitely. As Portelli remarks, 'there is no social system where consensus serves as the sole basis of hegemony, nor a state where the same social group can durably maintain its domination on the basis of pure coercion' (quoted in Morton, 2007: 107). This is partly because, despite being conditioned into habits of compliance, bureaucrats, police, and soldiers are not merely inert 'institutions' or 'resources' to be deployed at will; they are social forces that must be socially constituted, partly by cultivating consent. If state apparatchiks reject their missions as illegitimate, they may refuse to perform their assigned tasks, or even split and defect to the opposition. For example, the Portuguese military's revolt against colonial wars precipitated the 1974 Carnation Revolution, toppling the fascist Caetano regime and the entire Portuguese empire. Similarly, during the 2003 US invasion of Iraq it was assumed that the Iraqi state apparatus would continue to exist as a 'thing' that could simply be handed over to a successor government; in reality, most civil servants stayed at home, permitting the destruction of seventeen out of twenty-three ministries, while the army quickly dissolved into private militias that launched an insurgency against the state (Dodge, 2009: 266–7). State agents are a part of their own societies, with loyalties and interests beyond the state that all regimes must reckon with.

Accordingly, even the most unpleasant governments rely on a significant degree of active cooperation or at least passive acquiescence to constitute state power. As Finer (1985: 17) notes, 'autocracy', the term currently favoured by liberals to describe non-democratic regimes, is a logical contradiction. It literally means 'ruling out of itself', 'self-constituted, self-based rule'; yet, in reality, all regimes must cultivate societal support to survive. Governments rely not only on bureaucrats and soldiers performing their duties, but also on countless, routinized acts of everyday cooperation: following rules, paying taxes, and so on. As Agnew (2009: 89) argues, 'the power of states over their populations can be understood as resting largely on power "from below" . . . [the] state draws its power in capillary fashion from social groups and institutions rather than simply imposing itself on them'. Extreme repression often betrays an inability to attract such support: weakness, not strength. For example, contrary to the typical portrayal quoted above, the Myanmar state, 'while appearing domineering and pervasive . . . is [actually] a classic "weak" state, which has limited capacities to enforce many of its policies' (Ardeth Maung Thawnghmung, 2011: 645). Lack of popular consent meant that 'the bureaucracy has difficulty accomplishing even basic tasks necessary to maintain the regime, such as collecting revenue and supplying the army' (Englehart, 2005: 623).

Inverted liberals' failure to recognize that authoritarian regimes are sustained through legitimacy, not merely coercion, is highly problematic. Sanctions may actually bolster target regimes' popular standing, enabling them to resist sanctions (Grauvogel and von Soest, 2014). More importantly, all governments' intrinsic need for societal support means that no polity is guided solely by the personal preferences of a few hundred individuals. Because state power is socially constituted, leaders must always reckon with powerful societal interests. As Bueno de Mesquita and Smith (2011: ch. 1) insist: 'we must . . . stop thinking that leaders can lead unilaterally . . . that North Korea's Kim Jong Il can do whatever he wants . . . that Adolf Hitler or Joseph Stalin . . . or anyone else is in sole control'. Empirical evidence, even from the most unlikely settings, supports this view. In North Korea, for instance, interest groups like the military, the ruling party, the cabinet, the security apparatus, technocrats, and managers of export-processing zones are increasingly understood to play an important role (McEachern, 2008). Similarly, captured recordings of Saddam Hussein's meetings with subordinates revealed that

Iraqi decision making was never completely reducible to one man . . . responsibility for Iraqi policies was far more diffuse . . . [and officials] were able to disregard Saddam's directives in implementing policies. Even in Saddam's Iraq, a degree of volition remained inviolate (Woods et al., 2011: 326–7).

Accordingly, regimes are never autonomous from everyone apart from a few hundred individuals, as the first three of Crawford and Klotz's mechanisms and inverted liberals suggest. As Svolik (2012: 79, 88) observes, 'no dictator governs alone'; all 'must seek allies and...reward their support by sharing with them the spoils from joint rule'. Consequently, 'even established auto-crats are not free from constraints on their authority'. Power and resources may be so inequitably distributed in a given society that dominant groups may comprise only narrow oligarchies. However, these will always exceed a few hundred elites. Moreover, their dominance always depends on their relationship to other social forces, i.e. their ability to coerce or induce loyalty from subordinate groups. From this perspective, individual leaders are, ultim-ately, dispensable if they fail to sustain flows of resources to social groups capable of supporting a rival leader or regime. In Indonesia, for example, the socio-political coalitions of military, business, and bureaucratic elites that had underpinned President Suharto's authoritarian rule for three decades aban-doned him after the 1997 Asian financial crisis, embracing democratization to safeguard their interests (Robison and Hadiz, 2004).

Accordingly, 'decision-makers' are rarely free to simply alter their policies at will, no matter how much personal inconvenience they suffer as a result of targeted sanctions. Even at the most basic level, the targets are always likely to try to recoup their losses, by shunting the costs onto others or acquiring other resources in compensation. Whether they are able to do this, and thereby blunt the impact of targeted measures, clearly depends upon their relationship to wider society. 'Compellance' efforts that ignore this reality are doomed to fail. The same applies to 'normative communica-tion': no amount of 'signalling' to leaders can generate change unless domestic political dynamics also support it. For this reason, our analytical focus must be on those dynamics, not communicative action between sender and target elites.

The inverted liberal theory of 'smart' sanctions is thus more an attempt to salvage the use of sanctions as a policy instrument, and to salve the con-sciences of sender states' policymakers, than it is a robust guide to understand-ing how sanctions shape political outcomes in target states. As Major and McGann (2005: 341) observe, it cultivates the comforting belief that 'sanc-tions can be targeted against those we most dislike...while those we favour are shielded from harm'. 'Smart' sanctions are part of a wider—and arguably delusional—tendency to believe that 'targeted' governance can resolve com-plex social issues through technical means that bypass difficult political dynamics (see Valverde and Mopas, 2004). Targeted sanctions also pacified domestic centre-left critics, who opposed comprehensive sanctions but were prepared to support targeted ones, marginalizing far-left opponents of all sanctions (Rai, 2000).

Since the shift to targeted sanctions was based on a flawed theoretical premise, it has significantly undermined sanctions' efficacy: many studies show they are far less successful than comprehensive embargoes (Cortright and Lopez, 2002b; Elliott, 2002; Drezner, 2012; cf. CCDP 2011). This is because they rely on just one (highly dubious) mechanism, elite compellance, failing to activate others (Drezner 2012). Conversely, Major and McGann (2005) suggest that it is better to target 'innocent bystanders' than state elites: since the latter are already strongly committed to a policy, targeting the former, who are less committed, is more likely to activate political opposition. Whether this is true or not, it is clearly essential to ground our analysis in political realities, not moral judgements about civilian suffering. Normative evaluation must follow, not direct, empirical investigation.

The third, most sophisticated liberal theory of sanctions is *coalitional liberalism*. This emerged from liberal IR theory, which understands states' international behaviour as stemming from interaction among domestic interest groups (Moravcsik, 1997). A collection edited by Etel Solingen (2012b) has used this perspective to analyse sanctions imposed to counter nuclear proliferation. Unlike inverted liberals, Solingen acknowledges that all regimes are supported by interest group coalitions. She argues that sanctions 'work' by changing the balance between 'outward-looking' and 'inward-looking' coalitions, which favour different 'models of political economy': 'engagement with the global political economy' and 'protection[ism] and import substitution' respectively (Solingen, 2012a: 11–14). This reflects Solingen's long-standing assumption that *the* cleavage in domestic politics everywhere today is the question of how to respond to economic globalization, driving interest groups into 'liberalizing' and 'backlash' coalitions (Solingen, 1998). Solingen notes that sanctions' impact partly depends on the target's regime type (authoritarian regimes being more vulnerable than democracies), the type of sanctions deployed, and timing. But she argues that the most important factor is their 'distributional effects', i.e. which coalition benefits and which loses. Solingen argues that only inward-looking coalitions favour nuclear weapons, since they are associated with high military spending and state-led mega-projects; conversely, outward-looking ones favour stability and access to foreign markets and capital, which require privatization and low military spending (Solingen, 2012a: 12). Consequently, insofar as sanctions aid outward-looking groups and harm inward-looking ones, they should assist anti-proliferation efforts.

There is much to admire in this novel, relatively sophisticated contribution to understanding how sanctions work. Coalitional liberalism rightly avoids inverted liberals' naïve view of regimes as merely the property of a few hundred elites. Furthermore, it rightly insists on identifying the uneven impact of sanctions on different social groups as important for shaping political outcomes, a point previously underscored by Kirshner (1997, 2002). These crucial insights are incorporated into SCA.

However, coalitional liberalism also has serious limitations. Foremost is the modelling of domestic politics as involving just one struggle between two ideal-typical coalitions. First, it is not clear whether the inward-/outward-looking dichotomy is analytically valid. Solingen (2012a: 13) admits that these coalitions 'are only ideal types, whereas real types can be far more eclectic and hybrid'. However, when previously applying these ideal types to real-world cases in Southeast Asia, she found that *all* the regimes there were 'hybrids' (Solingen, 2004, 2005). In her new volume, Haggard and Noland (2012: 236–7) note that although North Korea may seem a 'textbook example' of an 'inward looking-coalition', it has actually displayed both reformist and anti-reformist tendencies. If even the world's leading 'hermit' state does not approximate either ideal type, the heuristic value of these categories seems low. Indeed, the widespread presence of 'hybridity' suggests that politics is not universally structured by groups' orientation to globalization. For example, Iraqi documents and policymakers suggest that the Ba'athist regime did not even discuss the end of the Cold War or how to position Iraq vis-à-vis globalization (Duelfer, 2004: ch. 1, 71). Reflecting the difficulty of making this reductionist model work, Solingen's own contributors do not really use it in their chapters.[2]

Secondly, it is not clear that these ideal types are necessarily associated with particular policy orientations, even in the narrowly defined domain of nuclear weapons. The assumption that outward-facing coalitions will eschew nuclear weapons and vice versa seems to reflect liberal faith that all supposedly 'good' things go together, rather than historical facts. The original nuclear weapons state is, of course, the US, generally considered the vanguard of globalization and yet consistently possessing the world's largest nuclear arsenal and highest military budget after 1945. Similarly, India acquired nuclear weapons not during its Nehruite phase of import-substituting industrialization (ISI) but after embracing globalization in the 1990s. Nor did this lead to its isolation from global markets. Solingen (2012a: 15) claims that South Africa denuclear-ized as part of its post-apartheid integration into the global economy. But South Africa had been integrated into the global economy since being colon-ized by Britain in the nineteenth century, becoming entirely dependent on commodity exports to and capital imports from the industrialized economies

---

[2] Kreps and Pasha (2012: 185) ostensibly adopt the dichotomous framework, but then deliberately ignore non-governmental actors, arguing they are uninvolved in foreign policy, i.e. they do not actually undertake coalitional analysis. Nader (2012) divides Iranian domestic coalitions into 'conservative', 'principalist', and 'reformist' factions. Haggard and Noland (2012), having noted its inapplicability to North Korea, ignore the framework. Palkki and Smith's (2012) treatment of Libya and Iraq does not mention the ideal types at all.

(Fine and Rustomjee, 1996). A more plausible explanation of its denucleariza-tion is the white minority government's concern to deny nuclear weapons to its black majority successor (Babbage, 2004). The apartheid regime clearly illustrates that an outward-facing economic model can be compatible with highly illiberal policies, vitiating the supposed link between economic and other policy preferences.

A final problem with coalitional liberalism is that the analytical framework stops with the specification of the distributional consequences of sanctions, failing to consider how domestic forces subsequently respond. The initial distributional burden of sanctions is just that—initial. Groups harmed by sanctions may react in diverse ways: passive resignation, changing their pref-erences, defecting to a rival coalition and so on. It is in *this* phase of sanctions that political outcomes are really determined, yet Solingen's framework says nothing whatsoever about it. The volume's contributors identify diverse the-oretical and empirical pathways following the introduction of sanctions; there is no obvious pattern or link to coalition types. In summarizing these mech-anisms, Solingen (2012a: 20–3) rightly argues that it is virtually impossible to specify them all in advance. However, the excessive parsimony of the coalitional liberal framework also offers no guidance on what to look for.

Liberal theory does not, therefore, furnish an adequate framework for ana-lysing sanctions' domestic impact, due to its questionable assumptions about state–society relations and politics. In its policy-oriented manifestations, it has swung from one extreme to another: assuming first that everyone affected by sanctions might contribute to political change; and then, in its 'inverted' stage, assuming that almost no one may. Most liberal scholars have limited their analysis of sanctions' concrete domestic effects to humanitarian conse-quences, rather than political dynamics (Weiss et al., 1997b; Cortright and Lopez, 2000). Coalitional liberalism avoids this analytical dead end, contain-ing important insights incorporated into the SCA. However, its theoretical model is too parsimonious to adequately capture the complexities of domestic politics and says little about strategic responses after the initial imposition of costs and benefits.

Public Choice Theories of Sanctions

Public choice theorists have produced the largest, most explicitly theorized literature on how external economic pressures impact domestic politics (Lundahl, 1984; Findlay and Lundahl, 1987; Cooper, 1989; Kaempfner and Lowenberg, 1992; Bonetti, 1997; Morgan and Schwebach, 1997; Major and McGann, 2005). Public choice theory (PCT) is superior to classical and inverted liberalism and overlaps with coalitional liberalism. It accepts that government policies stem from domestic groups' interactions, not simply leaders' personal preferences. PCT also recognizes that sanctions impact unevenly upon domestic groups, whose capacity to influence state policy also varies. Their effects thus depend on which groups are harmed and how this affects their political practices: the implied mechanism is 'political fracture'. Despite these significant insights, PCT has two major shortcomings. First, it uses a discredited pluralist state theory; second, its modelling of politics as a market-place involves weak explanations of why some groups are more powerful than others and of political motivation.

PCT analysis is rooted in an explicit, pluralist theory of state–society relations. It asserts that 'policy is shaped by individuals within nations, not by decisions made by anthropomorphised countries'; policies are the 'artefacts of collective choice processes driven by individual rational [utility-]maximising behaviour' (Kaempfner and Lowenberg, 1992: 6). Public choice analysis therefore begins by identifying interest groups in the targeted society. Because individuals' interests are assumed to be pecuniary, they are assumed to form 'rent-seeking' groups defined by their economic position, e.g. various producer and consumer groups—though some accounts also include groups based on political orientation and state employment (Kaempfner and Lowenberg, 1992: 30; Morgan, 1995). These groups interact in a 'political market', like consumers in a marketplace. Because they derive differential utility from any given policy, they have different 'demand curves' for it; for example, apartheid harms black workers' utility, but benefits white workers through higher wages. If the groups demanding a policy are 'more effective at producing political influence' than those opposing it, the 'market-clearing mechanism' results in an 'equilibrium' at which this policy is 'supplied' (Kaempfner and Lowenberg, 1988: 790).

PCT then models sanctions as impacting the 'political market' much as neoclassical economists might model exogenous shocks' effect on supply and demand in a commodity market (see also Rowe 2001: 21–9). If the groups demanding a policy experience a 'large negative income effect', this 'will cause a large downward shift of [their demand] curves', resulting in a lower equilib-rium and thus a lower 'supply' of the policy (Kaempfner and Lowenberg, 1988: 792). Additionally, or alternatively, sanctions may enhance the 'polit-ical efficiency' of opposition groups by 'reduc[ing] their incentive to free-ride in the collective production of political pressure'. This shifts their 'demand curves' for alternative policies upwards, generating a new 'equilibrium' at which lower levels of the offending policy are 'supplied' (Kaempfner and Lowenberg, 1988: 791–2). Morgan and Schwebach (1995) adopt a similar approach, but also factor in the salience of the issue for interest groups. Powerful groups may demand a policy but, if it has low salience for them and they are harmed by sanctions, they will not care enough to block a change in policy, allowing sanctions to succeed.

PCT offers significant advantages over inverted liberalism. Importantly, it does not assume that policies simply express the personal preferences of a few elites, such that targeting them alone will suffice. Instead, policies arise from struggles among social groups whose political power varies. Sanctions affect these groups differentially and thus condition the outcome of these struggles. These are important insights, reflected in SCA.

However, PCT has two serious flaws. The first is its use of a discredited pluralist theory of the state. Kaempfner and Lowenberg (1992: 30) conceptualize the state as a neutral arena for interest group lobbying, 'an impartial broker of wealth transfers between suppliers and demanders of policies'. There are three basic problems with this view. First, states are never 'neutral' among domestic interests. Even the progenitors of pluralist state theory have long conceded that states are not equally responsive to all interest groups. Dahl (1985: 55), for instance, admitted that uneven patterns of economic 'ownership and control' produced 'significant inequalities among citizens in their capacities and opportunities for participating as political equals in governing the state'. Going further, Gramscian theorists insist that states always exhibit 'strategic selectivity', favouring some interests and strategies while marginalizing others. Their institutional arrangements have

> unequal and asymmetrical effects on the ability of different social forces to realise their interests through political action . . . the structures of political representation and state intervention involve differential access to the state apparatuses and differential opportunities to realise specific effects in the course of state intervention (Jessop, 1990: 224).

Moreover, these structures change over time as social forces seek to mould state apparatuses to advance their interests and marginalize their rivals.

Another related drawback with conceptualizing states as 'neutral arbiters' is the problem of state officials' interests. The state's very existence generates new interest groups like bureaucracies and militaries. Kaempfner and Lowenberg (1992: 37) concede this just a few pages after claiming that the state is an 'honest broker', noting that government officials *could* be analysed as interest groups through a 'bureaucratic politics' approach. Indeed, public choice approaches more commonly present bureaucrats as self-interested groups lobbying to maximize their budgets (Udehn, 1996: 24–5). Although Kaempfner and Lowenburg brush past this possibility, Morgan (1995) does include government bureaucrats, the military, and the security–judicial apparatus as interest groups in his analysis. However, the state cannot *both* be populated by self-interested groups *and* serve as a 'neutral' broker among interest groups. If state officials are merely self-serving, who or what is left to 'clear the political market' (Kaempfner and Lowenberg, 1988: 788)?

27

A final aspect of this first flaw is the simplistic conception of how interest groups influence state policy. From a pluralist/PCT perspective, interest groups join 'political campaigns, lobby legislators, organize demonstrations or strikes, etc' and, given state neutrality, outcomes reflect fair competition between groups (Kaempfner and Lowenberg, 1991: 53). This implies that states and societies are separate entities, the former lobbying and pressuring the latter. However, this ignores myriad ways in which powerful interests shape the use of state power. For example, corporatist arrangements involve

> a much more closely knit nexus of state and interest organisation that is [expected by] pluralism. In corporatism, we don't see interest groups acting as pressure groups, but interest *organisations* disciplining their members in the interest of the state. Interest organisations are licensed by the state and attain a limited public status. They act as partners of the state, with one leg in civil society and the other in the state apparatus (Udehn, 1996: 55–6).

Indeed, while its form varies, state–society interpenetration is common to *all* state forms. For instance, with the crisis of capitalism in the 1970s, corporatist state forms were gradually dismantled, but while organized labour was expelled from state institutions, business interests maintained extensive influence through membership of policy networks, positions on oversight committees, and extensive access to political elites (Jessop, 1992). Any analytical attempt to divide state and society wrongly assumes there are 'clear and unambiguous boundaries between the state apparatus and society, state managers and social forces, and state power and societal power', when such boundaries are actually 'emergent, partial, unstable and variable' (Jessop, 2008: 64–5). Hence Gramsci's (1971: 263) concept of the 'integral state', which encompassed both 'political society' (governmental apparatuses) and 'civil society' (the formally private sphere where extensive governance and cultivation of political consent occurs).

The second major flaw in PCT concerns its explanation of why some interest groups are more powerful than others, and their motivations. In PCT, since the state's strategic selectivity is ignored, 'political influence' must be an attribute solely of groups themselves. Given PCT's rational choice perspective, individuals are seen as utility-maximizing, rational actors seeking 'pecuniary' benefits. Powerful interest groups are those whose members surmount collective action problems derived from the costs and benefits of mobilization and the problems of free-riding. These individuals can pool their resources and 'purchase political influence', which is conceived as a 'normal good' like any other (Kaempfner and Lowenberg, 1991: 53). This is a remarkably economically reductionist view of politics. Ideology is considered as a motivating factor only insofar as it 'provides the individual with a commodity... "piety"... [which] produces utility' (Kaempfner and Lowenberg, 1992: 139).

This arid conception of human motivation crucially underpins Kaempfner and Lowenberg's explanation of how sanctions produce political change. Beyond affecting income, which shifts demand curves directly, sanctions may also 'work' by signalling foreign approval of opposition to a given policy, with three consequences. First, foreign opposition 'probably . . . implies that a large proportion of their own population is opposed to the regime and is willing to take action against it'; it corrects 'preference falsification', thus lowering the costs of collective action. Second, it 'may raise the ability of interest groups to confer reputational utility by raising the probability of the group's success, encouraging activists to work harder, shifting up the adoption function, and encouraging non-activists to join'. Third, people might revise their private beliefs when they learn of foreign disapproval, because psychological studies show that popular beliefs attract more adherents (Kaempfner and Lowenberg, 1992: 153–9).

There are two major problems here. First, this approach is fundamentally indeterminate, with explanations dissolving into post hoc rationalization. There is no obvious reason, for example, why foreign opposition should imply that large parts of a target society agree with the goals of sanctions or furnish 'reputational utility'. Indeed, elsewhere Kaempfner and Lowenberg (1988: 791) suggest that domestic groups might 'regard sanctions as a foreign interference with national sovereignty, in which case they will "rally around the flag" and . . . expend more resources' to support the objectionable policy. Either outcome seems plausible, but since PCT essentially lacks any real appreciation of the ideological, social, and political character of the social forces at work, it offers no guidance as to which will actually occur. It provides only a reductionist language for analysts to frame post hoc accounts of either outcome. The same problem occurs when specifying the power of interest groups and explaining political outcomes. Political continuity or change can always be rationalized via reference to supposed increases or decreases in the 'political efficiency' of interest groups. However, since 'political efficiency' can only be measured indirectly, through political outputs, the argument becomes circular: outcome x occurred because group y became more politically efficient; we know y became more politically efficient because outcome x happened. Lacking any thicker notion of social power—e.g. as reflecting structural political economy inequalities, as Dahl suggests—PCT cannot explain the distribution of societal power and instead merely imputes it. In Morgan and Schwebach's study of sanctions against China, for example, the 'power weighting' of interest groups, their preferred policy positions, and the salience of issues are all crucial explanatory variables. However, they are all assigned values arbitrarily by the authors' research assistant via some entirely mysterious process. Unsurprisingly, their model proceeds to deliver 'some amazingly accurate predictions' (Morgan and Schwebach, 1995: 259).

The second, related problem concerns PCT's methodological individualism and its unconvincing account of political behaviour. Focusing only on individuals, who are assumed to be motivated solely by narrowly defined 'incentives', is thin and unacceptably reductionist. As noted, treating ideology as merely generating 'psychic returns' to supplement 'pecuniary' rewards is typical of this approach, which reduces all social and political interactions to exchange relations (Kaempfner and Lowenberg, 1991: 54–5). However, as Udehn (1996: 12) notes, the 'exchange of ideas is something completely different from the exchange of goods and services . . . The important difference is that people try to change, not to satisfy, the wants of other people'. Indeed, Kaempfner and Lowenberg implicitly concede this when mentioning that sanctions might change individuals' preferences. This suggests that ideology is not simply a 'commodity' that individuals want to consume; it actually (re)constitutes their preferences. Once this is conceded, rationalism and methodological individualism seem less appropriate than sociological approaches which see individuals and groups as partly constituted by their social environment. From this perspective, ideology has a far more profound function, leading people to 'develop collective identities and group solidarities that make them act to achieve common ends' (Udehn, 1996: 13).

Thus, despite offering considerable insight into how sanctions operate, PCT suffers from several debilitating weaknesses. Its main merit is the important recognition that political outcomes reflect domestic political processes and sanctions' effects depend on the necessarily uneven impact on the various participants. PCT's main limitation is its radical abstraction, which obscures the complex social, economic, and political conflicts into which sanctions intervene.

Institutionalist 'Regime Type' Approaches

Some more recent literature, while retaining PCT's rationalism, has tried to explain sanctions outcomes by reference to target states' 'regime type'. Briefly, different regime types are supposedly associated with different sizes of ruling coalition. The larger the coalition, the greater the chance that sanctions will harm a group whose support matters for the incumbent regime. Democracies are thus more vulnerable to sanctions than 'autocracies' because they involve broader coalitions (Bolks and Al-Sowayel, 2000; Brooks, 2002; McGillivray and Stam, 2004; Allen, 2005; Lektzian and Souva, 2007). This clearly improves on inverted liberalism in that it recognizes that even 'autocracies' answer to some domestic constituents, and on PCT insofar as it emphasizes that domestic institutions condition sanctions' impact. Ultimately, though, 'regime type' is not a persuasive explanatory 'variable'.

Two assumptions underpin the basic institutionalist argument that the success of sanctions correlates to the size of the target's ruling coalition. The first is that the absence of representative institutions in 'autocracies' prevents most people from influencing their governments. Framed in rational choice terms, 'autocracies' therefore have a narrower 'selectorate', making narrower coalitions possible (Allen, 2005: 123). Elites can therefore be insulated from even widespread societal suffering, so long as they continue funnelling resources to their supporters (Lektzian and Souva, 2007: 852–3). The second rationalist assumption is that political leaders engage in 'satisficing', resulting in 'minimum-winning' coalitions: they do not pursue the broadest possible coalition, only the absolute minimum required to win power (Lektzian and Souva, 2007: 853–4). A country's political institutions thus incentivize leaders to form particular sizes of coalition, shaping their vulnerability to sanctions. This approach, which emerged to explain when, not how, sanctions work, has generated some quite sophisticated literature on sanctions' duration and success.

However, this literature relies on a crude dichotomy between democracies and 'autocracies' (a term criticized earlier in this chapter). Using regime type as a proxy measurement for a government's coalitional base ignores the fact that 'no two "democracies" are alike and neither are any two "dictatorships" ... Indeed, they can be radically different' despite superficial similarities (Bueno de Mesquita and Smith, 2011: ch. 1). The dichotomous approach overlooks the existence of both narrowly based, oligarchic democracies, and widely based, popular 'autocracies'. Cambodia, for instance, is formally governed by a multiparty democracy instituted by UN intervention in 1993. In reality, it is ruled by a highly corrupt, hierarchical elite using a mixture of patronage and coercion to sustain its rule (Hughes, 2003). Conversely, despite lacking formal democratic institutions, Cuba's Castro regime survived US sanctions by mobilizing enormous popular support (Sylvan, 1983: esp. 227–32). Similarly, Geddes (2006: 153) notes that the few opinion polls that exist suggest 'widespread public support' for authoritarian coups. Moreover, post-coup regimes often seek the broadest coalitions possible, not 'minimum-winning' ones. This was certainly the case for Saddam Hussein (see chapter 4). Accordingly, Saddam was strongly concerned about sanctions' impact on the masses, as was Libya's Colonel Gaddafi (Palkki and Smith, 2012). Even Western democracies defy institutionalist assumptions. As one institutionalist concedes in a footnote, US presidents can be elected on just one quarter of the popular vote (McGillivray and Stam, 2004: 163, n. 8). Indeed, non-majoritarian outcomes are considered normal in many Western 'democracies'.

The dichotomous approach's weakness may explain the rather poor empirical support for this strand of institutionalism. For example, Allen's (2008a) statistical analysis apparently shows that sanctions are associated with higher levels of unrest, but the variation between sanctioned and non-sanctioned 'autocracies' is virtually zero, while, crucially, the difference between democracies and autocracies is substantively minimal.[3] Another quantitative analysis shows that democracies apparently do capitulate more readily to sanctions, but 'autocratic' or 'mixed' regimes do not behave as expected (Allen, 2008b). It seems that the autocratic/democratic dichotomy is not very helpful in explaining domestic responses to sanctions.

Some scholars have tried to improve the 'regime type' approach by specifying further subtypes, e.g. single-party, personalist, and military authoritarianism. This reflects growing recognition among Comparativists that 'different kinds of authoritarianism differ from each other as much as they differ from democracy', and their coalitional bases 'require empirical investigation and cannot be [specified] in the abstract' (Geddes, 1999: 121). Geddes (2009: 286) thus rejects a dichotomous analysis:

> Autocracies vary in terms of the most basic characteristics of leaders and the organizations through which they cooperate with each other, the economies from which they draw sustenance, the distribution of ability to influence political outcomes within the citizenry, and the international forces that buffet them. These differences... affect the likelihood of [regime] transition and how it occurs.

However, attempts to show that economic vulnerability varies by regime subtype have yielded unimpressive results. Geddes's (2004) finding that military and single-party regimes are somewhat more vulnerable than personalist or hybrid regimes lacks statistical significance, while the effects of sanctions on personalist and hybrid regimes are neither substantively nor statistically significant. Even these meagre results are contradicted by findings that dominant party regimes are robust during economic downturns (Svolik, 2012: 162).

Nonetheless, scholars have applied this approach to sanctions (Escribà-Folch and Wright, 2010; Escribà-Folch, 2012). Escribà-Folch and Wright (2010) argue that autocracies differ in their dependence on external revenues and in their ability to increase tax revenue and reallocate expenditures; consequently, sanctions have different effects on leadership stability in different autocracy subtypes. Personalist regimes are supposedly more vulnerable than military or single-party systems. The authors argue that when sanctions deprive personalist leaders of foreign aid that they use for patronage, they cannot compensate for this by increasing domestic taxation; consequently, they rely more heavily on repression to maintain power, heightening the risk of societal backlash. Hence, their likelihood of losing power more than doubles (Escribà-Folch and Wright, 2010: 350).

---

[3] Furthermore, there is no variation in unrest by sanctions type or cost, which undermines Allen's claim that sanctions cause unrest by fuelling relative deprivation.

These authors have simply swapped one dubious association (regime type and coalition size) for another (regime subtype and economic basis). There provide no reason to support their contention that personalist regimes are intrinsically more dependent on foreign aid or less able to raise domestic revenue, beyond suggesting that they have 'limited state capacity' (Escribà-Folch and Wright, 2010: 341). Why state capacity should vary by regime subtype is unclear. Their statistical 'proof' yields significant results only by excluding all 'hybrid' regimes (i.e. personalist-single-party or personalist-military). Even then, the degree of personalist regimes' dependence on foreign aid is only marginally higher than for other regime subtypes. Furthermore, changes in tax income under sanctions do not appear to vary straightforwardly by regime type, and the main blow to personalist regimes actually comes from lost 'non-tax revenue' (Escribà-Folch and Wright, 2010: 342). Their assumptions that regime subtypes are necessarily linked to particular political economy models and modes of rule are simply not supported by the evidence. Even if we discount all of this, their findings remain unimpressive. The probability of leadership change as a result of sanctions doubles, but from a very low base, from 4.1 per cent to between 9.3 and 11.1 per cent, depending on the model used. The risk of leadership change remains low in absolute terms, and it is still lower than the rate of change without any sanctions in military regimes, and little higher than that in single-party states. These meagre findings are not even statistically significant by conventional standards (Escribà-Folch and Wright, 2010: 348–50). Even then, all that occurs is leadership change, which need not actually involve wider regime change or even any policy changes. This is a classic example of how a quest for statistically significant correlations can generate highly complex studies yielding rather trivial results (Ziliak and McCloskey, 2011).[4]

Scholars' persistent inability to detect robust associations between regime (sub)types and sanctions outcomes suggests a fundamental flaw in the institutionalist approach. As noted above, scholars often recognize that many regimes are really 'hybrids', combining supposedly distinct regime subtypes. In fact, Svolik (2012: 26–32) argues, authoritarian polities exhibit such 'extraordinary scope and diversity' that there is 'no limit on the[ir] institutional heterogeneity'. His literature survey identifies no fewer than twenty-one subtypes, which, despite being conceptually muddled and overlapping, still fail to capture the full range of possibilities. 'Hybrids', as conventionally defined,

---

[4] Another example is Marinov's (2005) even more complex quantitative analysis, which purportedly shows that sanctions increase the risk of leadership turnover by 28 per cent. This apparently impressive result is nonetheless substantively trivial: the probability rises from 0.146 to just 0.183. Despite this (and other weaknesses), the '28 per cent' figure has become a 'factoid' in the sanctions literature and the article, published in a leading journal, is now widely cited. For a similar example, see von Soest and Wahman (2014).

account for 68 per cent of all cases (Svolik, 2012: 34), suggesting that these ideal-types are useless as hermeneutic devices. Other scholars concur, adding, moreover, that different subtypes often evolve into others (Gleditsch and Choung, 2004: 10–12; May et al., 2004: 6, 11–12). The categorization of democracies is no better, with Ljiphart identifying at least nine types (Shin, 1994: 148–9). Ultimately, rather than the infinite regress that 'regime type' approaches apparently require, it is better to analyse states in terms of their extant social power relations; that is, in terms of *what they are and how they actually operate*, rather than how well they conform to some idealized benchmark (Jayasuriya and Rodan, 2007).

Thus, while institutionalism rightly recognizes that domestic institutions mediate the impact of sanctions, it assigns far too much primacy to them in generating particular outcomes. The nature and composition of political regimes, their political economy context, and strategies of rule clearly cannot be read off regime type, particularly when it is reduced to a crude dichotomy.

The Neo-Weberian Theory of Sanctions

The neo-Weberian approach pioneered by Blanchard and Ripsman (1999, 2008) is the most sophisticated framework yet developed to analyse sanctions' domestic impact. Their basic argument is that sanctions outcomes depend on targets' 'stateness', i.e. their 'structural autonomy' from societal interests, its institutional capacities, and its legitimacy. Neo-Weberianism is thus also concerned with the 'political fracture' mechanism. It emphasizes that sanctions are mediated through state–society relations, and analyses sanctions episodes in an admirably nuanced, detailed, and historically sensitive fashion. However, the neo-Weberian concept of 'stateness' is inherently problematic, because it assumes that particular qualities like autonomy and capacity emanate from state institutions themselves, rather than emerging as relationships between social forces.

Neo-Weberians begin from assumptions similar to those of coalitional liberalism, PCT, and institutionalism. Blanchard and Ripsman (1999: 220–4) rightly insist that target governments care less about sanctions' aggregate economic impact than the 'political cost', which need not correlate to economic cost. They assume that all political leaders want to remain in power. To do so, they 'must keep key domestic groups happy to prevent them from overthrowing the government', and also defend the state externally. Leaders consequently 'focus on how decisions about compliance [with sanctions] will affect their re-election chances, their support among key constituencies, or the power of opposition groups'. Consequently, although sanctions could affect states directly through 'compellance', that influence is expected to be 'considerably less' than that generated via 'political fracture' mechanisms (Blanchard and Ripsman, 2008: 377–8). Analysis should therefore identify the impact of sanctions on important domestic groups.

Here, however, Blanchard and Ripsman depart from rival approaches by promoting a distinct, explicitly neo-Weberian view of state–society relations. Unlike PCT, neo-Weberianism does not assume that states are neutral and equally responsive to all interest groups. Rather, 'whether the...interest groups [mobilized by sanctions] have access to the state or whether the state can ignore their interests' varies, 'depend[ing] on the nature of the target state and its domestic political institutions' (Blanchard and Ripsman, 2008: 378). Rather than foregrounding 'regime type', though, they suggest that three institutional attributes—which vary within and across regime types— determine this capacity to ignore societal pressure, which they label 'state- ness'. The first, decision-making autonomy, is the 'structural ability of the foreign policy executive to select and implement policies when faced with domestic opposition...[which] derives from...institutional structures, decision-making procedures, and procedural norms'. The second is state cap- acity, i.e. the 'policy resources available...to co-opt or coerce key societal groups...[This] rests on the government's possession of financial resources, an adequate bureaucracy, the means of coercion, and diverse influence mech- anisms that can penetrate and, potentially, control its society'. The third is 'legitimacy', the 'degree to which domestic groups acknowledge the leader's right to rule, respect the authority of the state, and defer to it' (Blanchard and Ripsman, 2008: 378–9). Blanchard and Ripsman argue that targets with high 'stateness' can resist pressures caused by sanctions, and vice versa, illustrating this with sophisticated, historically nuanced case studies.[5]

This approach is clearly superior to the existing alternatives. Like other theories, neo-Weberianism focuses on how sanctions affect different domestic groups, and how these groups then proceed to effect political change (or not), but unlike them it rightly avoids reductionism or sweeping generalizations about coalitions and regime types. It identifies multiple bases of political power and agency—material, institutional, and ideational—and insists on careful, historical analysis of specific cases to capture the complexities of sanctions episodes.

Ultimately, however, neo-Weberianism is underpinned by a problematic state theory. The concept of 'stateness' is associated with the revival of statism in political science promoted by neo-Weberian scholars like Peter Evans, Stephen Krasner, and Theda Skocpol, several of whom Blanchard and Rips- man cite approvingly (see especially Evans et al., 1985). They work with an

---

[5] Again, as this implies, this approach is designed to explain when, not how, sanctions work.

ideal-typical notion of states as independent actors, autonomous from their societies. 'Stateness' measures the actual capacities that states enjoy to 'penetrate', dominate, 'ignore', etc., their societies. The key problem with the concept is that these capacities are seen to emerge directly from state institutions themselves, rather than as a relationship between social forces.

This is clear in Blanchard and Ripsman's discussion of decision-making autonomy, which is said to emanate from the norms and procedures of political decision-making. This is a circular thesis: the state's institutions are shielded from societal pressures because its institutional arrangements insulate it from society. Similarly circular is the view that the state's policy capacity flows from its 'possession' of resources, including human resources: the state has the capacity to overcome opposition because it has the resources to do so. Neo-Weberianism is thus so state-centric that institutional arrangements and capacities are presented as causing themselves. Blanchard and Ripsman do not explain how states develop these attributes because they are primarily concerned to explain *when* sanctions work, not how. They seek to identify a single variable, which can be read off empirical indicators, to explain success rates across many cases. But, at best, 'stateness' is not really an explanatory variable; it is a cluster of various unexplained dynamics given a single label.

From a Gramscian perspective, the attributes labelled 'stateness' do not inhere within state institutions but emerge historically and contingently from relationships among social forces, articulated within broader political and economic patterns. Consider, for example, a state's fiscal resources. If a state relies on taxation, it depends upon the ability and willingness of people to pay. Although tax-paying is now routinized in many Western states, this only occurred after centuries of power struggles to institutionalize what began as a form of forcible expropriation (Martin et al., 2009). Moreover, tax revenues do not simply reflect the bureaucratic capacity to collect revenue, as neo-Weberians suggest, but power relations among key social forces. As financial capital and associated wealthy groups grew increasingly powerful and transnationalized since the 1970s, while organized labour has weakened, the former have shunted the tax burden onto the latter, while using the threat or practice of offshore relocation to compel governments to cut taxes or not properly enforce taxation policies (Palan et al., 2010; Shaxson, 2012). From this perspective, capacities and resources are not something 'possessed' by the state; they emerge—and are (re)shaped and constrained by societal power relations (Block, 1977). The repeated failure of international statebuilding interventions to build up bureaucratic 'capacity', despite enormous investments of time and resources, also clearly illustrates how the emergence of state institutions depends on what local social relations permit (Jones, 2010).

Ditto, 'structural autonomy'. The state which best seems to embody the neo-Weberian ideal is Singapore, where an apparently autonomous, bureaucratic apparatus thoroughly penetrates and regiments society (Weiss, 1998). Insofar as this is true, this can only be explained by the defeat, forcible disorganization, and co-optation of all societal groups except the politico-bureaucratic elite of the People's Action Party, enabled by the specific historical conditions of the Cold War (Rodan, 2006). The Singaporean state's 'autonomy' thus expresses a specific relationship among social forces which generated particular institutional arrangements; it did not flow from those arrangements themselves. Moreover, as Jessop's (2008) concept of 'strategic selectivity' emphasizes, the state's autonomy is never total but rather highly uneven. The state is certainly not autonomous from the politico-bureaucratic elite that has captured it for over fifty years, which wields extensive control over the government-linked corporations and sovereign wealth funds dominating Singapore's political economy (Barr, 2014). Moreover, Singapore's structural dependence on foreign investment and trade has also led this elite to incorporate representatives of multinational capital directly into state apparatuses. For example, the National Wages Council includes representatives of the US, German, and Japanese chambers of commerce, and is designed to subordinate trade unions' wage demands to the requirements of 'long-term economic growth' (Lim 2014). This tight relationship could explain why the Singaporean government was highly responsive to US threats of banking sanctions after 2003 over its relationship with Myanmar's military junta (Jones, 2008: 285). The real question, then, in understanding political outcomes is not how autonomous a state is from society *in general*, captured as a single metric of 'stateness', but which specific forces enjoy access to state power and which do not. This will dictate whose interests are best reflected in policy outcomes, and thus which groups harmed by sanctions will be most likely to have political ramifications.

A second, related problem with 'stateness' is its inability to capture state transformation over time, which is particularly important when analysing sanctions. 'Stateness' is effectively a dichotomous variable, reflecting a neo-Weberian concern with so-called 'strong' and 'weak' states: a state with 'stateness' is 'strong', relative to its society, and 'weak' if it lacks it (Migdal, 1988). However, snapshot measurements of 'stateness' or 'strength' not only ignores the issue of strategic selectivity;[6] it also overlooks micro-level temporal changes. As Rowe (2001) shows, groups harmed by sanctions typically form new alliances and promote new institutions to offset their losses. In South Africa and Rhodesia, capitalist interests promoted ISI, compelling these states to acquire new economic functions. In Iraq, the state's developmental apparatuses

---

[6] Weberians tie themselves in knots trying to reconcile the notion of state 'strength' with the reality that any state's capacities and autonomy vary across policy domains. Evans's (1995) notion of 'embedded autonomy'—a contradiction in terms—is one example, as is the entirely unhelpful description of India as a 'strong-weak state' (Paul, 2010: 7). For a critique see Jayasuriya (2005).

collapsed, but the state developed new functions like rationing, oil smuggling, and agricultural promotion, reflecting emergent compacts between the regime, criminal merchants, agribusinesses, and tribal authorities (Bunton, 2008).

Net 'stateness' in such cases may decline, or stagnate, but this reveals little of what is actually happening: the social basis of a state and its institutional and ideological composition can change considerably beneath such a superficial measure. In turn, this could generate new social conflicts and vulnerabilities that sanctioners can exploit. For example, South Africa's ISI strategies produced a powerful nexus between national capital and the National Party regime, and generated a large black working class. The latter became the basis of a new generation of popular anti-apartheid resistance in the 1980s, led by the trade unions. The party–business nexus also meant that when sanctions exacerbated a government debt crisis in the mid-1980s (itself partly stemming from development spending), South African capitalists enjoyed political access to demand changes to the apartheid regime (Maloka, 1999). These dynamics are simply not captured by measuring 'stateness'.

Neo-Weberian analysis thus offers a significant step forward but is constrained by its state theory, which occludes strategic selectivity and temporal developments in state–society relations. What SCA adopts from this approach is its insistence on the primacy of political over economic costs, its focus on state–society relations, and its use of careful, historically nuanced case studies to trace the impact of sanctions on these relations. What we must discard is neo-Weberians' 'institutional fetishism', which leaves them

> unable to grasp how [state] capacities change in response to broader changes in the constellation of social and economic interests. What we require is a more constitutive conception of the state and policy capacity that recognises that the state is not an 'entity', but a complex and constituted set of relationships between frameworks of political authority and the international political economy, domestic social forces, and the broader ideational notions of authority or stateness (Jayasuriya, 2005: 383).

A Social Conflict Analysis of Sanctions

Having criticized the existing theoretical frameworks available to analyse how sanctions work, this section outlines my alternative: Social Conflict Analysis. SCA draws on Gramscian state theory, as developed by Poulantzas and Jessop. This conceptualizes states and regimes as being constituted by struggles for power and resources among coalitions of socio-political forces. From this perspective, sanctions 'work' by affecting these forces' composition, power, resources, alliances, and strategies, conditioning their struggles to control state power and thereby transforming target states, whether in ways desired by sanctions senders or not. SCA involves three steps. First, we identify the socio-political coalitions contesting state power and the political economy context that structure them. Secondly, we identify the economic impacts of sanctions and their distribution across societal groups. Thirdly, we examine the strategic response of key social forces and their political consequences.

SCA's Basic Foundations: Gramscian State Theory

As mentioned earlier, Gramscians have a far more expansive conception of statehood than mainstream state theories (see Morton, 2007: ch. 4; Martin, 1998: ch. 3). Gramsci (1971) emphasized that, in modern states, governance was not confined to the formal state apparatus but extended into 'civil society'. Indeed, it was in civil society that the hegemony of dominant social forces was actually secured through institutions like churches, trade unions, schools, and the media, which cultivated consent for a particular socio-political order among subordinated groups. Gramsci therefore argued that state power was not confined to 'political society' and the formal apparatus of government, but rather reflected broader social relationships, particularly class relations in the formally private sphere of the economy. Gramsci's insights were further developed by Nicos Poulantzas (1976) and Bob Jessop (1990, 2008). Both emphasize that state power is fundamentally a social relation. That is, rather than existing as a 'thing' independent of society, state institutions and capacities are condensations of historically specific, dynamically evolving relationships between social forces.

Gramscian theory thus focuses primarily on social forces, not state institutions, distinguishing it fundamentally from neo-Weberianism. Here there is some limited overlap with coalitional liberalism and institutionalism. *Contra* inverted liberalism, Gramscians do not understand regimes or their policies as the sole property of a few hundred elites. To capture, retain, and maintain state power, ruling elites must forge coalitions of socio-political forces that extend well beyond their immediate circle. Classes and class fractions are given particular emphasis here, given the importance of production in sustaining modern human societies, but ethnic, religious, and state-based groupings may also be crucial. For analytical convenience, we can identify incumbent alliances and their enemies as 'ruling' and 'opposition' coalitions. However, these coalitions are not synonymous with incumbent and opposition parties in, say, a liberal democracy. For Gramscians, all parliamentary parties could potentially be part of a wider ruling coalition underpinning a particular regime, with real opposition marginalized entirely from state institutions. Socio-political coalitions (or 'historic blocs', in Gramsci's terminology) are also hierarchical, prioritizing the interests and agendas of the most powerful groups, but they must secure the loyalty of subordinated groups through material concessions and ideological projects. This cultivation of consent is bolstered 'by the armour of coercion': force may always be used, particularly against recalcitrant groups outside the ruling bloc (Gramsci, 1971: 263).

Once state power is captured, dominant coalitions typically reconfigure its institutions and allocation of resources to lock in their supremacy and exclude their enemies. This again distinguishes Gramscian theory from rival approaches, because state institutions are not seen as neutral, determined by regime type, or autonomous, but rather as a historically evolving and dynamic 'expression of power' (Hewison et al., 1993: 3). The state's institutional materiality is constantly remoulded by socio-political struggles, generating its strategic selectivity—its systematic privileging of some groups and strategies over others (Jessop, 2008). State institutions and policies thus reflect the interests, ideologies, and strategies of the various social groups in conflict.

Gramscians also depart from institutionalists in understanding social groups and ruling coalitions' strategies as being closely related to economic forces, implying structural constraints on political action overlooked in mainstream approaches. Social forces are understood as being rooted in historically specific political economy contexts, notably as classes and class fractions located in different sectors. Gramscians also highlight potentially cross-cutting, non-class identities: divisions of ethnicity, religion, and so on are often critical to maintaining particular economic and political regimes (Hall, 1986). State-based groups—e.g. bureaucratic and military agencies—may also form part of ruling coalitions, though their interests vary and cannot be considered monolithically as 'the state'. Crucially, the evolving material context shapes these various groups' composition, size, and trajectory, as the aforementioned example of South Africa suggests.

This materially produced social context constrains the strategies that leading forces can use to build and maintain coalitions. State-centric institutionalists overlook this, suggesting that the narrow coalitional basis of authoritarian regimes means they can easily shift to different support bases where necessary (McGillivray and Stam, 2004). In reality, coalitional options are limited by the structure of the society in question. Moreover, the support of certain groups may be essential regardless of the regime in power. Scholars from many traditions observe that capitalist states are structurally dependent on capitalists to generate employment, tax income, and so on, which are essential for maintaining state apparatuses and providing material benefits to subordinate groups (Block, 1977; Przeworski and Wallerstein, 1988; Geddes, 2006: 165; Wilks, 2013). State managers acting on behalf of ruling coalitions are therefore constrained to develop political and economic strategies that reflect societal power relations; they cannot simply innovate at will. This insistence on relating political dynamics to economic ones makes Gramscianism particularly useful for analysing the impact of economic changes—like sanctions—on political outcomes.

Gramscian theory is also sensitive to the transnational constitution of societies, regimes, and states, making it helpful for analysing the impact of 'external' forces on 'domestic' outcomes. Mainstream political science tends unconsciously to adopt 'methodological nationalism', the assumption that the 'national' state or society is 'the natural social and political form of the modern world', and that political outcomes reflect overwhelmingly 'domestic' factors (Wimmer and Glick Schiller, 2002). Conversely, although Gramsci primarily analysed a particular national context—Italy—he observed how state-formation there was strongly conditioned by 'external' developments, such as periodic foreign invasions and the intervention of Anglo-American finance capital (Morton, 2007: 71–2). Subsequent developments and applications of Gramscian theory have emphasized how transnational capitalist development carries significant consequences for the composition of social forces, especially class forces, and the political and economic strategies that ruling groups can pursue (Cox, 1987; Robinson, 1996, 2003; Rodan et al., 2006).

For example, the 1970s oil crisis generated a petrodollar glut and plentiful cheap credit, fuelling developmental strategies among many postcolonial states. However, in the 1980s, recession in the West caused these states' commodity export revenues to collapse and interest rates to increase, precipitating a widespread debt crisis. This forced many governments to adopt IMF-designed structural adjustment policies that dismantled state-led development, destroying the socio-political coalitions that this strategy had produced and generating growing societal unrest (Morton, 2011). More recently, rapid Chinese development has fuelled booming commodity exports, enabling new strategies that have fashioned anti-neoliberal societal resistance into new ruling coalitions, such as those associated with Latin America's 'pink tide' (Beasley-Murray et al., 2009: 325).

'Domestic' social conflict is further articulated within and conditioned by broader transnational social formations and geopolitical relationships. Dominant groups backed militarily and/or economically by foreign states may pursue strategies of coercion and co-optation that would otherwise be impossible. For example, during the Cold War, Indonesia's Suharto dictatorship was able to massacre perhaps 1.5 million 'communists' and maintain a widespread network of state terror and patronage thanks to Western political backing, military equipment, and over US$50 billion in economic assistance (Robison, 1986; INFID, 2007). However, as the anti-communist imperative of supporting Suharto waned, these strategies became unsustainable. When anti-regime unrest emerged following the 1997–8 Asian financial crisis, massacres were no longer palatable to the Western powers, and their economic support was also made conditional upon the regime undertaking self-destructive reforms, hastening Suharto's demise (Anwar, 2002; Robison and Hadiz, 2006). The other side of the equation is that externally backed opposition groups can also (appear to) present a far greater threat to ruling forces. During the Cold War, for example, leftist oppositions were often seen by establishment forces as transnationally networked and resourced, provoking political reactions disproportionate to their size (Jones, 2013). Geopolitical relations thus have a constitutive effect on domestic developments that goes well beyond the sanctions literature's scant references to 'black knights' rescuing target states.

Social Conflict Analysis of Sanctions

The *first step* in analysing how sanctions work involves specifying the patterns of socio-political conflict in the target state immediately prior to sanctions being imposed. We need to identify the main lines of social conflict; the forces at work; and their relationship to the wider political economy.

The first goal is to identify the country's leading socio-political forces and the strategy they are using to maintain state power. Which subordinate forces do they seek to incorporate into their ruling coalition? How? Through what mixture of coercion, concessions, and consent? What resources does the regime use to sustain this strategy? Where does it get these resources from, i.e. what is its relationship to the economy and what development strategy is it pursuing? For analytical convenience, we can label these various relationships as the 'ruling coalition'.

The second goal is to identify the main forces struggling against the ruling coalition. What forces are involved and to what extent? What resources do they command and what is their relationship to the economy? What strategy are they pursuing to capture state power or compel changes in the ruling coalition, its strategy of rule, and/or its policies? Although for analytical convenience we can label these groups as the 'opposition coalition', the extent to which anti-regime groups actually cohere is an empirical question. There may be several opposition coalitions, or even no coalition at all, just a series of fragmented groups fighting the ruling coalition in isolation.

It is vital when undertaking this analysis not to make a priori assumptions about the orientation of particular forces. For example, scholars often complain when sanctions harm the 'middle classes', since they supposedly favour political and economic liberalization (e.g. Weiss et al., 1997b). Likewise, that capitalists collaborated with the Rhodesian regime, for example, is presented as counter-intuitive, and thus as evidence of states' neo-Weberian capacity to overwhelm societal forces (Rowe 2001: 96–7). This perspective is based on widely held but misleading assumptions. Historically, although Western capitalists sometimes promoted liberal democracy to advance their interests, as Bellin (2000) notes, in late developing countries, capitalists are highly 'contingent democrats', often working closely with authoritarian regimes where it advances their interests. In many post-colonial states, state-led development has generated state-linked bourgeoisies and professional middle classes that are highly *illiberal*, supporting authoritarianism to defend their privileges from the lower orders (Jones, 1998).[7] The idea that capitalist–state collusion is puzzling thus reflects a flawed assumption that capitalists normally prioritize liberal principles over profits. The opposite is true. As one Rhodesian businessman quoted by Rowe (2001: 128) states: 'it's hard to complain very loudly when you're making a fat profit'. Rhodesian capitalists only promoted a settlement with the black majority when the racist regime's capacity to maintain the social order upon which 'fat profits' depended was dwindling; the same is true in South Africa (see chapter 2). Moreover, this illiberal orientation clearly extends to capitalists outside postcolonial states. As one Dutch businessman remarked in relation to sanctions in Iraq: 'I really don't care if Hitler or Saddam rules Iraq. I have a clear task: to maximise my company's business . . . I am only answerable to my CEO and the shareholders' (Abu Gulal, 2001: 3029). The orientation of all social forces must therefore be subject to empirical investigation, not blithely assumed.

The *second step* in the SCA is to identify the immediate economic impact of sanctions on the target society. Importantly, this must go beyond aggregate measures of GDP decline and seek to specify the uneven impact on different societal groups. Table 1.1, which extends Kirshner's (1997: 46–9) suggestions, provides some basic guidance.

However, the analysis cannot simply stop here, as Kirshner (1997: 42) implies when he urges senders to simply select sanctions that will impact the 'core groups' supporting a target government. That sanctions harm a group tells us relatively little. Depending on its ideological orientation, its relationship to other forces, and its access to state institutions, it might resign itself passively to its losses, work with the government to offset them, or try to overthrow the regime. Just as the type of sanction does not automatically imply specific effects, there is no a priori way of knowing, in the abstract, how any given social group might respond to an embargo. This can only be grasped concretely in specific cases, which is why it is essential to ground our analysis in a historical understanding of social conflict within the target state (step one). Moreover, because the immediate distributional consequences of

[7] This was arguably part of many Western states' experience, too. Barrington Moore (1966) famously argued that in Germany an 'alliance of iron and rye' melded capitalist and aristocratic interests against those of the workers and peasants, retarding democratization.

Table 1.1 Sanctions types and impacted groups

Type	Groups likely to be affected
Trade	• Export sanctions: producer groups and exporters harmed. Multiplier effects likely in intermediate sectors. • Import sanctions: consumer groups (e.g. urban middle classes) and sectors reliant on imports harmed; import-competing industries may benefit. Embargoes on key commodities like oil may raise costs economy-wide. • Smugglers may receive windfall gains. • State agencies reliant on trade taxation may be harmed; revenues may also suffer if trade losses depress overall economic activity. • If sanctions cause exports to fall below imports, creating a balance of payments deficit, government intervention to depress import demand could slow economic activity, with further consequences.
Investment	• In the short term, local capitalists benefit because they may acquire departing foreign firms' assets cheaply, and since capital becomes more scarce, its returns increase. • In the longer term, lack of investment, technology transfer, and foreign expertise may depress productivity, profits, growth, and employment opportunities, particularly for skilled workers. Economy-wide multiplier effects are likely. • State apparatuses may be harmed directly if investment is an important source of foreign exchange, and indirectly if stunted growth damages tax revenues. • Disinvestment may depress demand for, and thus the value of, the local currency, depressing importers' purchasing power and increasing foreign debt repayment costs for both private and public borrowers.
Aid and Finance	• Directly harms groups dependent reliant on external aid/finance, e.g. for livelihoods or investment capital. Possible multiplier effects. • Directly harms state apparatuses dependent on overseas aid and loans; and indirectly the sectors upon which these resources would be spent.
Assets	• Harms those with assets frozen and their dependents.
Monetary (currency manipulation)	• Importers, exporters, and consumers (private and public) suffer from price volatility and alterations in buying power. • Private and public borrowers with foreign-denominated loans face higher repayment costs. • Government may suffer ideological blow if national currency has ideological resonance. • Non-tradable or subsistence sectors will be less affected.
Arms	• May constrain state's capacity for war or domestic coercion. • As with import embargoes more generally, potential windfall gains for domestic producers and smugglers.

sanctions may be transformed by the way local forces respond, this analysis can only be a prelude to the most important and final step of the SCA.

This *third step* involves exploring how the material effects of sanctions condition the socio-political conflicts identified in step one by altering the composition, power, interests, resources, ideologies, and strategies of the coalitions contesting state power, and how this generates political change (or fails to do so). The SCA's sequential steps thus foreground the target society's composition and conflicts as the main object of analysis, into which sanctions intervene. Step three analyses external coercive diplomacy not as an overriding determinant but merely 'as one aspect of the wider struggle' over state power (Gelb, 1988: 74). Consequently, like political action more broadly, local responses to sanctions will be structurally constrained by pre-existing social power relations and conflicts, and the wider economic and geopolitical dynamics in which they are articulated. Furthermore, the opportunity of groups harmed by sanctions to pursue redress will depend partly on whether the state's strategic selectivity favours their approach.

Sanctions may alter coalitional dynamics through at least two distinct but related mechanisms, their importance varying with the intensity of the effects identified in step two. First, particularly devastating sanctions could change a society's basic composition, destroying some sectors while giving rise to others. For example, Andreas (2005) shows that sanctions often generate nouveaux riches engaged in illicit smuggling, while weakening the salaried middle classes. Secondly, sanctions could alter—positively *or* negatively—the resources available to ruling groups for coercing, co-opting, or gaining consent from subordinated groups.

In turn, these mechanisms are likely to affect state managers' strategies. A regime losing societal support bases or necessary resources will likely be forced into significant strategic changes. If a regime is based among disintegrating urban middle classes, for instance, it may need to pursue new alliances with the criminal nouveaux riches, redirecting its scarcer resources to them. However, if a regime can exploit sanctions to increase available resources, this could assist in the realization of its existing strategy of rule, or even permit its amendment to cultivate a stronger or wider ruling coalition. Through conditioning ruling groups' strategies, sanctions can thereby indirectly alter the coalitional basis of the state, its institutional arrangements, its economic and ideological programmes, and its wider policies.

In the medium to long term, these two mechanisms, and ruling coalitions' strategic responses, may in turn also condition the composition, resources, and political opportunities of opposition forces. Again, the possibilities are diverse. If the ruling bloc narrows or contracts, this could in turn prompt defections to or from the opposition, tilting the balance of power between the rival coalitions. An embargo campaign could help inspire and unite a disparate opposition around a shared goal, as for example in Indian struggles against British rule (Purkayastha and Kidwai, 2013: 47), or it could exacerbate divisions and reduce the opposition's coherence, as in Iraq (see chapter 4). The deprivations inflicted by sanctions could prompt more people to mobilize for the opposition, as the 'naïve theory' suggests, or have a depoliticizing effect as people focus more on day-to-day survival (as in Iraq and Myanmar: see chapters 3 and 4). Changes in state institutions pursued by the ruling coalition could increase or decrease access points for political opposition as the state's strategic selectivity evolves. Finally, the long-term effects of ruling coalitions' economic strategies could generate new social forces that expand or contract the opposition's social base.

We can concretize these abstract possibilities by foreshadowing the analysis of Iraq in chapter 4. The oil embargo quickly destroyed much of the working and middle classes, prompting Iraqis to return to agriculture, expanding the peasantry and boosting tribal landlords. They also deprived the regime of the patronage resources it had used to pursue state-led development that created and sustained its broad societal base. Forced to abandon its erstwhile urban supporters, the regime sought to co-opt tribal chiefs and smuggling merchants into a revised support base, jettisoning its secular, nationalist developmentalism for tribalism and sectarianism (Bunton, 2008). This strategy generated considerable societal unrest and regime splits, but this did not substantially strengthen the opposition coalition, which instead suffered defections relating to sanctions busting and deepening ideological divisions. Although Iraq's evolving social conflict did not yield the regime change sought by the senders of sanctions, it nonetheless transformed the regime quite fundamentally, and it forced some key concessions around weapons of mass destruction. This underscores the importance of identifying what sanctions actually do, i.e. how they 'work' to create political effects, rather than describing what they do *not* do by merely evaluating their 'success' against their stated goals (though this is also possible).

As the foregoing suggests, analysis in step three must be historical and dialectical, reflecting the dynamic, evolving nature of social conflict in target states. Particularly in long-running sanctions episodes, regime survival strategies can rebound quite dramatically upon the development of social forces and conflict. South Africa's aforementioned resort to ISI to counter sanctions, for example, generated new economic sectors that expanded and solidified the ruling coalition in the short to medium term. However, in the longer term, the costs of this strategy, coupled with collapsing global commodity prices, precipitated a massive debt crisis in the 1980s, which powerfully undermined the apartheid regime and its ruling strategy. Furthermore, as noted earlier, ISI generated new social forces disposed towards political alternatives, particularly an Afrikaner big bourgeoisie and the black working class (see chapter 2).

As these highly variable outcomes suggest, it is extremely difficult to predict any given society's trajectory under sanctions because it depends very much upon the agency and strategies of local forces and their structural context. In this respect, SCA is certainly no worse than mainstream political science approaches, which have not generated a taxonomy of causal pathways for political change that withstand empirical scrutiny.[8] Indeed, SCA's emphasis

---

[8] For example, Stepan identifies as many as ten causal pathways in democratization (Shin, 1994: 149), but these are constantly found wanting by the sheer diversity of actual cases (Geddes, 1999).

on the constraints on rulers' political strategies and coalitions emanating from economic and social structures makes analysis more manageable, since it suggests that only a finite range of trajectories are possible or likely. As Marx (1852) famously observed, people 'make their own history, but they do not make it as they please; they do not make it under self-selected circumstances, but under circumstances existing already, given and transmitted from the past'.

The Rhodesian case illustrates the importance of these structural constraints. Despite being heavily based among tobacco farmers, the Rhodesian Front government only provided them with short-term support when its agricultural exports were embargoed. Rowe, a neo-Weberian, argues that this illustrates the state's autonomy from even powerful interest groups. However, as his own narrative reveals, support for farmers was actually constrained by the business community's refusal to keep financing agriculture, and by mercantile resistance to tobacco stockpiling (Rowe, 2001: 91, 109–11). The structural dominance of industry, commerce, and banking steered Rhodesian state managers towards a different strategic response to sanctions—ISI—that largely benefited these sectors, not agriculture (Rowe, 2001: ch. 5).

SCA thus offers a historical and sociological approach to understanding 'how sanctions work' (or do not work). Rooted in a distinct Gramscian theorization of states and regimes, it centres our analysis on the social conflicts animating political developments in the target state when sanctions are imposed, then explores how these conflicts are conditioned by sanctions' material effects. The key questions relate not to how much damage is inflicted, or even upon whom, but on societal groups' *strategic response* to sanctions, their composition and interrelations, and whether their strategies to control state power are aided, retarded, or transformed. This strategic analysis differs fundamentally from liberals' focus on sanctions' humanitarian implications, and from pro-sanctions activists who 'approach sanctions campaigns as moral crusades, rather than as *political* processes' (Gelb, 1988: 71).

Methodology

The principal method used in this book is historical-sociological analysis. This is a necessary departure from the positivist and quantitative approaches dominating the sanctions literature. Because the mechanisms I seek to uncover relate to evolving, dynamic social relationships, these can only be analysed historically. Gramscian state theory plays a heuristic role, focusing the analysis on the constitution and practices of dominant social forces, which can be identified through studying the political economy of target states. It also plays a conceptual role, helping us to interpret our findings. The book deploys SCA in three case studies. This method, despite its drawbacks, has considerable advantages for an exploratory study like this.

Historical-sociological analysis involves producing narrative explanations of sanctions' impact by identifying causal social mechanisms. Since, as we have already emphasized, the social processes involved in generating political change are interrelated, dynamic, and transforming, they cannot be grasped except through a historical, narrative format of explanation (Rosenberg, 1994: 103–4). However, this does not imply that we can merely describe the impact of sanctions, as is often the case in studies concerned with their humanitarian consequences. This is avoided by focusing the narrative on the identification of causal mechanisms (Mayntz, 2004: 241), i.e. the social and political processes through which sanctions are transmitted into the maintenance or transformation of the target regime. This focus on processes, or mechanisms, allows us 'step away from the description of regularities to[wards] their explanation' (Pawson, 2000: 288; see also Tilly, 2001; Falleti and Lynch, 2009). In such 'mechanismistic' analysis, historical narratives are used to describe how relevant contextual conditions combine with social mechanisms to produce specific outcomes (Bunge, 1997; Pawson, 2000).

This approach clearly departs from the large-n, quantitative, correlational analyses favoured by positivists and many students of sanctions. Many scholars have previously maintained that such approaches are unsuitable for tracing out the complex domestic dynamics through which sanctions 'work'. Indeed, correlational analyses are unhelpful for explaining or comparing macro-social phenomena like regime transformation because isolating the relevant variables and establishing their relative dependence or independence is practically impossible (Mayntz, 2004: 238; Gerring, 2007).

The factors relevant to this causal explanation are identified by theory (Falleti and Lynch, 2009: 1152–3). Gramscian state theory plays a heuristic role here, guiding analytical attention to the struggle between social forces and its impact on states and regimes. As with Marxist theory in general, the real legacy of Gramsci's work is not a set of timeless iron laws associated with capitalism or state formation, but the dialectical, historical materialist method of analysis, which explores how attempts to resolve conflicts in one time period subsequently generate new social contradictions (Ollman, 2003).

As the preceding section identified, SCA involves a three-step analytical process. The first step is to identify the main socio-political coalitions and conflicts in the target country at the time sanctions are imposed (see, e.g., Rodan et al., 2006). The second is to identify the immediate distributional material consequences of sanctions. In some cases this analysis may be necessarily brief because the burden is almost immediately altered by domestic strategic responses (step three), or because the sanctions are so comprehensive that the impact cannot meaningfully be disaggregated very far. In other cases, particularly where sanctions are incremental and piecemeal, this analysis may be detailed and complex, identifying specific sectors or sub-sectors where the damage is inflicted. The third step is to identify the impact of these material consequences for the strategies pursued by ruling and opposition coalitions. In the short term, the analysis focuses on how these material consequences affect the conditions necessary for existing strategies to succeed. In the medium term, it explores whether and how sanctions force coalitions to change their strategies, and how they affect the conditions for their realization. In very long-term episodes, the analysis loops back to exploring the recursive impact of these strategies on social, economic, and political development, and the implications for coalitional struggle.

The following chapters apply SCA to three case studies: South Africa, Myanmar, and Iraq. A key objection to the use of case studies, particularly when they are few in number, is that reasonable generalizations cannot be made from such a small sample. Insofar as this is true, the trade off is that case studies enable theoretical complexity and the identification of the conditions and mechanisms that generate particular outcomes; unlike large-n, quantitative studies, they are not limited to simply describing the frequency of outcomes (George and Bennett, 2005: 25, 30–1). Case studies are simply indispensible if we want to find out *how* sanctions work (or do not work), rather than *how often* they work. Furthermore, while careless generalization must be avoided, it is still possible to make cross-case comparisons and tentatively identify key factors, which could be used in larger-scale future research (Mahoney and Rueschemeyer, 2003). In any case, this book does not aspire to be the final word on how sanctions work. Rather, it seeks to propel a research agenda that others may pursue and refine.

Their drawbacks aside, case studies are nonetheless uniquely well suited to exploring causal mechanisms since they allow us to identify intervening factors and explore the conditions under which mechanisms operate (George and Bennett, 2005: 19–22). Indeed, 'only case studies provide the intensive empirical analysis that can find previously unknown causal factors and historical patterns' (Achen and Snidal, 1989: 167–8). They are therefore particularly well suited to exploratory studies like this one, where the mechanisms through which sanctions 'work' are not yet well understood. To mitigate the risk of selection bias, the cases chosen all involved the goal of regime change, but led to a variety of outcomes.[9] South Africa is widely thought of as *the* case of sanctions 'success'; Iraq is widely held up as a quintessential 'failure';

---

[9] Although regime change is arguably a maximalist goal with low expectations of success, nonetheless, measures to promote democratization are now the most frequent of all sanctions (von Soest and Wahman, 2014), accounting for 46 per cent of all cases from 1914 to 2000 (Hufbauer et al. 2007).

and Myanmar is an intermediate case, its recent transition from military rule a potential 'success' but very much understudied. Each case is sufficiently long-running to permit the study of mechanisms over time and, where applicable, the recursive impact of state strategies on coalitional struggles. The cases are also situated in different geographical and historical contexts, and involve a mixture of comprehensive and targeted sanctions instruments to enable the effects of different sanctions instruments to be explored.

There are also good pragmatic reasons to select these three particular cases. First, South Africa is now sufficiently distant from the apartheid era to permit interviews to be conducted with key figures in the apartheid establishment, providing data that was previously inaccessible. Moreover, while South Africa attracted a great deal of scholarly attention in the 1980s, the end of apartheid generated a few self-congratulatory pieces from sanctions advocates, then attention rapidly shifted elsewhere. There has been surprisingly little retro-spective assessment of what sanctions actually achieved in South Africa. An important new data source on Iraq has also emerged. Perhaps the only 'useful' outcome of the 2003 US invasion was the seizure of Iraq's state archives, including many recordings of Saddam Hussein's conversations with his sub-ordinates. Many of these sources, transcribed, translated, and archived at the Conflict Research Records Centre at the National Defense University in Wash-ington, D.C., now offers unprecedented insight into how a targeted regime responded to sanctions. Myanmar's liberalization since 2011 also afforded new opportunities for research, particularly a newfound freedom to conduct fieldwork interviews. The mass release of US diplomatic cables by Wikileaks in 2011 also provided new data on the impact of sanctions there.

Furthermore, these cases have strong political and ideological significance. Despite political scientists' caution about generalizing from small numbers of cases, political arguments often do precisely this. For example, Khong (1992) shows that policymakers repeatedly justify US wars as necessary to avoid 'appeasement', making persistent analogies to Western policy towards Ger-many in the 1930s. This 'analogical reasoning' is commonplace in discussions of sanctions. As what Weiss et al. (1997a: 215) describe as the 'only' 'major success', the South African case is frequently cited to 'prove' that sanctions 'work', thereby becoming the conceptual basis for their imposition elsewhere (Elliott, 1998: 58–9). Thus, for example, Myanmar was depicted as 'the South Africa of the 1990s', with Aung San Suu Kyi as the new Nelson Mandela (Thinan Myo Nyun, 2008: 477), and many anti-apartheid activists and strat-egies were redeployed towards Myanmar (Free Burma Coalition, 1997). Sanc-tions advocates like US Senator Mitch McConnell drew the analogy directly, claiming: 'sanctions worked in South Africa and they will in Burma too' (Pedersen, 2008: 33). Today, campaigners insist that since Israel is another 'apartheid state', it too should be targeted by boycotts, disinvestment, and sanctions, articulating a 'South Africa strategy for Palestine' (Barghouti, 2011: 63). If, however, our investigation suggests that sanctions 'worked' for reasons very specific to South Africa's society and state at a particular historical juncture, such arguments would clearly be undermined, creating a need for caution when extrapolating from one archetypal case to other contexts. The Myanmar case allows us to explore this analogical reasoning further. As of 2009, the most recent year for which solid data exist, Myanmar also had the largest number of entities subject to targeted sanctions over a sustained period, making it useful to explore their impact.[10]

Similarly, Iraq is the key case that drove the abandonment of comprehensive sanctions in favour of targeted measures. But does Iraq really show that comprehensive sanctions necessarily fail, or that they did not work for reasons specific to Iraq in the 1990s? Or, upon closer inspection, might they even have actually 'worked' in some ways, but not others? Until these questions are answered, the reasoning behind the move to 'smart' sanctions remains untested. Myanmar also allows us to explore the different dynamics behind comprehensive and targeted sanctions since different states imposed measures of varying scope.

Thus, whatever is lost in using case studies is more than compensated for in terms of political relevance, as well as being critical for causal analysis. Studies of national security policymakers' use of political research suggest that they generally eschew 'scientific' approaches involving complex modelling or large-n, quantitative methods as unhelpful, favouring those based on mid-range theory, history, and case studies (Avey and Desch, 2014). To be relevant to policymakers, the analysis of sanctions must critically scrutinize precisely those cases that are ideologically and politically central to the way they think about and practise sanctions.

---

[10] Serbia and Montenegro is the country with the largest number of entities ever targeted, but this occurred in a very short burst, rising from 279 in May 1999 to a peak of 811 in August 2000, then falling to thirteen in February 2001. Conversely, targeted sanctions began in Myanmar in 1996, with individually specified targets rising from 140 in April 2000 to 523 by April 2008—55 per cent of the total number of entities then targeted *worldwide* by UN and EU sanctions, and more than the number imposed on al-Qaida and its affiliates (Eriksson, 2011: 254–5, 264, 105–6).

2

South Africa

Sanctioning Apartheid

Although white minority rule in South Africa ended two decades ago, the case has dominated discussions of sanctions like no other. The dominant view, in scholarship and the public imagination, is that it is 'indisputable that... sanctions... forced the previously immovable and inflexible system of apartheid to recognize the necessity of change' (Davis, 1995: 181). Even sanctions sceptics argue that South Africa constitutes their 'only' 'major success' (Weiss et al., 1997a: 215). This judgement, coinciding with an 'ethical' turn in Western foreign policy, underpinned widespread optimism about sanctions' capacity to promote regime change in the 1990s (Elliott, 1998: 58–9). Reasoning by analogy, policymakers, activists, and scholars argued that since sanctions had toppled one abhorrent regime, they could do so elsewhere. Henceforth, 'nearly every theoretical argument about the potential impact of sanctions on a target was made with respect to South Africa' (Crawford, 1999b: 3). Myanmar, for example, was cast as 'the South Africa of the 1990s', with Aung San Suu Kyi substituting for Nelson Mandela (Thinan Myo Nyun, 2008: 477). In 2005, Palestinian campaigners issued a call for boycott, disinvestment, and sanctions (BDS) against Israel, similarly 'inspired by the struggle of South Africans against apartheid' (Barghouti, 2011: 240). BDS advocates argue they will work in Israel/Palestine because 'we've seen it all before in South Africa' (Barghouti, 2011: 223). Famous anti-apartheid campaigners like Archbishop Desmond Tutu became vocal advocates of sanctions in both Myanmar and Israel.

The trouble with this analogical reasoning is not simply the possible counterclaim that sanctions did *not* 'work' in South Africa as, for example, Pape (1997: 135) implies when describing apartheid's demise as being 'over-determined' by other factors. Many scholars accept that sanctions contributed to, rather than solely causing, this outcome. Even then, we must still ask *how* sanctions did so, and thus *why* they apparently 'succeeded'. Otherwise, analogical reasoning from this case to any other is simply flawed. There may well be factors specific to South Africa that enabled sanctions to work that are lacking in other target states.

After a voluminous literature on South Africa and sanctions in the 1980s, mostly debating their *prospective* utility, there was strikingly little analysis of their subsequent *effects* beyond superficial, self-congratulatory pieces celebrating the West's role in ending apartheid (e.g. Davis 1995). The major exception is the only extant investigation of how embargoes generate political change, Crawford and Klotz's (1999b) *How Sanctions Work: Lessons from South Africa*. However, as chapter 1 discussed, this analysis centred upon sanctions instruments, each chapter trying to show how a different type of sanctions could effect change. Accordingly, the generic features of particular instruments were accentuated to extract 'lessons' for their apparently unproblematic application elsewhere. Consequently, this work did not consider that factors specific to *this* society made sanctions 'work' as they did, which might powerfully condition the 'lessons' one can reasonably extract from South Africa. Our understanding of how sanctions worked in South Africa thus remains constrained, permitting simplistic claims that 'sanctions worked'.

This chapter deploys SCA to apartheid South Africa, exploring how sanctions shaped the development of socio-political struggles from the 1960s to the 1990s. Its basic argument is that the early economic embargoes—on oil and arms—were counterproductive in the short to medium term because they helped consolidate and broaden the ruling coalition, rather than undermining it. It was only in the 1980s, when South Africa's political economy had undergone considerable transformation and was undergoing a sustained crisis, largely unrelated to sanctions, that the long-term costs of these early measures, combined with debt and balance of payments crises, began to fragment the ruling coalition. Yet even this would not have ended apartheid without massive and sustained popular mobilization, which sanctions did not create and only modestly supplemented.

The chapter comprises three sections, reflecting the SCA methodology outlined in chapter 1. The first identifies the socio-political coalitions contesting state power and their political economy context. The second considers the distributional costs of sanctions in the 1960s and 1970s and their impact on socio-political conflict, while the third section performs this analysis for embargoes imposed in the 1980s.

South Africa's Coalitional Struggles

This section describes the historical evolution of South Africa's ruling and opposition coalitions. The first subsection, on 'classical apartheid', traces the origins of minority rule to the nineteenth-century development of a highly racialized form of colonial capitalism, particularly the requirements of the dominant mining and agricultural sectors, which remained largely unchanged until the 1970s. Legally enshrined after the National Party (NP) won the 1948 elections, white minority rule was secured through coercion and the monopolization of resources, with Afrikaners controlling the state and English-speaking whites dominating the economy. However, as the second subsection describes, from the 1970s, the contradictions of capitalist development generated a new trajectory of 'reform apartheid'. Responding to growing black urbanization and politicization, burgeoning Afrikaner big business, rising demand for skilled labour, and the emergence of a more 'enlightened' Afrikaner middle class, state managers pursued a more incorporative strategy, seeking to co-opt non-white elites into a broadened ruling bloc. The contradictions and limitations of this strategy generated increasing political fragmentation among whites and growing non-white resistance. South Africa also entered a sustained economic crisis, stemming partly from global economic changes, notably the oil crises and commodity price fluctuations. By the 1980s, the economy was increasingly unable to finance the black population's rising aspirations or the NP's strategy of coercion and co-optation to maintain the white-dominated social order. Massive unrest accelerated the ruling bloc's fragmentation while consolidating opposition forces under the ANC's nominal leadership.

Classical Apartheid: from Colonial Origins to the 1960s

South Africa's complex society is heavily shaped by the legacy of European colonialism. The territory was first settled by Dutch colonists, who established farms and trading companies by dispossessing indigenous African tribes ('blacks').[1] Their descendants, Afrikaners (or Boers), developed a distinctive culture and language, Afrikaans, initially created to communicate with slaves imported from Malaya. These slaves, along with the offspring of Afrikaner settlers and black Africans, became known as the 'coloured' population. Later migrants from the Indian subcontinent—some imported 'coolies', some successful traders and professionals—formed the 'Indian' minority. In the late nineteenth century, the discovery of gold and diamonds attracted British imperial interests, and English-speaking whites came to dominate an emerging extractive and industrial sector. Growing conflict over mineral resources

---

[1] The racial categories devised by the apartheid state, while obviously deplorable, are nonetheless adopted for the purpose of analysis because they marked major political divisions within South African society.

eventually precipitated the 1899–1902 Anglo-Boer War, through which Britain seized full sovereignty.

Apartheid's basic contours subsequently emerged as an accommodation between key white groups. White supremacy was already entrenched economically and politically by 1900. English mining interests and Afrikaner farmers relied on the hyper-exploitation of unskilled black labour and, while coloureds were enfranchised in the English-dominated Cape area, British governors were already restricting Indian merchants to protect whites from competition. After the Boer War, Afrikaner–English reconciliation was achieved by further entrenching white supremacy (Marx, 1997). The South African state, established in 1910, enfranchised only whites (except for Cape coloureds), and was initially ruled by the South Africa Party, an alliance of English and pragmatic Afrikaner elites. These elites faced armed rebellions and strike waves by white workers seeking protection from black competition. Although the uprisings were crushed militarily, white labour was subsequently incorporated into a more 'consensual order forged around... an interventionist state securing institutionalised minimum privileges for all whites regardless of their class position', at non-whites' expense (O'Meara, 1996: 44–5). This was expressed in the 1924–34 'pact' government, combining the Afrikaner NP and the Labour Party, and the NP–South African Party 'fusion' in 1934. Socio-political stability among whites was thus established on the basis of racial hierarchy.

Although this white unity did not last, struggles in the 1930s and 1940s further entrenched this hierarchy. The Great Depression devastated Afrikaner farmers and workers, spurring the growth of Afrikaner nationalism, which created tension within the ruling coalition. South Africa's entry into World War II on Britain's side drove some Afrikaners into armed rebellion and prompted the NP to quit government and recombine with hardliners who had defected over 'fusion'. The war also spurred industrial growth, fuelling black migration to the cities. Reflecting the English industrial bourgeoisie's power, the government did not impede this, but began lifting economic restrictions on blacks. In response, the NP expanded quickly, recruiting crypto-fascist anti-war elements, whites afraid of growing industrial unrest and black urbanization, a white petit bourgeoisie threatened by Indian competition, and farmers frustrated by low commodity prices (Beinart, 1994: 131–3). In 1948, the party won a parliamentary majority thanks to Afrikaners' numerical dominance and rural over-representation.

The NP's election led to the formal adoption of apartheid and cemented a division of power among whites. Under its *volkscapitalisme* platform, the NP seized total control of state power, using it to expand Afrikaners' stake in the English-dominated economy and protect Afrikaners culturally and economically against the English and blacks (O'Meara, 1983). It purged the predominantly English civil service, packing the bureaucracy with its Afrikaner supporters, and established a quasi-developmental state to provide business opportunities to the Afrikaner petit bourgeoisie that had bankrolled the party. The English were rapidly politically marginalized. However, despite initial government threats to nationalize the mines, the NP bought English acquiescence by not seriously challenging their economic control. It instead promoted Afrikaner capital via government contracts, agricultural subsidies, infrastructure projects, and state-brokered joint ventures with English companies (Fine and Rustomjee, 1996).

This ruling strategy ultimately depended on intensifying non-whites' economic exploitation and political exclusion. NP ideologists argued that South Africa's various races were incompatible and must live apart.[2] The Mixed Marriages and Immorality Acts banned interracial coupling, while the Group Areas Act carved South Africa into racial zones, reserving the cities and best agricultural land for whites, and confining blacks to impoverished tribal 'reserves'. Non-whites were designated non-citizens and were legally disenfranchised. However, the practical application of apartheid ultimately reflected the requirements of capital accumulation. Expelling blacks from urban areas helped disrupt labour unionization, shifting resistance into the countryside where it was easier to control. Coupled with harsh restrictions on rural black mobility, it also directed workers to white-owned farms and mines. Furthermore, white workers were protected from competition, particularly in skilled jobs, stimulating Fordist employment and consumption patterns. Yet industry's requirements for a large, settled workforce ensured that apartheid was never completely enforced. Blacks were permitted to remain in peri-urban areas, though they were classified as temporary workers from their tribal 'homelands' and subject to pass laws.

The material benefits flowing from these arrangements solidified the ruling coalition. Its hegemonic force was the Afrikaner bourgeoisie that financed and organized the NP. Key companies like Volkskas, Sanlam, and Rembrandt received disproportionate government patronage, burgeoning into massive conglomerates rivalling their English counterparts by the 1970s. Despite the NP's petit bourgeois ideology and voter base, smaller businesses were comparatively neglected (Fine and Rustomjee, 1996: 148–51, 157–9, 192–3; Saul and Gelb, 1986: 65, 74). Cheap rural labour, infrastructure spending, and regulated, high commodity prices enabled some farmers to establish massive agribusiness empires and diversify into other sectors, notably finance (Fine and Rustomjee, 1996: 148–51, 185–8; Beinart, 1994: 172–3). English capital also benefited substantially. Mining houses remained private, secured pliable

---

[2] *Apartheid* is Afrikaans for 'apartness'.

labour at below subsistence rates, and benefited from infrastructure development and protectionism (Saul and Gelb, 1986: 68; Cohen, 1986: 38–48).
South Africa's predominantly English industrialists were lesser beneficiaries.
They gained from the suppression of black unions and wages, the stabilization
of a skilled, white workforce, and the expanding consumption this facilitated.
However, apartheid limited domestic consumption and labour markets,
increasing their costs and producing skills shortages by the 1960s (Saul
and Gelb, 1986: 46–7, 71–2; Lipton, 1986: 21–5). Nonetheless, apartheid
broadly benefited South African capitalists until the 1970s. Aided by global
support for Keynesianism and World Bank infrastructure funding, a sustained
economic boom ensued. Profit rates soared and foreign investment tripled
from the 1930s to the 1960s (Singh, 1992–3: 131). White workers and small
businessmen also secured protection against non-white competitors, enjoying
preferential access to housing and employment, and rising wages. By 1970,
white employment was concentrated in the secondary and tertiary sectors and
in skilled, white-collar occupations, dramatically narrowing the Afrikaner–
English income gap (Lipton, 1986: 37; Beinart, 1994: 172–3).

Some non-whites were also incorporated into the ruling coalition, but in a
firmly subordinate position. Coloureds and Indians, despite being disenfranchised, were nonetheless more privileged than blacks, being allowed to continue providing goods and services to their own communities in demarcated
urban areas. A thin sliver of urban and rural blacks also benefited somewhat
from apartheid. Pretoria bolstered the authority of compliant black chiefs over
the populations of rural 'reserves', gradually dispensing 'development' assistance that chiefs used to enrich themselves and their followers by funding
state-linked businesses. Likewise, local advisory boards provided an outlet for
aspirant urban blacks willing to cooperate with the regime (Beinart, 1994:
181–7). Black wages also tripled from 1916 to 1970, but this was from a
miserably low base (Lipton, 1986: 44). The vast bulk of the black population
was marginalized and horribly oppressed.

Opposition to the ruling coalition was racially divided, fragmented, and
episodic in this period. Among whites, the NP faced considerable parliamentary and extra-parliamentary opposition into the 1950s. However, economic
growth expanded the NP's base, and the continuity between apartheid and
earlier racialism left English parties unable to formulate realistic alternatives.
The Liberal Party, for example, split in 1959 over whether to support a universal franchise. There were negligible links between white and non-white
oppositionists. The remnants of the black working class resumed labour
organizing, influenced by communism and Garveyism, and there was some
rural resistance to white land-grabs and the reimposition of chiefly rule.
However, these movements were fragmented and the main political resistance organization, the African National Congress (ANC), was dominated by

relatively conservative black professionals. This changed during the 1950s as the youth wing, headed by Nelson Mandela, began reaching out to black workers and radicalizing the ANC. The burgeoning resistance peaked in 1960 with a rural uprising in Pondoland and a wave of urban strikes and ANC-led, anti-Pass Law demonstrations. These rebellions were brutally suppressed, with the massacre of sixty-nine people at Sharpeville drawing international condemnation, and 18,000 people were detained during a subsequent state of emergency. The internal resistance, too fragmented and disorganized to withstand the crackdown, was quelled for the next sixteen years. The ANC, the Pan-African Congress (PAC), and the South African Communist Party (SACP) were banned, their leaders imprisoned or forced into exile, where they became dependent on support from China, the Soviet Union, the Organization for African Unity (OAU), and the Non-Aligned Movement. Anti-apartheid resistance was thus driven abroad, prompting the ANC's first calls for international economic sanctions.

Importantly, sanctions were part of a relatively coherent and comprehensive ANC strategy for overthrowing apartheid. The ANC's alliance and overlapping membership with the SACP fostered a Marxist analysis of apartheid as a 'special form of colonialism' involving both racial and class domination (ANC, 1985). Reflecting Marxist praxis, its strategy focused on splitting the bloc of social forces underpinning this regime, whilst unifying other social groups around itself (ANC, 1969). International solidarity, including sanctions, was just one 'pillar' of this strategy, alongside mass mobilization, underground organization, and armed struggle—which the ANC's armed wing, Umkhonto we Sizwe (MK), launched from bases in Zambia and Tanzania with assistance from Moscow. Mass mobilization was generally seen as the most important 'pillar', with sanctions playing a strictly supplementary role (Kasrils, 2013: 20). The ANC's representative in London, Abdul Minty, who fostered the Anti-Apartheid Movement and led the call for sanctions, asserted: 'victory will come through the struggle of the people . . . sanctions must be regarded as a complement to that struggle and not as an alternative' (GPAAWC, 2007: 129). My opposition interviewees consistently stated that sanctions made sense only in support of a domestic rebellion.

Reflecting the ANC's Marxist analysis of politics as a struggle between contending socio-political blocs, they believed that sanctions could help by 'restraining the regime's capacity; dividing the alliance of forces behind the apartheid state; [and] uniting and broadening the anti-apartheid support base within the country and externally' (Maharaj, 2011). The regime's repressive apparatus was seen as partially financed by foreign trade, investment, technology, and weaponry. Consequently, ANC President Oliver Tambo argued, blocking these flows could 'weaken the system and make it less capable of resisting our struggle' (Starnberger Institute, 1989: 49–50; Orkin, 1989a: 26).

Sanctions could work directly, by removing these external 'props', and indirectly, by restricting the regime's tax base (Lekota, 2011). Tambo's aide, Thabo Mbeki, also explained that sanctions, alongside the other 'pillars', were aimed at 'breaking up the power structure' by encouraging key forces to break from the regime. 'Out of this', he argued, 'you will get a realignment of forces' favourable to the opposition (Lodge, 1988: 250–1). Sanctions might, Mbeki suggested, 'generate, from even within white South Africa itself, very many forces which . . . would say: "but we can't stand by and allow this country to be destroyed . . . " . . . the price has now become too high' (Hanlon and Omond, 1987: 26). The ANC did not seek sanctions to help mobilize opposition by, for example, increasing black unemployment (Lodge, 1989: 38–9). This was the task of the other 'pillars'. By the 1980s, the ANC's strategic understanding of sanctions was widely shared by the broad anti-apartheid opposition within South Africa.[3]

Initially, however, there was no serious change in the ruling coalition, even when confronted by serious domestic unrest. The 1960 crackdown initially precipitated serious capital flight, halving South Africa's gold reserves by May 1961, prompting some calls for reform from big business (Marks and Trapido, 1987: 52). Two of South Africa's six dominant conglomerates—Anglo-American Corporation, owned by the Anglophone Oppenheimer dynasty, and Rembrandt, owned by the Afrikaner Rupert family—founded the South Africa Foundation, a group designed to protect South African business's links with major trading partners in Europe and North America by advocating cautious domestic reforms. Little ensued in the short term. The government imposed capital controls, benefiting big business, particularly Anglo-American, which stepped in to stabilize local capital markets, and emerging Afrikaner business empires, which took over distressed firms (Marks and Trapido, 1987: 53; Fine and Rustomjee, 1996: 160–1). Foreign investment also quickly returned, rising sevenfold from 1965 to 1975 (Singh, 1992–3: 136). The subsequent collapse of the gold standard also benefited South Africa as the price of gold, its predominant export, soared, boosting mining and government revenues, generating ever greater flows of benefits to NP supporters.

'Reform Apartheid': from the 1970s to the 1980s

From the late 1960s, profound changes in South Africa's social structure and renewed anti-apartheid resistance began transforming the country's coalitional

---

[3] This was reflected in the remarkably consistent views of many interviewees from trade unions (Erwin, 2011; Mufamadi, 2011; Mkhize, 2011), resistance organizations (Evans, 2011; Cooper, 2011), and civic and religious groups affiliated with the United Democratic Front (Coleman, 2011; Coovadia, 2011; Boesak, 2011; Crawford-Browne, 2011).

conflict. Coupled with a mounting economic crisis caused partly by transformations in the international political economy, and with geopolitical changes in southern Africa, they set the state on a course of 'reform apartheid' designed to recast white hegemony.

Ironically, the ruling coalition's first fissures emerged from contradictions generated by the very success of apartheid capitalist development, particularly within the labour market. By the late 1960s, full white employment, coupled with blacks' exclusion from skilled jobs, was causing rising labour costs, falling international competitiveness, and severe skills shortages (Lipton, 1986: 85–254). Initially confined to manufacturing, this problem spread to the emerging commercial and financial sectors, and even to large-scale agribusinesses as they became mechanized. The mines, traditionally reliant on low-skilled, black, migrant labour, were less affected, but rising capital intensity also generated increased demand for skilled mineworkers. Mine owners experimented with using settled, black, skilled labour, creating tension with white labour unions. Thus, while smaller-scale, labour-intensive enterprises and white workers still favoured apartheid, larger-scale, capital-intensive businesses began favouring its relaxation.

The potential for sectoral divisions over this was dampened by South Africa's remarkable degree of capital concentration. Mining and agriculture remained less dependent on skilled labour than industry, commerce, and finance. However, by 1970 British colonialism and NP patronage had together concentrated South African capital into massive conglomerates with interests spanning multiple sectors. By the early 1980s, the *Financial Mail* reported, twenty of South Africa's top 100 industrial firms controlled 61 per cent of total assets. Of this portion, 39 per cent was held by Old Mutual, 28 per cent by Anglo-American, and 10 per cent by Sanlam. Furthermore, all of the top twenty firms were connected to each other, and to mining and finance, by interlocking directorships. Finance displayed even greater concentration, with 2.7 per cent of firms controlling half of the turnover, 6.3 per cent employing 54 per cent of workers, and 6 per cent controlling 85 per cent of all fixed assets (ANC, 1985).

Crucially, due to structural changes in South African society, reform demands now emanated from Afrikaner as well as English communities, and from non-business circles. Thanks to government patronage, many Afrikaner businesses had become large-scale enterprises, interpenetrated with Anglophone interests through joint ventures, mergers, and acquisitions. They now faced similar pressures to English big businesses and consequently became increasingly vocal proponents of gradual reform. That Afrikaner conglomerates were outgrowing their NP-provided incubator was dramatically symbolized by *The Assault on Private Enterprise* (Wassenaar, 1977), a polemic against government regulation by Sanlam's chairman, Andreas Wassenaar. Government patronage had also generated an urbanized, educated, Afrikaner middle class which, feeling more socially and economically secure, began questioning apartheid, broadening the basis for reform beyond the bourgeoisie. By the late 1960s, Afrikaners were increasingly divided between these *verligtes* ('enlightened ones') and rural and working-class *verkramptes* (conservatives). This split was expressed in all the key Afrikaner cultural institutions, notably the Dutch Reformed Church, the Broederbond, and the NP itself (Lipton, 1986: 44).

Verligte requests initially prompted modest revisions to classical apartheid. Demands for labour flexibility from peak business organizations like the Association of Chambers of Commerce (ASSOCOM) and the Federated Chambers of Industry (FCI) found a sympathetic audience among elements of the economic planning bureaucracy. A new 'coalition of capital' also started financing the opposition Progressive Federal Party (PFP) to promote reform from within parliament (Hackland, 1987). The NP government responded modestly, increasing funding for black education and moderating the 'colour bar' to admit more blacks to semi-skilled occupations in 1973. The regime's gradual capitulation to the needs of capital accumulation was also reflected in lax enforcement of apartheid laws: by 1970, 46 per cent of blacks lived in South Africa's 'white' cities (Lipton, 1986: 44).

However, a more serious shift towards 'reform apartheid' was driven by the revival of black opposition. Ironically, government-funded education fostered an educated generation of black youths which became radicalized by the 'Black Consciousness' movement, becoming the vanguard of renewed anti-apartheid resistance. In June 1976, tens of thousands of these youths staged protests in the Johannesburg township of Soweto. The police massacred demonstrators, sparking widespread violence in which hundreds were killed. The massacre attracted overseas criticism and sanctions (discussed in the later section 'The Impact of Early Sanctions: Oil and Arms'), but the domestic repercussions were even more powerful. For blacks, Soweto became a new focus for resistance. The crackdown spurred recruitment to MK, introducing a new generation to the ANC for the first time. It also signalled to whites that black quiescence was over, necessitating changes to maintain social order. By the late 1970s, *verligte* intellectuals and big businesses were openly demanding reform. The Afrikaanse Handelinstituut, the principal Afrikaner business association, publicly criticized policies like influx control. Warning that black unemployment created fertile conditions for communism, it urged the government to provide housing and economic opportunities to cultivate 'stabilised elements' among workers, and an 'African middle class' to secure 'the trust and loyalty of the blacks in a system of free enterprise' (Greenberg, 1987: 396–7). Anglo-American and Rembrandt also founded the Urban Foundation, an NGO working to improve living conditions for urban blacks and fostering a black middle class with a stake in the system (Cohen, 1986: 58; Saul and Gelb, 1986: 72).

This fearful, defensive response to renewed domestic black resistance was partly shaped by the latter's articulation within wider geopolitical developments. The collapse of the Portuguese empire after a left-wing coup in Lisbon in 1974 had isolated South Africa and Rhodesia as the last white minority governments in Africa. To widespread rejoicing among South African blacks, Mozambique and Angola's colonial administrations, which had been friendly to Pretoria, were replaced by anti-apartheid, Marxist regimes. MK bases relocated to these countries, hundreds of miles closer to South Africa, enabling them to launch cross-border raids. The Mozambican and Angolan governments, backed by the OAU, also supported the liberation of Namibia, which South Africa had occupied since 1919, initially under a League of Nations mandate. Given these dramatic changes, paranoid Afrikaner securocrats saw the Soweto uprisings as part of a black communist 'total onslaught' directed from Moscow.

A final driver for reform apartheid was a structural crisis in the South African economy emanating partly from global upheavals, particularly the 1973 oil crisis and the 1971 dismantling of the gold standard. Despite expanding considerably, South Africa's economy had not significantly diversified beyond the dominant 'minerals-energy complex' (Fine and Rustomjee, 1996). It remained dependent on imports for around 40 per cent of its capital goods, while raw and semi-processed materials still comprised about 80 per cent of its exports, around half of which was gold. This trade structure determined South Africa's balance of payments—the difference between total trade and investment flows to and from an economy. During growth periods, capital goods imports increased, typically faster than exports, creating a balance of payments deficit. While this could partially be covered through borrowing and investment in the expectation of future growth and exports, the government was increasingly forced to artificially suppress growth in order to curtail imports. The situation worsened after the gold standard collapsed, since South Africa's export revenues began fluctuating wildly. The 1973 oil crisis further compounded the problem. Although rising gold revenues partly offset higher oil prices, the crisis induced stagflation in developed Western economies, increasing the cost of South Africa's capital imports. Collectively, these trends produced a structural break in South Africa's economic performance. \Its average growth rate declined from 4.9 per cent in 1947–74 to just 1.8 per cent in 1974–87. Its terms of trade fell by two thirds from 1975 to 1992. Inflation climbed to 10 per cent and remained persistently high. Private savings and investment slumped, and annual job creation slowed from 157,000 in 1960–74 to just 54,000 thereafter (Levy, 1999: 416; Lowenberg, 1997: 68; Gelb, 1991: 6).

This stagnation left South Africa increasingly dependent on foreign investment to cover its structural balance of payments deficit, heightening its external vulnerability. By 1975, one quarter of its total investment came from overseas (Davis, 1995: 175). After Soweto, the vulnerability this exposure produced was clearly displayed: facing rapid capital flight, Pretoria had to seek IMF loans and pursue savage deflation to improve the balance of payments; it was forced to request IMF assistance again in 1982. Though cushioned somewhat by rising gold prices, South Africa was entering a debt crisis similar to those engulfing other developing countries. It still attracted foreign investment, since it was perceived as less risky. However, this changed as socio-political instability mounted in the mid-1980s (discussed in the later section 'Later Sanctions: Disinvestment, Finance, and Trade'). Investors hiked interest rates and shortened the length of their loans; consequently, by 1985, two thirds of South Africa's foreign debt was short term, requiring payment or renewal within six months (Carim et al., 1999: 163). This left the economy dangerously exposed should lenders decline to 'roll over' (renew) these loans.

These structural transformations drove significant changes in South Africa's ruling coalition and its strategy, creating the era of 'reform apartheid'. This began under Prime Minister John Vorster (1966–78) but climaxed under his successor P. W. Botha (1978–89), who famously told his compatriots to 'adapt or die'. Responding to social changes and growing demands for reform, Vorster successfully courted big business, *verligte* Afrikaners, and English voters by relaxing some socio-economic aspects of apartheid. NP *verkramptes* resisted, expressing growing white divisions. They were eventually expelled in 1969, becoming the base for the new opposition Reconstituted National Party.

Vorster's major innovation was the policy of 'separate development', which pushed black 'tribal homelands' towards formal 'independent statehood'. This sought to provide internationally recognized avenues for black political representation and economic advancement outside of South Africa itself, thereby displacing political contestation. Thus, Transkei, Bophuthatswana, Venda, and Ciskei were made independent in 1976, 1977, 1979, and 1981 respectively. However, the new 'states' were economically unviable, dependent on South African 'aid', and lacked real autonomy. The 'Bantustans' were widely seen as impoverished holding areas for black labourers, who were forced to 'commute' to 'white' cities, and dumping grounds for the unemployed, aged, and infirm. South African capitalists refused to relocate industries to the Bantustans' outskirts to help remedy these problems, and international recognition was also withheld. Nonetheless, 'separate development' was a significant shift towards incorporating black elites into a revised ruling coalition. Development assistance to homeland regimes created employment and business opportunities that deliberately—and successfully—cultivated a black middle class to help stabilize those territories (Cohen, 1986: 22–3; Saul and Gelb, 1986: 102, 178–86).

P. W. Botha massively accelerated 'reform apartheid' by forging a new alliance between security officials and big business. Botha had cultivated a power base in the military and internal security establishment whilst serving as defence minister. By the mid-1970s, the security forces were already seen as more powerful than parliament. Botha entrenched this, creating the securocrat-led State Security Council (SSC), which acquired a dominant role vis-à-vis other state bureaucracies (Alden, 1998). This reconfiguration of state apparatuses helped Botha reorient foreign and domestic policy around an overriding logic of counter-insurgency. Against the 'total onslaught', the military had adopted a 'total strategy': domestic counter-insurgency coupled with raids against ANC bases and hostile neighbouring governments. However, counter-insurgency ultimately depends upon ameliorating the conditions fuelling an insurgency. Accordingly, Botha now pursued socio-economic reforms to undercut black opposition and satisfy big businesses' demands. He purged the bureaucracy, promoting reformist technocrats who justified relaxing apartheid using neoliberal ideology (Greenberg, 1987; Posel, 1987). The finance ministry, for instance, came under strong monetarist influence due to the deliberate recruitment of overseas-trained economists, including former IMF and World Bank employees (Mullins, 2011; Du Plessis, 2011; Durr, 2011). Botha courted big business, promising them deregulation and inviting business leaders to join commissions and cabinet subcommittees to shape government policy (Fine and Rustomjee, 1996: 98; Mann, 1988: 55, 62–3, 78–9).

Reflecting Botha's counter-insurgency approach, his new strategy combined repression with a 'hearts and minds' campaign. Botha responded to growing black unrest and business pressure by legalizing black trade unions, improving urban living conditions, and permitting blacks to own property and start businesses, deliberately cultivating an anti-communist 'middle class'. A tricameral parliament was established in 1983, with chambers for Coloureds and Indians. Blacks still had to exercise their political 'rights' mostly in the Bantustans, but local community councils were established in black townships, along with multiracial provincial regional services councils, which were intended to be self-financing through rent and service charges. Such efforts to cultivate wider popular consent were coupled with coercion for those who resisted: hardline domestic policing and escalating foreign interventions. Initially with US backing, South Africa launched covert attacks on Mozambique and Angola. Angola sought aid from Moscow and Cuba and, by the mid-1980s, South Africa was embroiled in one of the Cold War's hottest conflicts.

Reflecting white South Africans' growing diversity, these relatively modest reforms split the NP. By rapidly elevating *verligte* social forces' interests and preferences, Botha had transformed the NP 'from a populist movement to a party of the bourgeoisie' (Saul and Gelb, 1986: 88). Thereby, 'large-scale Afrikaner capital established itself as the hegemonic element in Afrikaner nationalism' (Mann, 1988: 55). The NP essentially abandoned its traditional base among Afrikaner workers and farmers. Eventually, hardliners again defected, forming the Conservative Party in 1982, which attracted extensive support from these disgruntled social groups (Saul and Gelb, 1986: 90). Resistance also emerged among lower-ranked bureaucrats, especially within apparatuses created to enforce apartheid. However, the SSC's deliberately crafted autonomy insulated reform apartheid from these forces.

More importantly, reform apartheid's new institutions failed to cultivate non-white consent, instead becoming lightning rods for mounting opposition. In 1984, non-white opposition to the tricameral parliament led to the formation of the United Democratic Front (UDF) to campaign for an electoral boycott. The UDF united an unprecedented number of civic, cultural, religious, and political groups from across racial and urban/rural divides in a historically unprecedented, popular anti-apartheid front. Although not ANC-led, the UDF adopted the ANC's Freedom Charter as its platform, demanding non-racial democracy and wealth redistribution. The UDF's campaign was so successful that turnout for the parliamentary and local black council elections was just 12 to 18 per cent (Beinart, 1994: 237). Without popular consent, these institutions were inoperable. Local councils were unable to collect the rent and service charges they needed to operate as boycotts and protests swept the townships from September to November 1984, encouraging the hitherto reticent black trade unions to stage a two-day strike. Although troop deployments briefly quelled the unrest, from January to July 1985, protests resumed, escalating into a national movement to render the townships 'ungovernable'. In most areas, local councils collapsed and UDF street committees seized control. In December, the Congress of South African Trade Unions (COSATU) was formed, uniting the vast majority of black unions. COSATU aligned itself to the UDF, and implicitly to the ANC, declaring its opposition to both apartheid and capitalism—heightening whites' fear of revolutionary upheaval (Saul and Gelb, 1986: 42).

Botha nonetheless persisted with his strategy, intensifying coercion by declaring a partial state of emergency in July 1985. This prompted international condemnation and capital flight, with Western banks refusing to roll over their loans. With South Africa's debt totalling US$23.7 billion, half of its GDP, it was forced to default. Within a week, R11 billion was wiped off the Johannesburg stock exchange and the rand collapsed by nearly a fifth (Carim et al., 1999: 164–6). With little more to lose, Botha imposed a full state of emergency from June 1986 to December 1987. The army and police were deployed to smash the UDF and restore public order, enabling the local councils to resume operation. Reflecting the counterinsurgency approach, efforts to improve township housing and services were also intensified. However, despite tens of thousands of arrests and a superficial restoration of stability within six months, the regime still could not foster popular consent for reform apartheid (Alden, 1998: 217–33). Although opposition forces failed to topple the regime, Botha had also failed to recast white hegemony. Stalemate had emerged.

The Impact of Early Sanctions: Oil and Arms

We can now explore the impact of sanctions on the social conflict just described. Sanctions were imposed on South Africa in several waves, largely reacting to its domestic crises, notably the 1960 Sharpeville massacre, the 1976 Soweto uprising, and the mid-1980s states of emergency (see Table 2.1). Thus, contrary to the 'naïve theory' of sanctions, domestic unrest drove the imposition of sanctions, rather than vice versa (Lowenberg, 1997: 69). Furthermore, unlike today's sanctions, these measures were largely propelled by civil society actors—principally the ANC and allied campaigns—not governments. While most non-aligned states were vocally anti-apartheid, South Africa's major trading and investment partners in the West saw Pretoria as a Cold War ally. Worried about the 'communist' ANC and increasing Soviet

Table 2.1 Main sanctions imposed on South Africa

Date	Measure
August 1963	UNSC imposes voluntary arms embargo.
November 1963	UN General Assembly urges all states to stop supplying petroleum to South Africa. The OAU and the Organization of Arab Petroleum Exporting Countries impose oil embargoes in 1964 and 1973. Iran defies the ban until 1979, when Norway and Britain also join the embargo.
November 1977	UNSC imposes a mandatory arms embargo.
March 1983	The IMF is effectively barred from lending to South Africa by a US Congressional amendment.
June 1985	Following unilateral measures by non-aligned and European states, UNSC calls on all states to adopt voluntary embargoes on new investment, transport links, gold coin sales, and sporting and cultural relations. Many states impose some sanctions.
September 1985	EEC strengthens military and oil embargoes and pledges to assist anti-apartheid groups.
October 1985	British Commonwealth, minus Britain, adopts wide-ranging trade, investment, and tourism embargoes.
September 1986	EEC bans imports of South African coal, steel, and gold coins, and bans new investments. Japan bans imports of South African iron and steel.
October 1986	US bans new investments in South Africa; bars imports of South African uranium, coal, textiles, agricultural products, iron, steel, sugar, and parastatals' products; suspends air links.
October–November 1986	Grass-roots disinvestment campaign climaxes. Major firms like IBM, General Motors, and Barclays withdraw from South Africa.
1987–9	Several European states adopt unilateral comprehensive sanctions. Pressure on the US and British governments to follow suit is resisted.

influence in southern Africa, they resisted sanctions, often imposing them, half-heartedly, to deflect calls for more comprehensive measures.

Reflecting this, early consumer boycott campaigns were not principally aimed at the apartheid regime. Rather, they 'sought to mobilise... [Western citizens to] force their government to take a position' (Maharaj, 2011). Ronnie Kasrils, a senior ANC figure, describes this as a two-stage strategy, first 'focusing on easier targets', then reorienting the campaign towards 'banking and the nerve centres of business once a critical mass had been achieved'. This was part of the ANC's overall strategy of 'isolating the centre of reaction' by 'reaching out to sections of the oppressor's social base, both nationally and internationally, in order to neutralise or win them over' (Kasrils, 2013: 25, 27).

Since consumer boycotts were not directly aimed at South Africa, this section explores the earliest sanctions that were: the oil and arms embargoes. While modestly successful in mobilizing international opinion, in the short to medium term, these embargoes were largely counterproductive in their stated goal of dividing the apartheid power bloc. They were successfully evaded, with sanctions-busting strategies complementing the regime's ruling strategy, broadening and strengthening the ruling coalition. Few negative effects were felt until the multidimensional crisis of the mid-1980s.

The Oil Embargo

Oil was initially seen as South Africa's Achilles heel because it was entirely dependent on imports for this vital commodity. Oil and petroleum products are essential in all modern societies, fuelling transportation and power generation and being essential to many industrial production processes. The distributional consequences of an oil embargo might therefore be imagined to be widespread, affecting every economic sector, either directly or via multiplier effects.

However, the government began adapting to an anticipated embargo during the 1960s, shifting these consequences before they even materialized. It established vast strategic stockpiles in exhausted mines and a state-owned enterprise, Sasol, which created large oil-from-coal plants to enhance South Africa's self-sufficiency. These import-substitution efforts reduced the country's import dependency to around 40 per cent for petroleum and 20 per cent for petroleum products by the 1980s (IRRC, 1990: 17). South Africa acquired these imports without severe difficulties, initially from sanctions-evading countries and later through black markets, which involved costlier premiums. The regime thereby vastly reduced the embargo's potential economic cost. By financing the sanctions busting, it also dispersed the residual cost throughout the economy, via increased prices and taxation, diffusing any potential reaction.

By provoking this strategic response, the oil embargo strengthened the ruling coalition, rather than weakening it. It did not undermine but rather complemented the NP's strategy of state-assisted development through import substitution, and created a nexus of interests around domestic oil production. Sasol employed many Afrikaner managers and officials whose interests were tied to sanctions busting. Sasol also boosted demand for coal, pleasing the mine owners. Moreover, as a former top executive of a civil engineering company recalls, such infrastructure projects 'created opportunities for business... [and] caused the business community and government to get closer together' (Brink, 2011). A more sinister consequence was the state apparatus's partial criminalization. Sasol and the bureaucracies tasked with sanctions busting necessarily developed close relations with criminal middlemen who flocked to South Africa en masse, especially after the 1973 oil crisis. Despite intense secrecy, allegations of corruption and kickbacks surfaced. These were quickly suppressed for 'security' reasons, granting perpetrators impunity (Hengeveld and Rodenburg, 1995c; Scholtz, 1995). Big business was also drawn into these networks. For example, the Reserve Bank connected sanctions busters with Afrikaner financiers like Nedbank to secure them credit, deepening the 'symbiotic relationship' between business and the regime (Crawford-Browne, 2011). Multinational oil firms also played a critical role, supplying crude oil, for which they initially received government subsidies, and maintaining South Africa's domestic petroleum distribution systems (Hengeveld and Rodenburg, 1995b: 21–2).

The oil embargo, and the ruling coalition's response, also shaped the opposition's strategy, with mixed consequences. After Soweto, MK had escalated its guerrilla attacks inside South Africa; the embargo apparently channelled these towards oil installations. As one MK cadre recalls, Sasol plants were targeted because '[we] were very conscious of the contribution of the international community to our struggle. We felt it was our duty to reciprocate in kind... to express our appreciation of their support and show them what we were capable of doing for our own liberation' (Hengeveld and Rodenburg, 1995d: 32, see also 47–8). The most successful attacks were the bombings of the Sasol I and II plants and the Natref refinery in June 1980. ANC cadre Frene Ginwala argues these 'spectacular' attacks were 'tremendously important' since they 'shattered the myth of white invulnerability. It was not about the quantity of oil that was lost... it was that column of smoke that was important. Sasol was a symbol of power' (Hengeveld and Rodenburg, 1995d: 36). A leading Black Consciousness activist concurs that this 'armed propaganda' had a 'phenomenal' impact in mobilizing black youths behind the ANC (Cooper, 2011). Despite these claims, MK remained relatively small, with under 10,000 guerrillas, and while its operations became more frequent, by 1986 under 500 had been undertaken. This was clearly insufficient to compel a well-armed state to surrender. At best, it perhaps reminded non-whites that resistance was possible and elevated the ANC to prominence (Lodge, 1988: 230, 235), helping to give 'the people the will and the inspiration to do their bit', as SACP leader Joe Slovo later suggested (Waldmeir, 1998: 48).

In the short term, however, MK attacks arguably solidified the hegemonic bloc. While they perhaps deepened reformists' concern, the majority apparently hardened their attitudes. Most whites retained faith in the security services' capacity to combat black 'terrorism', supporting the escalating security restrictions that followed (Eglin, 2011). These measures, particularly the 1980 National Key Points Act, drew business and the state even closer together, underscoring their shared interest in order and 'security'. Sasol employees had already formed a commando unit, equipped and trained by the army, to defend their installations. Now private firms were required to host arsenals; to form militias, which were given military training and integrated into regional defence plans; and to become military bases during emergencies (Hengeveld and Rodenburg, 1995d: 39). The oil embargo thus reinforced the burgeoning military-industrial complex that eventually undergirded the Botha regime.

The Arms Embargo

Initially, South Africa also appeared vulnerable to an arms embargo, since it relied overwhelming on (largely British) imports. One might therefore anticipate either 'resource denial' or at least the imposition of higher costs as the target is forced into the black market. The regime's strategic response involved the second route, which, like the oil embargo, ironically expanded and entrenched the ruling coalition in the short to medium term.

Following the voluntary UNSC arms embargo in 1963, the government began promoting domestic self-sufficiency. It established an Armaments Production Board in 1964 to manage the supply and regulate the production of weapons. In 1976, anticipating a mandatory embargo, the Armaments Development and Production Corporation (Armscor) was created. Armscor acquired the state's ordinance and munitions factories and several private sector enterprises, and established new production and research and development facilities. It also coordinated and promoted private sector arms firms, setting standards and managing procurement. Black market networks enabled continued access to overseas technology—at a 20 to 100 per cent premium—enabling South African firms to pirate foreign inventions or incorporate them into their own products, some of which became world leading (Manby, 1992: 207). By the 1980s, Armscor provided three quarters of South Africa's arms requirements and had become one of the country's largest corporations, subcontracting to a network of 6,000 private firms employing

135,000 workers (Saul and Gelb, 1986: 142; Evans and Phillips, 1988: 122). Indeed, South Africa had become a major arms *exporter*.

Like the oil embargo, then, arms sanctions reinforced rather than challenged the NP's coalitional strategy. Armscor became an important funnel for government patronage and business opportunities, especially for Afrikaner but also English businesses (Fine and Rustomjee, 1996: 166). Given the conglomeration of South African business, most leading firms were involved, either directly or through subsidiaries. Moreover, corporations were again drawn directly into state apparatuses. Business leaders sat alongside senior generals on the Defence Advisory Council, established in 1973, and alongside military and labour ministry officials on the Defence Manpower Liaison Committee (Evans and Phillips, 1988: 122). Under P. W. Botha, businessmen also served with army officers on cabinet subcommittees and the joint management committees established as part of the National Security Management System, tasked with managing civil unrest (Mann, 1988: 55; Alden, 1998: 73–9). The state's shifting strategic selectivity had political consequences later. According to one minister, these business interests—which thrived under sanctions—pressed officials to decelerate reforms during the 1980s (Durr, 2011).

Moreover, given the context of the 'total onslaught', the embargo further elevated the military's position and deepened the state's criminalization. Reflecting growing unrest and the SSC's ascendancy, defence spending had already risen from 7 to 20 per cent of the government budget from 1959 to 1974 (Schieber, 1976: 35–7). The strategic response to the arms embargo apparently removed any remaining self-restraint. General Magnus Malan, defence minister and chief of the South African Defence Forces (SADF), argued that Armscor had granted South Africa total autonomy, destroying foreign powers' capacity to 'prescribe to or blackmail [us]', 'guarantee[ing] internal political independence and negat[ing] any coercion' (Malan, 2006: 226). The military secured massive secret funding to develop conventional, nuclear, chemical, and biological weapons. Malan (2006: 222) argued that South Africa 'was compelled to go down the path of nuclear armaments because sanctions made it impossible to approach the traditional arms suppliers in the West' to counter the growing 'communist threat'. In the process, bureaucratic and military corruption deepened. Armscor personnel became involved in sanctions busting, paying 'backhanders' to suppliers with Malan's approval (Malan, 2006: 228–9, 237). The chemical and biological weapons programme was run by a particularly 'nepotistic, self-serving and self-enriching group' (TRC, 1998: 520). Headed by a SADF-linked smuggler, it used other sanctions busters to procure and pay for supplies (Gould and Folb, 2002: 48, 66, 183–5, 237). Through these channels, it also imported large quantities of narcotics, allegedly to weaponize for use in crowd control, but more likely for domestic retail (TRC, 1998: 515–6).

In the medium term, then, the oil and arms embargoes expanded and consolidated the apartheid ruling coalition, complementing 'reform apartheid'. This was expressed directly in the 1977 general election, when sanctions helped fuel a 'war psychosis' among whites, generating unprecedented English support for the NP and its biggest electoral victory yet (De Villiers, 1995: 58). This was not, however, a simplistic 'rally round the flag' backlash, as the sanctions literature might suggest. As explained above, part of Vorster's appeal to English-speaking whites was his cautious reform programme, and 1977 also saw the relatively liberal Progressive Party replace the United Party as the official opposition. Thus, sanctions played into, rather than reversing or significantly changing, the overall evolution of South Africa's social conflict. However, in the longer run, these embargoes took a more serious toll.

The Long-Term Consequences

The regime's sanctions-busting projects were costly. Such expenditure was bearable, even beneficial, during the first few post-war decades, when strong domestic growth and the international economic and political environment supported dirigiste economic strategies. However, when these conditions changed in the mid-1970s, these strategies were increasingly seen as a drag on economic growth by big business interests and neoliberal technocrats. Most importantly, resources devoted to sanctions busting could not be utilized to finance the reform apartheid strategy. Some authors also suggest the arms embargo eroded South Africa's military capacities, though this is hotly disputed.

The total cost of evading the oil and arms embargoes, whilst difficult to establish, was undoubtedly high. The most comprehensive estimate for the oil embargo, including the costs of constructing and subsidizing Sasol and related installations, middlemen's premiums, and the opportunity costs of stockpiling, but excluding security measures, sabotage costs, lost coal export earnings, and environmental damage, is US$34.6 billion (Hengeveld and Rodenburg, 1995a: 199). Assessing the cost of the arms embargo is virtually impossible given its inseparability from general defence spending, which was predominantly determined by regional and domestic developments. However, the Truth and Reconciliation Commission found that secret project expenditure and the 'defence special account', used to finance sanctions-busting projects, totalled R52.4 billion (US$15.2 billion). The precise figure is not necessarily important. Sanctions enthusiasts too often quote such figures as evidence that sanctions 'worked', as if imposing costs equates to 'success'. In reality, these colossal costs were willingly borne for several decades until the social, economic, and political context changed.

One key change was the aforementioned structural transformations that generated growing opposition to direct government intervention in the economy. Leading business interests and economic managers increasingly depicted Sasol and Armscor as examples of the 'inefficient' distortions created by political 'interference'. By the early 1980s, Armscor was struggling with rising production costs, partly caused by sanctions, necessitating significant restructuring, and began to be seen as a burden on an already struggling economy (Batchelor, 1998: 111–13). Likewise, by 1987, Finance Minister Barend Du Plessis was denouncing the millions 'squandered on building up the country's strategic reserves of oil' (Hengeveld and Rodenburg, 1995a: 200). The *Financial Mail* criticized further government sanctions-busting plans, involving the construction of liquid natural gas plants (Mossgas), as 'imposing sanctions on ourselves'; such opposition substantially curtailed the project (Lipton, 1990: 22–3). F. W. De Klerk, himself a former energy minister, later described Sasol as a 'very unproductive form of investment that has contributed to the unfavourable course of economic growth and job creation' (Hengeveld and Rodenburg, 1995a: 203). Thus, sanctions busting, once a guarantor of white prosperity and political independence, was increasingly seen as a threat to economic growth and socio-political stability in the straitened circumstances of the 1980s.

However, particularly given the powerful state and business interests bound up in these projects, criticism of Sasol and Armscor's 'inefficiency' would not have generated significant change without the escalation of popular anti-apartheid resistance. The crucial point for understanding how *all* sanctions 'worked' in South Africa during the 1980s is that growing popular demand for economic, social, and political empowerment required resources to ameliorate/and or suppress—resources that were being drained by structural economic decline, the debt crisis, and by sanctions busting. The strategy of reform apartheid required very high levels of spending on both security and welfare improvements to successfully coerce or persuade non-whites to accept neo-apartheid. This was impeded by the costs of sanctions busting. Mossgas, for instance, was projected to cost R11 billion—equal to a decade's worth of expenditure on black housing (Waldmeir, 1998: 119). As Finance Minister Du Plessis (2011) recalls: 'the price of countering sanctions . . . [was] cancelling out our ability to invest politically and socially in our solution to our internal problems . . . we foresaw a revolutionary type of situation developing, where we would not [even] have been able to deal with conflict control . . . Sanctions would diminish that [capacity], and it would undoubtedly result in an eruption.'

Arguably, the regime's earlier response to the oil embargo indirectly contributed to this proto-revolutionary upheaval. Sasol's reliance on domestic coal supplies deepened South Africa's dependence on black mineworkers. Over time, this supported the emergence of the National Union of Mineworkers, which became a vanguard anti-apartheid force in the late 1980s. As Mitchell (2009) documents, historically, coal mining unions—in league with railway workers—have often played a critical role in political struggles and democratization thanks to their capacity to paralyse vital energy supplies. This is untrue in oil-powered economies because oil production is capital- rather than labour-intensive, and oil is more easily transportable. Accordingly, the apartheid regime's sanctions busting contributed to the emergence of its own grave-diggers.

Some authors also argue that the arms embargo directly drained the regime's coercive capacity, but this seems highly dubious. Many assert that it degraded South Africa's technological superiority, costing the SADF air superiority in Angola when confronted by Angolan, Cuban, and Soviet pilots flying cutting-edge MiGs. This is said to have caused South Africa's defeat at Cuito Cuanavale in 1988, devastating the military and strengthening those demanding a peaceful settlement in Namibia and South Africa itself (e.g. Davies, 1989; Commonwealth Secretariat, 1989b: 43; Crawford, 1999a: 63–5). Insofar as South Africa was actually 'defeated', the primary cause of this outcome was not sanctions but the massive Soviet–Cuban intervention in Angola, without which Pretoria would never have been outclassed. However, whether it *was* in fact outclassed is hotly contested. The sanctions literature uncritically adopts the viewpoint of Cuba and the ANC, but entirely ignores the opposite interpretation provided by South African historians and generals (e.g. Steenkamp, 1989; Geldenhuys, 2009). This intensely politicized historiography precludes decisive judgement, but one of the most even-handed surveys suggests both that the SADF were *not* militarily defeated, *and* that the battle's political outcome was, nonetheless, widespread recognition of the need for a settlement (Mills and Williams, 2006: 167–88).

The crucial development was apparently not a single battle, but rather Cuba's escalating intervention, which reinforced the SADF's long-standing view that the Angolan war was not militarily winnable. Cuba had increased its troop strength to 25,000, against Pretoria's 3,000-strong expeditionary force. As the then director-general of South Africa's foreign ministry recalls, this signalled that the conflict had 'escalated to a point where both sides . . . felt that we couldn't go on like this'. The SADF insisted it was undefeated, that 'we gave them a run for our money', but 'Cuito Cuanavale demonstrated to us . . . that we must do whatever else we can to bring the situation under control' (Van Heerden, 2011). More importantly, the SADF never believed that the war could be won militarily. The purpose of South Africa's intervention had always been to manufacture a favourable *political* settlement in Angola and Namibia. Reflecting its counterinsurgency ethos, the SADF consistently told politicians that it was 'not a war we can win; the only way to win and normalise the situation is politically' (Viljoen, 2011). Virtually all of my interviewees then conversant with military officers reported that the SADF's 'formula' for a settlement was 'eighty percent political and twenty percent security', with many soldiers describing their role as 'buying time'. As one minister recalls: 'the military people themselves were yearning, and begging, and screaming for a political solution' (Wessels, 2011). This suggests that emphasizing Cuito Cuanavale as a decisive military defeat is misguided. Its real significance was to signal to Pretoria what it already knew, and this had little to do with sanctions.

Arguably the most important constraint on the war emanated, once again, from inside South African society. The apparent inability of political leaders to create a settlement in Angola and Namibia prompted the SADF to demand more resources simply to hold the line (Du Plessis, 2011). Again, this was impossible to finance alongside the internal requirements of reform apartheid. Botha was forced to cut black welfare spending to meet the SADF's demands, prompting reformist ministers to warn that this 'will cost you dearly in the long run' (Wessels, 2011). The finance minister warned his colleagues: 'we are using virtually all of our concrete [resources] on conflict control, and there is very little to invest in . . . the elimination of the basic reasons for conflict' (Du Plessis, 2011). A lesser, but significant, constraint on the war was growing white resistance, led by the End Conscription Campaign, a member of the UDF. Available data also suggests crumbling white morale. In 1985, 25 to 40 per cent of conscripts failed to report for duty, and from 1985 to 1988 the annual number of attempted suicides within the SADF tripled to 344 (Davis, 1991: 76).

Eventually, these internal developments interfaced with geopolitical changes to enable South Africa's withdrawal from Angola and Namibia. In pursuit of detente with the US, the USSR sharply reduced its involvement in regional conflicts after 1986, including southern Africa, pushing its erstwhile allies into peace talks. Washington also applied growing pressure on South Africa to negotiate. When talks began, the pro-settlement foreign ministry, long sidelined by the military in the SSC, increasingly asserted control over Pretoria's Angolan policy (Van Heerden, 2011). The 1989 peace settlement delivered South Africa's key goals. The Soviets and Cubans withdrew. The Namibian settlement contained safeguards to protect the white minority from persecution or economic expropriation, despite losing political power. This illustrated how negotiations might secure certain white interests in South Africa itself, reinforcing the eventual shift towards talks with the ANC. This outcome was clearly generated by the complex intersection of international and domestic dynamics, with sanctions playing a relatively small role.

To conclude, the oil and arms embargoes initially had counterproductive effects, expanding and consolidating apartheid's ruling coalition rather than

weakening it. Sanctions-busting costs were shouldered as the price of Afrikaner domination and actually complemented the regime's ruling strategy. It
was only amidst the mid-1980s social, political, and economic crises that these
embargoes began directly undermining the regime by limiting the resources
available to finance reform apartheid. Without the popular resistance that
necessitated reform apartheid, these sanctions would simply not have 'worked'
in this way.

Later Sanctions: Disinvestment, Finance, and Trade

In the mid-1980s, South Africa faced a new wave of sanctions. Grass-roots
campaigns, particularly in Britain and the US, successfully pressured multinational firms to disinvest from South Africa. Major trading partners barred
some South African exports from entering their markets and, after most
Western banks withdrew their lines of credit, several governments cemented
this by banning new investments in South Africa. The following sections
explore the impact of these measures.

Disinvestment

Under pressure from anti-apartheid campaigners in their home countries, one
third of foreign companies withdrew from South Africa in the 1980s. However, identifying any immediate distributional costs is difficult because disinvestment was more apparent than real, and the costs were immediately
shaped by struggles between capital and labour. Generally speaking, disinvestment can benefit local capitalists in the short to medium term by allowing
them to acquire departing firms' assets cheaply and increasing the returns to
increasingly scarce capital. Conversely, it might harm local employees of the
departing firms, through job losses or worsening terms and conditions. In the
longer term, however, businesses in the affected sectors are likely to suffer
lower productivity owing to the loss of overseas capital, technology, and
technical expertise. This general pattern is observable in South Africa, except
that organized labour successfully struggled to shift costs onto employers.

Many authors argue that foreign disinvestment from South Africa was more
apparent than real. Despite selling their subsidiaries, multinationals often
conducted business as usual through convoluted ownership arrangements,
product and technology licences, and buy-back agreements (Innes, 1989).
Thus, many concluded that disinvestment had either negligible or negative
consequences for anti-apartheid forces, particularly for workers who now
faced less favourable employment prospects. Conversely, many local subsidiaries were sold cheaply to South African firms or managers, creating a windfall

for local capitalists (Lipton, 1990: 7). Anglo-American's control of shares on the Johannesburg stock exchange, for example, rose to 60 per cent as it acquired Barclays bank and other foreign firms (Innes, 1989: 234).

The real picture seems more complex. To offset domestic pressure, many multinationals had earlier adopted corporate codes of conduct like the Sulli-van Code in the 1970s, agreeing to improve black workers' pay and conditions and to recognize and negotiate with their trade unions. According to Rodman (1994: 330), the new South African owners reversed these concessions and further undermined black unions by cutting jobs to rationalize production. Arguably, however, the very fakery of multinational disinvestment provided leverage for unions. COSATU interpreted multinationals' scams as signalling their reluctance to withdraw from a profitable market, but also their need to distance themselves from the apartheid regime. This created what senior COSATU official Alec Erwin calls 'pullout leverage', which, he recalls, 'dramat-ically increase[d] our bargaining power'. Unions threatened further cam-paigns, to force multinationals to genuinely disinvest, in order to extract concessions from employers. Some firms agreed to minimize redundancies; raise pay; lobby the governments of South Africa and their home states; recognize black unions, helping COSATU to strengthen its 'organisational base'; and place some disinvestment proceeds into a 'massive fund' for work-ers (Erwin, 2011). Another senior trade unionist concurs that unions success-fully imposed 'conditionalities' on multinationals' disguised presence, which helped 'massify [sic] the numbers of those who were already onboard' with COSATU's political demands (Mkhize, 2011).

Although this strategy was not universally successful, overall it did help to fragment the apartheid ruling bloc in ways that strengthened the opposition. Some firms resisted the 'pullout leverage', ignoring strikes and sacking work-ers, particularly in car manufacturing. However, most remaining multination-als became more vocal proponents of reform and more responsive to black demands (Van Heerden, 1990b). A prominent example was Shell, formerly a close government ally in sanctions busting. Shell introduced corporate social responsibility programmes, offered its employees shares, and placed a front-page advertisement with the *Weekly Mail* expressing support for a free press, freedom of assembly and movement, and democratic rights. Ford gave an employees' trust a 24 per cent stake in Samcor, its local subsidiary; the trust nominated two company directors and used its dividends to benefit workers (Joffe, 1989: 62). Reflecting the potential long-term effects of disinvestment, even conglomerates that benefited from disinvestment, like Anglo-American, openly bemoaned the threats it posed to managerial and technological links with the West and to long-term competitiveness (Murray, 1986: 26). COSATU's assistant general-secretary regarded such outcomes as 'an important achieve-ment': 'employers joined our side and said, "we don't want to disinvest but we want this government to know that we don't support its programme of repression" ... they were beginning to take a stance which weakens the resolve of the other side to maintain the status quo ... fragmenting the ruling bloc' (Mufamadi, 2011). Importantly, this included the representatives of South Africa's powerful local conglomerates. Indeed, Erwin argues that 'the real target [of sanctions] was internal capital ... [we wanted] them to break their links with the NP regime ... even ... to get them to [engage in] forms of civil disobedience ... and that worked: it was national capital that began to break ranks' (Erwin, 2011). This is explored later in this section.

Thus, notwithstanding its limited economic consequences, disinvestment had some impact on social conflict. Despite losses, organized labour did not suffer greatly but in some cases gained bargaining power. The unions solidified their organizational bases in the factories, helping them to survive the states of emergency, subsequently re-emerging to assume a vanguard role in the opposition after the UDF's suppression. Disinvestment also indicated to far-sighted businesses that apartheid posed an increasing threat to their interests, encouraging them to demand more significant reform. There was no decisive break: capital did not suddenly defect from the apartheid bloc to the opposition. But disinvestment contributed to a gradual realignment that ultimately helped pave the way for regime change.

Finance and Trade

Financial and trade sanctions on South Africa were also partial and limited. However, when combined with the long-term effects of earlier sanctions and, most importantly, growing popular resistance, they weakened the ruling coalition while strengthening opposition forces, in three ways. They generated struggles within the state over the appropriate strategic response, which strengthened pro-reform elements; they undermined the reform apartheid strategy; and they hastened the ruling coalition's fragmentation as key elements of big business further distanced themselves from the regime.

We must distinguish financial sanctions from private companies' market-based investment decisions, which were taken independently of sanctions. The two are typically, and misleadingly, conflated as 'banking sanctions'. As discussed above, South Africa's mid-1980s financial crisis was caused by structural contradictions arising from its historical development, not by sanctions. South Africa had become dependent on overseas borrowing, and mounting unrest made its loans costlier and shorter-term. Accordingly, as Figure 2.1 shows, investment was already declining well before 1985. In 1984, Citibank lamented that 'South Africa's external finances are in total chaos' because the Reserve Bank was paying 'no regard whatsoever ... to the maturity structure of the debt' (Hirsch, 1989: 273). The clustering of repayment dates around

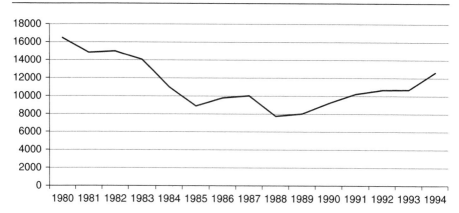

Figure 2.1 South Africa's foreign direct investment stock (US$ millions, current exchange rates)

Source: UNCTAD (2012)

August 1985 was risky because, if just one bank would not renew their loan, this could compromise South Africa's ability to repay the rest. Investment risk was also exacerbated by township unrest, which had triggered massive capital flight in 1960 and 1976, and investors and ratings agencies began downgrading South Africa's creditworthiness in response to the UDF's anti-parliament protests. Subsequently, the rand depreciated by a third from June 1984 to June 1985; there was substantial capital flight in late 1984; and one British bank recalled its loans in early 1985 (Commonwealth Secretariat, 1989a: 44–8). The rand's collapse exacerbated the problem by vastly increasing the cost of servicing South Africa's dollar-denominated debt. This all occurred before Botha's state of emergency prompted Chase Manhattan to refuse to roll over its loans in July 1985, prompting Western banks to recall their loans en masse—let alone before any actual sanctions. It was thus a set of commercial decisions, responding to South Africa's internal situation, not sanctions, that triggered the debt crisis and its economic effects.

Governmental sanctions contributed only indirectly and marginally by influencing investors' risk assessments. Because the IMF had been barred from providing bridging loans to South Africa in 1983, banks could not anticipate IMF-led restructuring of debt repayments in the event of a default. Shortly before Chase Manhattan's decision, France also restricted new investments in South Africa, increasing the climate of uncertainty. Nonetheless, as banks stated publicly, they reacted to safeguard their capital, not to promote political change (De Villiers, 1995: 86; Bethlehem, 1988: 73). Indeed, with their home country governments, they dismissed calls from anti-apartheid leaders like Desmond Tutu to seize South Africa's overseas assets or exploit their leverage to promote democratic change. Instead, Pretoria encouraged

Western concern that it might entirely renounce its debt to negotiate a favourable repayment schedule (Harris, 1986).

Virtually all governmental embargoes on new investment were imposed only *after* these events. Since private investors had already fled and were unlikely to reinvest anyway, identifying any effect from these sanctions is difficult. They mainly underscored that resumed access to international capital now depended upon a political settlement. This was important insofar as it undermined the regime's previous strategy—used in 1960 and 1976—of restoring order by force then luring investors back. Arguably this strengthened reformist forces, as we shall see.

The subsequent trade embargoes were obviously politically motivated sanctions. However, their modest scope excluded most South African exports. The targeted sectors—notably iron, steel, coal, uranium, and fruit—took non-trivial hits, harming conglomerates' interests in mining and agriculture. In 1987, for example, iron and steel exports fell 27 per cent, while coal exports fell by three million tons from 1985 to 1987, despite a market discount of US$5 per ton, costing the industry R900 million (Lipton, 1990: 16; Commonwealth Secretariat, 1989b: 51–2, 78). Ironically, however, because the rand's value had collapsed, South African exports actually became more competitive. Consequently, its exports volumes actually increased by 26 per cent from 1985 to 1989, generating substantial trade *surpluses* (Lipton, 1990: 14).

Although the rand's collapse complicates identifying their overall costs, sanctions clearly did not bring the economy to its knees. Examining South Africa's trade figures in dollars is a harsh measure because, since the rand depreciated by 70 per cent from 1980 to 1990, even a doubling of trade in rand terms would register as an overall decrease when converted to dollars. Nonetheless, as Figure 2.2 shows, even when denominated in dollars at contemporary exchange rates, South Africa's trade *increased*, and its trade surplus—crucial for repaying its foreign debt—doubled from 1984 to 1994. This remarkable performance was achieved by discounting, dumping, redirecting some trade from Western markets towards Africa and East Asia, and concealing the origins of South African goods. Overall, having contracted by 32 per cent from 1983 to 1985, the economy actually experienced *stronger* growth under sanctions than beforehand, with GDP increasing by 60 per cent from 1983 to 1994.

However, presenting the data like this does not account for inflation, which ran at 12–16 per cent during this period (UNCTAD, 2012). Presented in rand, and adjusted for inflation, South Africa's GDP stagnated for longer in the mid-1980s and re-entered recession from 1989 to 1992 (see Figure 2.3). Nonetheless, although this reveals that South Africa's economic growth was more stuttering than Figure 2.2 suggests, it still expanded dramatically in real

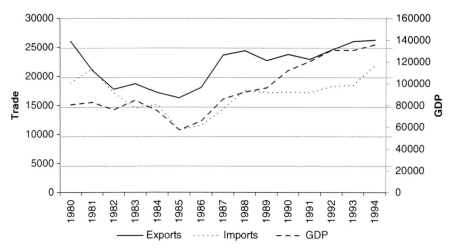

Figure 2.2 South African trade and GDP (US$ millions, current exchange rates)
Source: UNCTAD (2012)

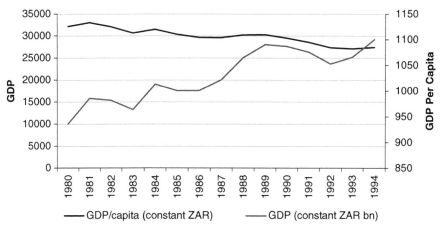

Figure 2.3 South Africa's GDP and GDP per capita (constant South African Rand, base year 2013)
Source: Economy Watch (2013)

terms over the decade. Again, this suggests that the impact of sanctions is not best sought in their relatively modest economic costs, but rather in terms of their impact on socio-political conflict. Hence, the crucial point to note here—explored further below—is that, despite substantial growth in overall GDP, rapid demographic expansion nonetheless caused real incomes per capita to shrink.

Impact on Social Conflict

Combined, these sanctions impacted South Africa's ruling coalition in three main ways. *First*, it triggered a struggle within the apartheid bloc over the appropriate strategic response that sharpened *verkrampte/verligte* divisions and reinforced the ascendancy of reformist technocrats and big business.

Anti-reform forces, led politically by the Conservative Party, advocated a 'siege economy', urging the government to renounce its debts, promote self-sufficiency through 'inward industrialization' (ISI), and ignore international pressure. Some domestically oriented businesses hoping for an 'autarky boom' supported this (Starnberger Institute, 1989: 30; Hayes, 1987: 28–9). So did some military officials, who proposed attacking neighbouring states that supported sanctions and the ANC, and revising regional trade agreements to benefit South Africa (Durr, 2011). These forces were initially succoured by P. W. Botha's infamous August 1985 'Rubicon' speech which, despite promising significant reforms, was so defiantly expressed that it prompted widespread capital flight.

Pro-reform forces—particularly large-scale, internationally oriented capital and the economic technocracy—opposed the 'siege economy' strategy, warning it would only deepen South Africa's crisis. Anglo-American's chief executive, Gavin Relly, cautioned that industrialization required 'deregulation'; a 'siege economy' approach would cause South Africa to

> revert to a stumbling rural economy ... South Africa can't live in a vacuum ... In the short run, one can create a totally artificial environment which can give the semblance of a boom. But the dangers of isolation are long-run ... A country which falls radically behind in modern technology, in human thinking and ingenuity is simply going to become a slum ... [black] political frustration will ... be constantly erupting ... In that sort of scenario, you can't have change peacefully, you can only have it by revolution (Murray, 1986: 24–6).

Many Afrikaner capitalists concurred. One leading businessman insisted that 'the South African economy needs links with the rest of the world. There is a limit to the amount of capital the country can generate internally to finance growth' (Innes, 1989: 238). The chairman of Standard Bank Investment Corporation stated that 'in this day and age there is no such thing as economic self-sufficiency ... South Africa needs the world. It needs markets. It needs skills. It needs technology and above all it needs capital ... It is imperative that we do not adopt poses of defiance and bluster' (Davis, 1991: 78). The foreign missions of business organizations like ASSOCOM and the South Africa Foundation served as transmission belts for international pressure, warning the government not to trigger further sanctions (Van Heerden, 1990a: 201; Hirsch, 1989: 278–9).

These views were shared by reformist technocrats in the economic and foreign affairs ministries, producing a split among state agencies, which illustrates the unhelpfulness of monolithic understandings of states or regimes. The head of the Development Bank warned that any retreat to a 'siege economy' would 'impair South Africa's long-term development'. Successful industrialization required access to regional markets, not the destabilization of neighbouring states (Davies, 1989: 202). Similarly, the Reserve Bank governor, Gerhard De Kock, argued that since 80 per cent of South Africa's imports were non-substitutable capital and intermediate goods, a siege economy was impractical (Stoneman, 1990: 185). With Finance Minister Du Plessis, De Kock exploited the crisis to accelerate structural adjustment towards export-oriented industrialization, a long-standing goal, in line with neoliberal programmes being imposed elsewhere in Africa by the IMF (Lipton, 1990: 31). The foreign ministry also replicated business organizations' role in serving as a transmission belt for international pressure, 'bring[ing] international realism to the debate' by warning of the 'international consequences' of any violent response to sanctions (Van Heerden, 2011).

The pro-reform coalition's preferences largely became government strategy, reflecting its ascendancy and access to state power in the era of reform apartheid. Botha's January 1986 'Rubicon II' speech announced reforms to placate external creditors, prioritizing debt repayment to recover access to international capital markets. To amass the large annual trade surpluses required to finance debt repayments, exports would be promoted. The government also accelerated the deregulation and privatization of state assets. Business leaders were invited to a major conference in November 1986 to discuss the draft economic strategy, and joined the Private Sector Export Advisory Committee to help implement it. A cabinet subcommittee on sanctions was also established. Chaired by the neoliberal, Anglophone deputy finance minister, Kent Durr, who was close to leading business magnates, this was the main body in which the impact of sanctions was evaluated and policy responses developed. Defence and foreign affairs officials were included but, unlike SSC committees, which the military dominated, economic technocrats successfully struggled for primacy. Durr and his officials had 'to fight off the security establishment' who 'wanted to take retaliatory action, and we would have to explain ... [why] they couldn't' (Durr, 2011).

Reformist influence over the state's response to sanctions ultimately strengthened demands for *political* change, which reformists saw as the only long-term solution to the crisis. The sanctions committee's assessment was that while they could be evaded in the short term, 'in the longer term, sanctions would ... become a major economic problem', with investment and trade restrictions producing economic stagnation and an 'ungovernable country' (Krogh, 2011). Sanctions busting was just 'a holding operation';

ultimately a 'political answer' to South Africa's crisis was imperative (Durr, 2011). This view was echoed by the president's Economic Analysis Unit, which argued that 'we can't go on forever—we always said... "we buy time"... something will have to be done in the political sphere so as to come to an agreement [with opposition forces]' (Mullins, 2011). Big business argued similarly. Anglo-American's 1986 chairman's statement essentially echoed the UDF's demands, calling for the unbanning of political parties, the freeing of political prisoners, the repeal of apartheid laws, and the negotiation of a new democratic constitution (Pallister et al., 1987: 212). In January 1986, the FCI issued its *Business Charter of Social, Economic and Political Rights*, the most ambitious and liberal proposals yet issued by business elites. This was later endorsed by associations representing three quarters of South African employers, including the Afrikaanse Handelinstituut.

Sanctions' *second* major impact was to constrain the resources available to finance 'reform apartheid', thereby aiding its defeat. To amass funds to repay its creditors, South Africa required a considerable balance of payments surplus. However, given the economy's reliance on capital goods imports, boosting growth and exports also increased imports, risking a balance of payments deficit. Consequently, whenever GDP growth exceeded about 2.5 per cent, deflationary measures were required to maintain the surplus, which subsequently depressed economic growth. This 'growth ceiling' constrained government revenues, which were urgently required to finance reform apartheid's coercive and welfare measures. Sanctions did not cause this problem, but did exacerbate it. Sanctions busting increased import costs and reduced export revenues for the same volume of economic activity; directed scarce funds towards the oil and arms industries; and hampered new borrowing to repay existing debts. Finance Minister Du Plessis (1991) estimated that 'financial sanctions' prevented the government spending R6 billion on urban improvements in 1991 alone.

A critical by-product of the growth ceiling, and of sanctions more generally, was increased black unemployment. By the mid-1980s, black demographic expansion was such that annual GDP growth of 4.5 per cent was thought necessary merely to prevent black unemployment rising beyond an already dangerous level, estimated at between 1.8 and 3 million (Starnberger Institute, 1989: 18–19; Meth, 1989: 245). Sanctions only exacerbated unemployment, with ASSOCOM and FCI estimating potential job losses at 200,000 to 1.4 million over five years (Meth, 1989: 247–51), and real incomes continuing to fall (see Figure 2.3). While this would obviously frustrate the reform apartheid goal of co-opting blacks through offering them socio-economic advancement, it also harmed blacks themselves—a point stressed by anti-sanctions Western and South African politicians and businessmen.

This had a real potential to divide opposition forces. On the one hand, sanctions appealed to anti-apartheid forces eager to avoid a violent resolution of the conflict, like religious organizations. Sanctions were easier for churches and other NGOs to support than armed struggle, allowing them to join and support the UDF (Boesak, 2011). However, South Africa's 'moderate' black forces, which self-identified as anti-apartheid but which Botha hoped to co-opt, were typically anti-sanctions. Black councils denounced sanctions for encouraging revolutionary violence against them (Hanlon and Omond, 1987: 39). Chief Mangosuthu Buthelezi, ruler of the KwaZulu Natal 'home-land', and the ANC's most prominent conservative rival for black leadership, was also opposed. Buthelezi, his political front, Inkatha, and its allied trade unions all argued that sanctions would only harm blacks and strengthen white conservatives (Hanlon and Omond, 1987: 42–3). While ANC–Inkatha relations were never easy, this disagreement over sanctions (and armed struggle) 'heightened tensions', precipitating a 'breakdown of relations, which … led to the escalation of black-on-black violence that followed in the [late] 1980s' (Zondi, 2011). As subsequent chapters show, this divisive effect of sanctions is not unique to this case.

Ultimately, however, ANC/UDF-aligned opposition forces were sufficiently united and organized to overcome this non-white dissent and any short-term welfare losses. The crucial political dimension here was somewhat lost in the 1980s sanctions debate. To counter anti-sanctions criticism, ANC supporters typically downplayed estimates of job losses, or produced opinion polls showing black support for sanctions, which reduced the debate to one about data-gathering methodology (see Orkin, 1989b). From a strategic perspective, the important question is not 'will unemployment rise?', but 'what impact will this have on the forces contesting state power, and prospects of political change?' These questions cannot be answered in abstraction. There is nothing intrinsic about unemployment that drives people to revolt against a government; passive resignation is an equally plausible response (as subsequent chapters illustrate). Two crucial characteristics of the South African context, however, meant that black unemployment would support, not constrain, political change.

First, by the 1980s, the non-white masses had been extensively politicized and radicalized by decades of grass-roots mobilization. They largely blamed the apartheid regime for their poverty and would also blame it if their circumstances worsened. More importantly, sufficient numbers now believed that economic advancement was not a substitute for, and actually depended upon, their political liberation, for which many were prepared to endure short-term economic sacrifices. This was not a given, but emerged from years of political struggle and ideological development: the Black Consciousness leader Steve Biko, for example, had originally encouraged investment to support black economic empowerment (Hanlon and Omond, 1987: 28–31). Secondly, the non-white masses—including the unemployed—had now built organizations able to politically channel popular anger and withstand state repression. Jobless youths were a huge component of the UDF groups that rendered the townships ungovernable in 1985–6, while COSATU had organized an unemployed workers' union. Although the 1985–8 states of emergency severely weakened the UDF, the unions survived because the government dared not risk crippling the economy by attacking them. Indeed, despite the economic crisis and rising layoffs, labour militancy actually *rose* to unprecedented levels. From 1986–7, workers won average pay increases of 18 per cent and the days lost to strike action increased from 1.1 million to over 9 million (Bethlehem, 1988: 303, 305). This active struggle, stemming from decades of political organization, prevented sanctions merely impoverishing and demobilizing the masses.

Crucially, this struggle caught the apartheid regime in an inescapable dilemma. Without the debt crisis and sanctions, perhaps it could have financed sufficient repression and welfare spending to quell the unrest. Alternatively, without popular rebellion, this spending would have been unnecessary, enabling resources to be devoted to debt repayment and economic restructuring. But the regime could not manage both crises simultaneously. The only foreseeable trajectory was escalating social conflict. This is why P. W. Botha condemned sanctioners for 'encourag[ing] . . . militant revolutionaries in South Africa to continue with their violence and intimidation' (Bethlehem, 1988: 72). As Finance Minister Du Plessis recalls, 'unless you were able to get the economy to grow at least as much as the number of entrants into the job market every year, you were sitting on a time bomb . . . that would have been ticking louder and louder all the time' (Du Plessis, 2011). Another cabinet minister concurred that without rapid growth 'we've got no hope because then the whole atmosphere will be conducive of revolutions' (Delport, 1991). And indeed, as Figure 2.3 shows, despite an impressive performance, apartheid South Africa could simply not generate sufficient growth to prevent real incomes falling. This was reflected in widespread despair among whites by the late 1980s, revealed in opinion polls (Manzo and McGowan, 1992). As De Klerk later commented, sanctions helped make 'people realise we were in a dead-end street' (Waldmeir, 1998: 119). This partly reflected a perception that sanctions would only escalate over time, fuelled particularly by constant agitation in the US Congress. Whites increasingly realized that 'reform apartheid' was failing, and a more radical solution was required. As the managing director of the Trust Bank of Africa stated in 1988:

South Africa simply cannot accept . . . [economic growth] of only 2.5 percent per annum . . . [This would create] abject poverty, rising social violence, increasing political instability and inevitable economic ruin . . . The tide of growing isolation must be turned in the interest of all South Africans. An important step in this direction will be the achievement of a legitimate consensus between white and black leaders. A dramatic breakthrough is required (Davis, 1991: 77–8).

The *third*, related, impact of sanctions on South Africa's ruling coalition was that it stimulated big business to pursue such 'breakthroughs', distancing it from the NP regime. Business had feebly attempted this after Sharpeville and Soweto, reflecting their evolving interests. As before, there was no decisive or immediate break. According to one minister, while many businesses urged faster reform, some businesses continued to benefit from apartheid and complained that reform was too fast (Durr, 2011). Moreover, even business leaders who, in the Anglo-American chairman's evocative phrase, wanted 'apartheid to be expelled from the bowels of our country' were cautious (Murray, 1986: 24). South Africa's opposition was widely seen as 'communist' due to the ANC's relationship with the SACP and Moscow, and Freedom Charter's demands for democratic economic management and wealth redistribution. Township violence also profoundly alarmed many whites, as UDF and ANC supporters turned on regime 'collaborators' like local black councillors and fought Chief Buthelezi's Inkatha movement. Thus, while far-sighted business leaders increasingly felt that the existing order could not hold, they feared what might replace it.

These limitations led some analysts to suggest that sanctions and the political backlash they generated were counterproductive, reducing 'business activism' and forcing business and the state closer together for sanctions-busting activities (Adam and Moodley, 1993: 57; van Wyck, 1988: 84–5; Lipton, 1990: 35–6). Rowe's (2001) neo-Weberian study of Rhodesia similarly suggests that states become more dominant during sanctions busting, subordinating business interests. However, while this may have characterized South Africa's earlier sanctions busting, the reformist coalition that had since captured the state ensured that 1980s sanctions busting largely reflected their deregulatory preferences. The government was largely confined to rubber-stamping corporate plans to, for example, establish front companies abroad or mislabel or mix goods to conceal their origin. The state's role in sanctions busting actually decreased: subsidies and tax relief for companies stockpiling spare parts, for example, were scrapped as part of general economic deregulation (Durr, 2011). This suited big business. As one senior Anglo-American executive (2011) recalls, when sanctions busting, 'the last person you want[ed] to have any close association with [was] the people that [were] being punished'. As noted earlier, business elites condemned any dirigiste sanctions-busting projects, like Mossgas, as wasteful government interventions in the economy. Accordingly, sanctions busting did not restore the earlier cosiness between the Botha government and big business. Although there was no 'neat break', business instead began 'to read the future...to gradually distance itself, reading the wind, and...to begin to align itself with the future' (Maharaj, 2011).

This distancing involved three interrelated types of activity. First, business elites lobbied the NP government to accelerate reform. As noted above, business leaders and associations issued public calls for political liberalization to reduce economic pressure on South Africa. Although these public demands withered under the state of emergency and with P. W. Botha's often dismissive responses, business leaders continued urging reform privately. Afrikaner capitalists typically enjoyed better access to NP politicians through shared cultural and social networks. Figures like Anton Rupert of Rembrandt and Fred Du Plessis of Sanlam used this access to demand faster political change (Durr, 2011; Fourie, 2011). However, Botha's courting of big business had also created greater access for English businessmen, through fundraising events, for instance, where they also conveyed pro-reform messages to ministers (Fourie, 2011). Moreover, according to prominent English businessman David Brink (2011), 'sanctions created an environment whereby government had to start listening to business . . . [particularly] English speaking businessmen'. Forming a group called 'There Must Be a Better Way', he sent a delegation to urge P. W. Botha to release Nelson Mandela and accelerate reforms in 1987.

These pressures arguably helped keep reform afloat despite the brutal crackdown and severe political challenges to the NP. During the June 1986–December 1988 national state of emergency, enormous police and military coercion was used to restore order in the townships, with UDF groups banned and tens of thousands of activists imprisoned. Simultaneously, however, efforts continued to improve urban living conditions and remove some apartheid strictures. In 1985, miscegenation was legalized. In August 1986, the NP's federal congress resolved to adopt a single citizenship and a universal franchise for all South Africans and create a means for black participation in government. Botha apparently envisioned a loose confederal system wherein each racial group would continue to govern their 'own affairs', with mixed-race democratic institutions governing 'general affairs'. This would involve black leaders joining a multiracial 'national council', and potentially the establishment of a fourth, black, parliamentary chamber.

Botha's inability to break from the basic contours of reform apartheid, despite its obvious failure to secure long-term capitalist social order, let alone white domination, ultimately produced his demise. His difficulty stemmed partly from fear of a white backlash: the Conservative Party's share of the vote had increased from 17 per cent to 29 per cent from 1981 to 1987, displacing the liberal PFP as South Africa's official opposition (Lipton, 1990: 38). But in 1988, reform apartheid halted entirely as 'moderate' black leaders' refused to join the national council and Indian parliamentarians refused to enact further reform measures until apartheid legislation was repealed. Business leaders increasingly realized that Botha's removal was required to restore sociopolitical stability. Anglophone capitalists approached the *verligte* finance minister,

Barend Du Plessis, offering to bankroll a campaign 'to try to make [him] state president, when P. W. [Botha] goes, or in order to get him to go' (Du Plessis, 2011). Following a cabinet revolt in February 1989, which compelled Botha to relinquish the NP leadership, Du Plessis ran to succeed him, losing only narrowly to F. W. De Klerk. Later that year, some Afrikaner business interests also claimed to have 'tied their contributions to the NP's election fund specifically to a speeding up of reform and increased efforts at negotiation', even insisting 'that their contributions be paid in instalments over the next year as progress was made' (Lipton, 1990: 36). Business thus intervened directly to reinforce the NP's increasingly dominant *verligte* elements, even in the face of mounting parliamentary resistance.

The second form of business activism involved reaching out to opposition forces, which accelerated as Botha's inability to win black acquiescence for reform apartheid became evident. In September 1985, Anglo-American led a business delegation to meet ANC leaders, despite ferocious government criticism. This 'trek to Lusaka' legitimized contact between the white establishment and the liberation movement, and various civil society organizations launched a dozen similar expeditions. Meanwhile, Consolidated Goldfields, a British firm with mining interests in South Africa, initiated secret talks between the ANC and Afrikaner intellectuals at Mells Park in Britain. The apartheid intelligence service used these to establish indirect communications with the liberation movement, supplementing secret discussions being held with Nelson Mandela. Eventually, the Mells Park talks included F. W. De Klerk's brother, providing a direct line to the presidency after De Klerk succeeded Botha in August 1989 (Harvey, 2001). These discussions became an important channel to explore a possible peace settlement.

These talks were mirrored by domestic business initiatives to court opposition activists. The 'trek to Lusaka' persuaded Anglo-American's chairman that ANC leaders were not die-hard adherents of 'crummy Marxism', but only 'want[ed] to flatten the pyramid a little . . . they were people who can be talked to' (Pallister et al., 1987: 196–7). South African capitalists began realizing that their economic interests might not be threatened by an ANC-led government, particularly as Soviet backing for the ANC waned after 1986. To explore this possibility, the Consultative Business Movement (CBM) was formed in mid-1988. The CBM organized 'encounters' between business leaders and members of the UDF, the ANC, trade unions, the PAC, Inkatha, and others, to identify their respective positions and concerns and to promote dialogue about the future. These discussions later broadened to include senior state officials and NP ministers, including reformist politicians like Roelf Meyer, Leon Wessels, and even F. W. De Klerk. They provided opportunities for business leaders to divide reformist opposition activists from their radical brethren, to encourage 'moderation' and 'develop a sense of realism in the opposition circles' (Evans, 2011).

Business leaders gradually accepted that a deal was possible with these supposed 'communists': 'they were actually Christian, peace-loving South Africans who wanted non-racialism, who wanted whites to play a role, who wanted a prosperous economy, and believed in market mechanisms' (Coleman, 2011). CBM participants 'spread the gospel' to their networks, spawning similar initiatives (Brink, 2011), and prompting much collective and individual lobbying of the government for change. Particularly important was the recruitment of Afrikaner businessmen like Marinus Darling of Sanlam who 'became messengers for [the CBM]', telling NP leaders 'we've got to start talking [to the opposition] and here are some honest brokers who can really do this job' (Leading South African Businessman, 2011). Eventually, the CBM became the secretariat of the Convention for a Democratic South Africa (CODESA), the negotiating forum for a new democratic constitution, which was thus quite literally brokered in a space created by capital.

The third set of business initiatives comprised interventions in civil society to create an ideological climate favourable to change. Reformist businessmen made public statements supporting political reforms, sometimes attracting death threats in response. In meetings of the Broederbond—the highly influential Afrikaner cultural organization, which included many NP politicians— businessmen urged their compatriots to recognize that, 'in the long run, there's no way we can survive the economic sanctions', and to embrace political change (Delport, 2011). In June 1986, the American Chamber of Commerce in South Africa distributed a document entitled *Civil Disobedience*, produced by Desmond Tutu's Get Ahead Foundation, which advised people on how to defy apartheid laws. It suggested that blacks should move into white areas and pledged legal assistance if difficulties arose. General Motors also pledged legal and financial assistance to employees wishing to violate the laws banning them from 'white' beaches in Port Elizabeth (De Villiers, 1995: 135). The Urban Foundation, despite its central role in reform apartheid, also launched a campaign against the pass laws. Perhaps the most influential initiative was Clem Sunter's 'scenario planning' exercise, financed by Anglo-American. This engaged a cross-section of South African society to identify potential future scenarios, which were then presented to hundreds of audiences nationwide. They popularized the notion of a 'high road' of negotiations—leading to sanctions being lifted, rapid economic growth, deregulation, and social peace—and the 'low road' of no negotiations—leading to escalating sanctions, economic stagnation, civil unrest, and eventually a 'wasteland' (Sunter, 1987). These presentations shaped public debate and government thinking. In 1986–7, for example, the deputy minister of police invited Sunter to speak to 'the top hierarchy of the police', recalling that 'very few' were not 'persuaded of what could happen if we don't start the process of change . . . it was certainly an important factor in people's minds' (Meyer, 2011).

These initiatives were not solely prompted by sanctions, nor did they suffice to terminate apartheid. Business leaders were responding to a growing range of threats to their interests, the most significant being the growing risk of revolutionary, non-white violence. However, sanctions arguably heightened capitalists' sense of 'urgency' (Leading South African Businessman, 2011; Evans, 2011). Business did not bring down the apartheid state; it had no interest in doing so. But its less myopic elements clearly did promote change, distancing themselves from the regime, realigning themselves towards the opposition, and groping towards an alternative political settlement—as the ANC had long hoped for.

In summary, given the crucial context of structural economic crisis and growing anti-apartheid resistance, the sanctions imposed on South Africa in the 1980s had important consequences for the forces contesting state power. On the opposition side, they increased the trade unions' leverage and helped them survive the state of emergency intact. They also accelerated the fragmentation of the socio-political bloc underpinning the apartheid regime, intensifying *verligte/verkrampte* divisions and boosting reformists. Sanctions constrained the resources available to finance the regime's strategy of reform apartheid, making a more fundamental transformation increasingly necessary and likely. As reform apartheid stalled, sanctions encouraged business to begin leaving the apartheid coalition and support a negotiated solution.

Conclusion

In February 1990, President F. W. De Klerk unbanned the ANC and SACP and pledged to repeal all apartheid legislation and negotiate a new, democratic constitution with opposition forces. As this chapter shows, the reasons behind this apparently sudden decision were complex and long-term, stemming from transformations in Afrikaner society, the contradictions between apartheid and economic growth, Soviet withdrawal from Africa, and, above all else, escalating popular resistance. Sanctions did *not* force a 'previously immovable and inflexible' system to move. They intervened into a society that was in constant motion; indeed, had it not been evolving, sanctions would not have 'worked' as they did. While early anti-apartheid sanctions largely consolidated the socio-political bloc underpinning it, with changed socio-political and economic conditions from the mid-1970s, they began contributing to its fragmentation, and rendering neo-apartheid solutions increasingly unfeasible. Ultimately, De Klerk (2004) was probably right that 'the government would have been able to maintain control of the country for at least [another] ten or twenty years'. By then, however, South Africa would have been in ruins: white domination could only have been maintained by destroying the wealth and security it was designed to protect. Accordingly, De Klerk sought to preserve as much white power and privilege as possible through negotiations, seizing the opportunity of a post-Cold War climate where the 'Washington consensus' would reinforce pressures towards a free-market, democratic settlement.

Following the unbanning of the ANC, sanctions played an increasingly minimal role. Despite the ANC insisting on maintaining sanctions in case the NP reneged, the most significant measures were all lifted during 1991, before formal negotiations began. Western states instead responded to De Klerk's call for South Africa to be 'rewarded' for steps towards democracy. Perhaps this modestly helped the NP to muster white support for CODESA. But the major impetus was the collective desire to avoid escalating social unrest or even civil war. By the time CODESA convened in December 1991, sanctions were no longer a major issue: the parties were overwhelmingly focused on maximizing their position in the emerging dispensation. Interviewees from all sides reported that sanctions did not affect the proceedings. External powers sought to influence the talks in other ways, particularly encouraging the ANC to protect private property and avoid widespread nationalization.

Sanctions' role in South Africa was thus highly contingent upon local dynamics. They had very different effects over time, reflecting profound changes in the target state's social, political, and economic context. Three in particular stand out: the emergence of cross-communal, anti-dirigiste, large-scale business interests; the rise of sustained popular resistance to apartheid; and the mid-1980s economic crisis.

Without the first element, sanctions tended to broaden and consolidate the ruling coalition by providing lucrative business opportunities that tied the state and business closer together. Had the sanctions of the 1980s been imposed in the 1960s, this dynamic would arguably have been reinforced. However, when increasingly powerful conglomerates—especially Afrikaner business groups—had outgrown state patronage, become more internationally oriented, and begun chafing against the dirigiste restrictions of apartheid, sanctions were more threatening to capitalist interests, spurring them towards political alternatives.

Without popular resistance, though, the need to seek these alternatives would simply not have existed. Unrest in 1960 and 1976 was swiftly repressed, and capitalists—whatever their qualms—supported the government in restoring social order and quickly resumed business as usual. Only when coercion faltered amidst sustained, countrywide unrest from 1984 onwards did apartheid appear unsustainable. Moreover, popular mobilization powerfully shaped the effects of sanctions by making it impossible for the regime to simply displace their effects onto the oppressed majority, since doing so would only fuel unrest, undermining reform apartheid. Had the non-white masses been disorganized and passive, reform apartheid might have successfully co-opted the emerging black middle class and homeland leaders into Botha's neo-apartheid structures. That they were not is testament to decades of grass-roots organizing and mobilization.

Finally, without South Africa's structural economic crisis from the mid-1970s, sanctions would also have had very different results. During apartheid's boom decades, sanctions were endured as the price of Afrikaner advancement. By the 1980s, much of this advancement had been achieved, and the costs of sanctions busting were increasingly seen as threatening Afrikaner prosperity and security. Moreover, sanctions only exacerbated the mid-1980s debt crisis; it did not caused it. The crisis created temporally unique vulnerabilities, without which modest Western sanctions would arguably have had negligible effects.

Thus, although South Africa is frequently touted as the ultimate success story of sanctions and used to justify their imposition elsewhere, their contribution to ending apartheid was actually rather modest and ultimately determined by contextual factors, which should caution us against extrapolating from one case to others. Their effects were not determined by the attributes of the measures themselves, like their scope, intensity, or degree of enforcement. Indeed, the data show that their economic impact was modest. Their effects were instead determined by the socio-political environment into which they intervened, which was in turn part of an evolving economic and geopolitical context. They 'worked' insofar as they reinforced pressures for change emanating principally from within South African society itself. Where target states lack these pressures, we cannot expect even identical sanctions to yield the same outcomes.

3

Myanmar

Sanctioning Military Rule

The apparent success of sanctions against South Africa fuelled a dramatic upsurge in their use in the 1990s. Prominent among the new targets was Myanmar (Burma).[1] In 1988, the sclerotic Burmese Socialist Programme Party (BSPP) regime collapsed amidst widespread popular protests, precipitating a bloody military coup. Although relatively free elections were held in 1990, the junta refused to transfer power to the winners, the National League for Democracy (NLD). Instead, it remained in control, suppressing the opposition and jailing NLD leader Aung San Suu Kyi. Western campaigners subsequently depicted Myanmar as 'the South Africa of the 1990s', presenting the NLD as the new ANC, casting Suu Kyi in the role of Nelson Mandela, and launching campaigns modelled explicitly on the anti-apartheid movement (Free Burma Coalition, 1997). Veteran campaigners like Archbishop Desmond Tutu urged the world to 'do for Burma what it did for South Africa', whilst advocates like US Senator Mitch McConnell claimed that 'sanctions worked in South Africa and they will in Burma too' (Pedersen, 2008: 49–50, 33). Many sanctions followed, including an arms embargo, trade and investment restrictions, and targeted sanctions against regime officials and businessmen. In 2010, Myanmar held its first elections since 1990. During 2011–12, the new administration embarked on political and economic reforms and the NLD comprehensively won by-elections which saw Aung San Suu Kyi elected to parliament. Many Western leaders now ascribe these events, in part, to sanctions (e.g. US Embassy, 2009a; Liddington, 2012). Suu Kyi also claims that Myanmar's experience shows 'sanctions work' (*New York Times*, 2012). One scholar also claims that 'sanctions played a key role in paving the way for the

---

[1] I use 'Burma' to refer to the country before 1989, and 'Myanmar' thereafter, as the state's official name was changed.

[transition] ... The ruling class, after twenty years of isolation ... realised that they would be in a better position by opening the country to foreign investments and trade' (Giumelli, 2013a: 31).[2]

How far did sanctions actually undermine military rule? Contrary to these rosy assessments, before 2010 most Myanmar experts argued that sanctions had a negligible impact. They maintained that only the people, not the regime, suffered, and that sanctions only stiffened the generals' resistance (e.g. Badgley, 2004; Pedersen, 2008). This chapter advances a more nuanced argument. By damaging and retarding Myanmar's economy, sanctions undoubtedly hampered the military regime's transition strategy, within which economic development was very important. Sanctions constrained the regime's capacity to co-opt opponents, broaden its support base, and cultivate consent for its preferred political order. Sanctions also encouraged the opposition to resist, helping it to thwart the regime's transition strategy in the 1990s. Yet they did not empower opposition forces—which lacked a compelling strategy for seizing power—to widen its coalition or displace the junta. Thus, sanctions ultimately prolonged a fruitless political stalemate. Ultimately, moreover, the balance of power shifted towards the regime, enabling it to impose its preferred settlement. Sanctions therefore only delayed the eventual outcome and needlessly delayed Myanmar's transition from direct military rule.

The analysis comprises three sections. The first describes the political economy context, the coalitions contesting state power in Myanmar, and their transition strategies. The second analyses the scope and impact of key sanctions imposed on Myanmar, identifying the principal sectors and groups affected. The third explores the consequences for the ruling and opposition coalitions and their strategies.

Myanmar's Coalitional Struggles

Myanmar's post-1988 trajectory was strongly influenced by the legacy of military and one-party rule in Burma from 1962 to 1988, which systematically weakened and disorganized all non-state forces. Accordingly, unlike South Africa, where societal mobilization peaked in the 1980s, Burma's 1988 protests were largely spontaneous, and opposition groups did not surmount their fragmentation and organizational weakness. The state remained dominated by the military, which has cultivated support from bureaucrats, crony capitalists,

---

[2] No evidence is presented and, rather strangely, the same author elsewhere suggests sanctions played a 'marginal role' with the junta 'enjoy[ing] complete internal freedom' (Giumelli and Ivan, 2013: 32).

former rebel leaders, and government-organized NGOs, and pursued a managed transition to 'disciplined democracy'. Opposition forces, a weak, fragmentary collection of middle-class pro-democracy activists and some ethnic minority resistance groups, were persistently weakened by regime coercion and co-optation. Unlike the ANC, the NLD's transition strategy has prioritized survival and moral opposition over popular mobilization. Sanctions fit rather vaguely into this approach.

Social Conflict in Myanmar from Independence to 1990

Burma has endured civil war virtually since independence in 1948, entrenching societal fragmentation, narrowing the state's social basis, and making governance heavily reliant on coercion. To achieve British support for rapid decolonization, the main pro-independence force, the Anti-Fascist People's Freedom League (AFPFL), expelled its leftist elements and broke from the powerful Communist Party of Burma (CPB). The CPB launched an armed insurrection, depriving the AFPFL government of its mass base among the peasantry. Fearing the loss of the quasi-autonomy they had enjoyed under British rule, several ethnic minority groups in Burma's borderlands joined this rebellion, while others extracted constitutional concessions on autonomy and secession rights. The new state's fragile integrity was further undermined when in 1949 a defeated Guomindang army retreated from China into Burma and, backed by the US and Thailand, established a quasi-state, trafficking in opium to finance its raids into China. By the 1950s, the government had lost control of most of its borders and its survival depended heavily on the army. The military expanded, assuming extensive state-building duties and ever greater powers vis-à-vis the central government (Callahan, 2007a). Following an intra-AFPFL split, the army forced elected politicians to accept a military 'caretaker government' from 1958 to 1960. In 1962, citing continued governmental instability and mounting separatist threats to Burma's territorial integrity, the army seized control permanently.

The army's subsequent attempts to establish a more coherent, integrationist political order actually exacerbated societal divisions and further weakened the state's social basis. After ruling directly from 1962 to 1974, the military transferred authority to the BSPP. Under this one-party state, all rival power centres were forcibly disorganized. Political parties were abolished, the bureaucracy purged, the Buddhist sangha (clergy) nationalized, universities and business groups kept 'fragmented, controlled and/or rigidly restrained' (Steinberg, 2001: 49–52), while other civil society organizations survived only as underground fragments (Kyaw Yin Hlaing, 2007). The BSPP pursued an autarkic import-substitution industrialization strategy and nationalized all significant businesses, spurring 300,000 ethnic Indian business owners to emigrate and forcing the remaining Burmese petit bourgeoisie into the black market. The legacy of this, in stark contrast to South Africa, is strong state involvement in the economy, including the widespread presence of military-controlled firms, and the extreme weakness of the Burmese business class. Although the BSPP cultivated support from state-backed workers' and peasants' organizations, these lacked autonomy and quickly became sclerotic. Moreover, the CPB and all ethnic minority groups returned to armed insurrection, financed by cross-border trafficking in opium, timber, and gemstones. The army, now almost exclusively drawn from the majority Bamar ethnic group, became locked into an endless series of counter-insurgency campaigns against ethnic-minority rebels, fusing war and state-making (Callahan, 2007a).

This violent societal fragmentation and political disorganization had clear consequences when the BSPP regime fell amidst mass unrest in 1988. The uprising stemmed from the failure of the BSPP's development model. By 1987 the economy was rapidly shrinking and the state virtually bankrupt. The protests, which were precipitated by a currency devaluation and led by middle-class students, disaffected ex-BSPP personnel, and veteran democratic politicians, erupted in August 1988 and spread quickly to many Bamar cities. However, these groups were heavily factionalized and unable to agree on a unified strategy. Moreover, anti-government forces in the borderlands were alienated from this intra-Bamar conflict. Ethnic minority rebels did not escalate their armed struggle; indeed, they proceeded to fight amongst themselves, with an inter-ethnic alliance headed by the CPB dissolving during 1989 following disputes over opium trafficking. These opposition divisions allowed Burma's most unified political force—the military—to seize power via a bloody crackdown in 1988, which it presented as necessary to defuse a plot between 'internal and external destructionists' that would tear Burma apart (Jones, 2014a).

The post-coup junta, the State Law and Order Restoration Council (SLORC; renamed in 1997 as the State Peace and Development Council, SPDC), initially promised to hold multiparty elections in 1990 then return the army to its barracks. However, as the situation stabilized, SLORC increasingly recognized the risks of simply handing control to the victors. The BSPP constitution had been dissolved, providing no predictable framework for a future government. Insurgencies continued in the borderlands, raising the spectre of unacceptable concessions to the minorities, which had prompted military intervention in the 1950s and 1960s. Moreover, the NLD had floated the possibility of Nuremburg-style trials for leading generals, threatening their personal security. Consequently, during 1989 SLORC announced that the 1990 polls would elect a constituent assembly to draft a new constitution, not a government. However, when the NLD won 60 per cent of the vote and 81 per cent of the seats, emboldened by popular and Western support, it demanded the immediate transfer of power (Tonkin, 2007). Fearing political chaos and for their own security, the generals refused and cracked down on the opposition, initiating a twenty-two-year political confrontation.

The Military Regime's Coalitional and Transition Strategy

The military regime's post-1990 strategy involved creating a strictly managed transition to a limited democracy that would protect the country's territorial integrity and sovereignty, ensure socio-political stability, and safeguard military interests. Faced with opposition resistance to this in the 1990s, the regime entrenched itself, seeking to reorganize society to create the conditions necessary for its plans to succeed. The military cultivated alliances with former ethnic minority rebel leaders and emerging crony capitalists whilst intervening to weaken and disorganize the opposition.

After the 1990 crisis, SLORC groped towards a more organized transition strategy. Importantly, like most military regimes, SLORC did not intend to retain power indefinitely, but rather sought to create the conditions necessary for a successor regime to protect the political order preferred by the army leadership. It described the end goal as 'disciplined' or 'discipline-flourishing democracy': a nominally democratic and civilian regime operating within clear constitutional safeguards that would prevent any recurrence of the civilian political disarray, violent disorder, and threats to national sovereignty allegedly present in 1988 and Burma's earlier democratic era (Jones, 2014a). To pursue this, the regime convened the National Convention (NC), a constituent assembly held from 1992 to 1996. Uncooperative representatives elected in 1990 were diluted by selected delegates from other groups, including the ethnic minorities. SLORC established non-debatable 'basic principles' for the NC. Myanmar would be a unitary state with limited regional autonomy, to constrain ethnic minority separatism. It would have a strong executive, with the president having military experience and no ties to foreign countries, to ensure the government was in 'safe hands' and deliberately exclude Aung San Suu Kyi. The commander-in-chief, drawn from the military, would be constitutionally empowered to take control should Myanmar's sovereignty and integrity be threatened. Finally, one quarter of parliamentary seats were to be reserved for military representatives, providing a de facto veto over constitutional change, which would require 75 per cent approval. Through the NC, SLORC attempted to cultivate support for its preferred political settlement.

SLORC bolstered this process by building up a supportive coalition while coercing and co-opting opposition forces. In support of its 'national causes', which emphasized the 'non-disintegration of the Union' and the 'consolidation of national sovereignty', the regime's publicly stated objectives announced a state-building programme designed to produce 'peace and stability' and 'development', while 'wip[ing] out those inciting unrest and violence'.[3] An expanded coercive state apparatus was central to this project. The army doubled in size to around 400,000 soldiers in the decade after 1990; the police also expanded; and an extensive military intelligence apparatus was established to infiltrate opposition groups. Military committees were established to govern all levels of society, with a purged bureaucracy mapped onto this structure. This apparatus was tasked with harassing and disorganizing the democracy movement, with thousands of activists being imprisoned.

The regime also established the Union Solidarity and Development Association (USDA), a mass organization designed to rally popular support and funnel patronage, which claimed twenty-three million members by the mid-2000s. SLORC also courted the sangha, renovating pagodas and lavishing patronage on conservative abbots to enhance its legitimacy among the majority Buddhist population. As one general remarked, 'it is better to have people go to monasteries to pray and meditate, following the country leaders' example, than to let them go around throwing stones' (Koh 2011: 160).

More innovatively, SLORC sought to incorporate ethnic minority groups into its coalition. The regime seized upon the CPB's implosion to pursue ceasefires in the borderlands. In exchange for suspending their insurrections, rebel leaders were permitted to retain some territory, control over resources, and smuggling routes, while the government would initiate development projects and joint business ventures in the war-weary borderlands. As more groups signed ceasefires, the army was concentrated against the holdouts. Moreover, unlike in South Africa, the regime benefited from increasingly favourable geopolitical circumstances. With the Cold War over, China and Thailand stopped supporting Myanmar's rebel groups, promoting ceasefires instead to help their domestic business interests gain access to Myanmar's natural resources. Moreover, notwithstanding their halting efforts to accelerate the regime's transition to democracy, the other member states of the Association of Southeast Asian Nations (ASEAN), which Myanmar joined in 1997, were generally supportive of the junta's state-consolidating efforts, and opposed Western sanctions (Jones, 2012: ch. 8). Thus, by the mid-1990s, fourteen major ceasefires had been signed, encompassing all but two major rebel groups. Their leaders often joined the NC and became 'subcontract[ors]' for the regime in their domains (Taylor, 2009: 450). Soldiers, bureaucrats, and government-aligned NGOs and Buddhist clerics entered the borderlands, often for the first time, gradually extending state control (Callahan, 2007b).

---

[3] This programme was printed on the front page of every government-approved publication until 2013.

This coalitional strategy was undergirded by a new economic strategy designed to direct benefits to supportive groups. To avert government bankruptcy, SLORC embarked on crash liberalization in 1988, opening Myanmar to foreign investment and trade and partially dismantling state monopolies. This created a boom in commodity exports and construction, with permits and contracts being distributed to supportive business interests. In the borderlands, joint ventures were launched around logging, mining, and other extractive industries, with 'ceasefire capitalism' underpinning new alliances between local elites and regional army commanders (Woods, 2011; Jones, 2014a: 8–11). A senior minister explains that, by selectively allocating business opportunities, SLORC hoped to 'enhance the centripetal forces holding the country together by . . . nullify[ing] the centrifugal forces . . . the secession-seeking minority/national races, insurgents, narcotics groups and even the straggling communists, by inviting them back to the legal fold' (Koh, 2011: 67). These groups were even permitted to launder proceeds from smuggling and drug trafficking through government banks and invest in legitimate national businesses, which then received further patronage. SLORC thereby created a new, state-dependent class of 'crony capitalists', with interests spanning banking, real estate, tourism, mining, logging, manufacturing, construction, transport, and telecommunications (Jones, 2014b: 5–8). Army-linked firms were also prioritized, and the military absorbed between a third and a half of government spending in the 1990s, providing employment and daily necessities to its members and their families (Steinberg, 2001: 75–7). More broadly, SLORC hoped that 'consolidating the masses for economic development' would prevent them 'being carried away by various political inspirations' (Abel, 2012), dampening calls for political change, 'as seen in China and some successful ASEAN states' (Koh, 2011: 201).

Notwithstanding its more integrationist trappings, the regime's overall strategy was highly uneven in relation to Myanmar's major ethnic and social groups. The prime beneficiaries were the country's Bamar population. Military rule secured their collective but always tenuous political dominance, and provided resources and avenues for employment and social advancement (Callahan, 2000: 31–2). However, there were also beneficiaries among ethnic minority ceasefire group elites. Furthermore, even some of the regime's most brutal policies attracted some support. For example, Rohingya Muslims in Rakhine state endured exceptionally harsh treatment, including attempts to forcibly deport vast numbers in the early 1990s. As renewed attacks on Muslims since mid-2012 have shown, these policies did not just reflect the cruelty of a few generals. Rather, they responded to (and further encouraged) popular resentment of a group seen as culturally unacceptable illegal immigrants posing a demographic threat to Buddhists. Despite also suffering mistreatment by the regime, Buddhist members of the Rakhine ethnic minority nonetheless supported this policy (Hla Saw, 2012). Even the most brutal divide-and-rule approaches could therefore bolster support for military rule.

The Opposition Coalition and Transition Strategy

Reflecting the legacy of BSPP rule, Myanmar's opposition forces—primarily the NLD-led democratic movement and the ethnic minority resistance groups—are relatively weak and fragmented. Unlike the ruling coalition, which expanded during the 1990s, the opposition coalition contracted, struggling to survive regime crackdowns, let alone mobilize support. Its transition strategy was thin, lacking clear political analysis, failing to specify how the opposition might seize power, and being confined largely to symbolic opposition. Sanctions occupied an ambiguous place within this strategy.

Even before 1990, pro-democracy forces were clearly fragmented. The most popular, vanguard force, the NLD, was a loose alliance of retired generals expelled from the BSPP, middle-class intellectuals and pro-democracy activists, and ex-military businessmen, clustered around Aung San Suu Kyi, daughter of Burma's revered pro-independence leader, General Aung San. The business group defected even before 1990, protesting 'radical' influences. The so-called '88 Generation of Students, who had led the street protests, were also heavily factionalized and unable to unite. Over one hundred parties contested the 1990 elections as different personalist factions vied for power. SLORC's crackdown exacerbated these weaknesses, with many students and intellectuals, including Suu Kyi, being imprisoned, and most parties being outlawed. The NLD was left largely in the hands of ex-BSPP personnel, lacking political nous and despised by many military officers. Successive crackdowns prompted mass defections from the party and the closure of all NLD offices outside of Yangon by the late 1990s. While the 1988 crackdown had prompted thousands of students to join the ethnic minority insurgencies in the borderlands, their relations with the rebels were poor and, unlike the ANC, they could not attract external support for armed revolution. They were gradually defeated by disease, malnutrition, and counter-insurgency, the survivors fleeing abroad to establish various NGOs, fractiously competing for Western funding. Their inability to influence subsequent events inside Myanmar was symbolized by their entirely unsuccessful calls for mass insurrection in September 1999.

The Bamar opposition's relations with ethnic minority groups have also been tenuous, whilst many former resistance groups have essentially defected to the ruling coalition. Despite their initial disconnection in 1988, after 1990 the NLD allied with the United Nationalities League for Democracy, a coalition of nineteen ethnic minority parties. The Ethnic Nationalities Council, another umbrella group, also tacitly supported the NLD's leading role by demanding 'tripartite dialogue' with them and the regime. However, this relationship was eroded by SLORC's 'divide and rule' ceasefire strategy, which picked off various rebel groups and dramatically reduced the main threat to the regime's survival. Although most ceasefire groups remained mistrustful of the regime, many also perceived the NLD as a Bamar party that neglected minority issues and prioritized rapid democratization over their political, economic, and social grievances. Coupled with state repression, these factors largely impeded effective inter-ethnic cooperation among opposition leaders.

The opposition's mass base was also weak. While hundreds of thousands, perhaps millions, participated in the spontaneous 1988 uprising, the only mass unrest thereafter was in 2007, when around 10,000 Buddhist monks and 30,000 sympathizers marched in major cities to protest the rising cost of living (Taylor, 2009: 424–5). Despite attracting massive international media attention, in reality most people remained passive and the unrest was quelled within three days (Zöllner, 2009). This passivity is partly rooted in the political economy context. The failure of Burma's post-independence development and the repressive environment means that Myanmar remains overwhelmingly rural and agrarian. Urbanization is under 30 per cent, and only 10 per cent of GDP comes from industry, versus 60 per cent from agriculture, which supports around 70 per cent of the population (European Commission, 2007: 27). The working class is commensurately small and, until 2011, trade unions were outlawed. Workers are mostly fragmented across small-scale private factories, with larger concentrations confined to state-owned enterprises where activism could easily lead to dismissal, or worse. Subsistence agriculture also affords a (grim) survival strategy for many Myanmar. Moreover, as many as five million people have moved to work abroad. This has provided both a release valve for the regime, which need not confront rising domestic joblessness, and a survival mechanism for ordinary people through overseas remittances. This again contrasts starkly with South Africa. There, blacks were displaced from their land and forced into daily struggles for survival in the cities, spurring the formation of trade unions and civic associations, even under repressive conditions. Moreover, with an economy partially dependent on imported migrant labour, South Africa could not 'export' its social problems to neighbouring states as these were poor, labour-exporting countries.

Political developments have also deprived Myanmar's poor of political outlets. The CPB's collapse and the demobilization of ethnic minority resistance groups deprived the peasantry of political organization, whilst bloody crackdowns against demonstrations in 1976, 1988, and 2007 made spontaneous protests very risky. The anthropologist Christina Fink (2007: 116) finds that Myanmar parents transmit their experience of repression inter-generationally, discouraging their children from becoming politically active. A 2010 survey underscored the efficacy of state coercion: only 8 per cent of respondents were prepared to join protests, but 80 per cent said they would do so if they were not suppressed (Kyaw Yin Hlaing, 2012: 203).

Far more contentiously, virtually all of my interviewees, of all political stripes, identified Buddhism as a pacifying factor. However, from a Gramscian perspective, like any ideology, no religion is *necessarily* conservative or radical; what matters is how political forces use and adapt the ideas. Thus, conservatives may use Christianity to encourage 'meekness', but radicals developed liberation theology to support social change. Likewise, Buddhism is not monolithic in Myanmar. Anthropological research shows that many people have indeed coupled passive cooperation with the regime with a retreat into Buddhist mysticism, astrology, and other superstitions (Skidmore, 2004). The BSPP's nationalization of the sangha and SLORC's patronage has entrenched a generally reactionary religious establishment promoting a conservative 'official Buddhism'. As one SLORC minister approvingly notes, karma is used to legitimize contemporary suffering as reflecting misdeeds in past lives, not government misrule; *metta* (loving kindness) is invoked to encourage tolerance over vengeful behaviour; and 'greed' is discouraged to promote acceptance of one's meagre lot. This interpretation 'preaches contentment . . . So, if they have a decent meal twice a day, that's enough. They don't want riches' (Abel, 2012). As one (Christian) ethnic minority activist argues, this interpretation of karma is 'politically very degrading, because you say, "this is my fate, I was destined to be ruled by the rulers" . . . People don't see themselves as subjects, they see themselves as objects of fate . . . [It is] very demobilising' (Alan Saw U, 2012). This contrasts starkly with South Africa, where ruling elites confronted a crisis of rising expectations and churches played leading roles in organizing mass resistance. A Buddhist Bamar activist argues that official Buddhism also encourages people to 'seek a saviour', to look for 'divine' intervention rather than mobilizing to fight injustice (Prominent Myanmar Pro-Democracy Activist, 2012). Commensurately, Aung San Suu Kyi is popularly seen as a *nat* (angel) who will save the people (Houtman, 2005). Although this refraction of political conflict through religion may reinforce mass passivity, it also illustrates how official Buddhism is contested for anti-regime purposes. Similarly, the idea that Buddhism is universally demobilizing is obviously contradicted by the role of some monks in protests in 1988 and 2007 (discussed further in 'Sanctions' Impact on Coalitional Struggles'), and in promoting anti-Muslim pogroms after 2011. Furthermore, because Myanmar's ethnic minorities are in some cases non-Buddhist or maintain their own local variants of Buddhism, they often resented the regime's promotion of 'official Buddhism'. Thus, while Buddhism may have been used intentionally to depoliticize Myanmar's masses, this has also been contested. The effects of Buddhist doctrine reflect this struggle, rather than simply the nature of the religion itself.

Any leaders facing this socio-political configuration might struggle to devise a viable strategy for democratization, but the NLD did particularly poorly. This reflects the repressive environment; the domination of the Central Executive Committee (CEC) by aged, rigid, ex-military personnel, unresponsive to the broader membership and lacking any idea of how to build a transformatory political movement; and widespread deference to the patrician Aung San Suu Kyi, whose moral fibre is apparently unmatched by strategic nous. Unlike the ANC, the NLD has no articulated analysis of Myanmar society or the regime's power bloc, nor has it generated any concrete platform akin to the Freedom Charter capable of unifying Myanmar's fragmented opposition. Many NLD activists and sympathizers argue the party had no transition strategy whatsoever. One former CEC member recalls: 'the NLD had no clear strategy...[we] were doing politics ad hoc...no strategy or tactics, what to do or how to go...we did not make any progress as a political movement' (Khin Maung Swe, 2012). A current CEC member says the NLD's 'strategy has been to survive legally' and avoid total suppression; 'just to stand firm and not move—that's all' (Han Tha Myint, 2012).

Viewed more generously, the NLD's transition strategy has been described as 'pressure and compromise', i.e. to pressurize the regime to force it to compromise with the opposition (Ko Ko Gyi, 2012). Taylor (2009: 414–15) argues this involved three strands: educating people about democracy to discourage them from pursuing mere self-enrichment; resisting SLORC/SPDC's new constitution by withholding cooperation, insisting that the 1990 election results be honoured and challenging the regime's legitimacy; and hampering the regime's economic strategy to weaken the state's fiscal basis and provoke popular dissatisfaction and/or intra-regime splits. Whether the strategy was ever this coherent is debatable. Although Suu Kyi delivered speeches on democracy, a former close colleague denies this was a conscious strategy of mass education, let alone mobilization (Prominent Myanmar Pro-Democracy Activist, 2012). A CEC member concurs: 'there was not activism from the NLD' (Han Tha Myint, 2012). Far greater emphasis was placed on the second strand: confronting the regime, seeking to 'veto' any move towards 'disciplined democracy'. Accordingly the NLD walked out of the NC in 1995, boycotting its resumption in 2003 and the 2010 elections, repeatedly insisting that the military transfer power in accordance with the 1990 elections. Since the NLD had no means to compel the regime to comply, its struggle was primarily moral, not political.

As for the third strand, the NLD never clearly specified how sanctions were supposed to assist their transition strategy. To retain its legal status, the NLD could not openly request foreign intervention; its leaders consequently deny ever requesting sanctions, despite contrary evidence, claiming it was a choice for Western governments (Han Tha Myint, 2012; cf. Bangkok Post, 1989).

Conversely, Western governments largely based their policies around Suu Kyi's assumed wishes.[4] This dual abrogation of responsibility precluded any strategizing over how sanctions would assist political change, beyond vague hopes of increased 'pressure' on SLORC/SPDC (Khin Maung Swe, 2012). Suu Kyi argued against investment in Myanmar because it benefited only a 'privileged elite' whilst 'encouraging the present military regime to persist in its intransigence' (Free Burma Coalition, 1997: 59). This was a moral argument against economic engagement with an illegitimate regime, not a description of how sanctions might affect the regime materially. Indeed, the NLD (2011) insists that 'economic conditions...have not been affected by sanctions to any notable degree'. Instead, it apparently viewed sanctions as a tool of 'normative communication' (Crawford and Klotz, 1999a), suggesting they 'serve as a warning' that human rights violations 'cannot be committed with impunity' and thereby 'discourage the military government from oppressing the people' (NLD, 2011). Hence, sanctions seemed to be part of the opposition's primarily *moral* struggle against the regime. '88 Generation leader Ko Ko Gyi (2012) suggests that sanctions sought to deny the regime international legitimacy. Similarly, NLD CEC member Han Tha Myint (2012) argues they were meant to offer moral support, to 'convince our people that the world has not abandoned us...We have been working only on our moral principles...it might not be very useful for us [politically], but it's very useful for us spiritually'. In various vague ways, the NLD thus hoped that sanctions might restrain the regime and strengthen moral opposition to its rule.

Clearly, Myanmar's opposition coalition was (and remains) rather weak. Reflecting the disorganizing effects of BSPP rule, opposition forces are fragmented, divided, and isolated, lacking active mass support. The NLD struggled to build meaningful ties with ethnic minority opposition groups, who increasingly defected by signing peace deals with the regime. It did not identify a viable transition strategy, merely seeking to block the military's designs. Sanctions were apparently sought to help delegitimize military rule rather than affect its power bloc. We can now examine what sanctions achieved, by first specifying their scope and material impact, then their consequences for coalitional struggle.

The Material and Distributional Consequences of Sanctions

This section identifies the main sanctions imposed on Myanmar (summarized in Table 3.1) and the scope and distribution of material consequences.

[4] For an example of Western diplomats attempting to divine these wishes, and Suu Kyi declining to identify them, see US Embassy (2009c).

Myanmar's famously unreliable national statistics vitiate real accuracy here, but broad patterns are identifiable. Overall, the material impact was modest. Sanctioned only by the West, Myanmar's economy largely reoriented towards Asia and continued to grow. From 1988 to 2010, Myanmar's GDP increased from US$12.6 billion to US$45.4 billion, imports rose from US$246 million to US$4.8 billion, exports grew from US$167 million to US$8.7 billion, and foreign investment increased from US$4 million to US$8.3 billion (IMF, 2011; UNCTAD, 2012). Thus, the main impact of sanctions was to help concentrate growth in extractive industries and larger firms able to absorb higher transactions costs. This largely benefited state-linked enterprises while undermining the petit bourgeoisie and the working class.

Trade: Reorientation Towards Asia

Trade sanctions did not curtail Myanmar's total exports, which have grown substantially. Rather, they oriented the economy towards Asia and concentrated trade in primary sectors controlled by the state and its allies.

Table 3.1 Main sanctions imposed on Myanmar

Date	Measure
1988	US and Canada impose arms embargo. Canada suspends aid.
1989	US revokes Generalized System of Preferences benefits.
1990–1	EU imposes arms embargo, suspends all defence cooperation, and confines aid to humanitarian purposes.
1994	US Congress withholds funding to international organizations aiding Myanmar.
1996	US suspends all non-humanitarian aid; vetoes all further assistance from international financial institutions; imposes visa ban on Myanmar government officials; prohibits new US investment.
	EU imposes visa ban on senior government officials.
1997	EU and Canada revoke Generalized System of Preferences benefits.
1998	EU extends travel ban; freezes financial assets of officials; restricts exports of items useful for repression.
2000	EU extends travel ban and asset freezes to 140 named individuals.
2003	Canada excludes Myanmar from Least Developed Country Market Access Initiative; imposes visa ban on officials.
	Japan suspends all non-humanitarian aid.
	US bans all imports from Myanmar; bans Myanmar financial transactions in dollars; freezes regime assets in US; expands visa ban.
	EU extends visa ban.
2004–8	US and EU extend visa ban and asset freeze to lower-ranking officials and regime's business associates.
2007–8	Australia imposes and extends financial sanctions on regime officials.
2007	Canada imposes total trade, investment, and financial services embargo; freezes assets of regime and USDA members and their families; bans Myanmar shipping and aircraft from Canada.
	EU bans wood imports from Myanmar.
2008	US bans import of Myanmar rubies and jade; expands visa bans and asset freezes.

Reflecting its weak development under the BSPP, Myanmar largely exports primary commodities and imports capital and consumer goods. In the 1990s its leading exports were agricultural and aquacultural commodities (around one third) and timber (around a fifth). In the 2000s, this shifted as offshore gas fields came online (accounting for over 30 per cent of exports), agriculture and fishery's share declined (to around 13 per cent), as did timber (to about 10 per cent), whilst a fledgling garments industry had also grown (comprising about 10 per cent of exports). Myanmar's imports comprise capital and intermediate goods (around two thirds) and consumer items (about one third) (IMF, 1999: 68–9; U Myint, 2010: 32; Alamgir, 2008: 982). Myanmar's imports always came overwhelmingly from Asia, but from the late 1990s its exports began entering Western markets—largely led by garments. This was then curtailed by sanctions after 2003 (see Table 3.2 and Figure 3.1). Notwithstanding a brief dip thereafter, the total value of Myanmar's trade has risen substantially, largely thanks to booming gas exports.

Thus, Western sanctions mainly reoriented the economy eastwards, the proportion of its trade with Asia rising from 67 to 82 per cent from 2000 to 2005 (Alamgir, 2008: 987). Reflecting the nature of demand from Myanmar's rapidly industrializing neighbours, this concentrated growth in primary sectors—

Table 3.2 Myanmar's top five export destinations

1990		2000		2010	
Thailand	15%	US	27%	Thailand	30%
Singapore	14%	EU	20%	India	12%
India	14%	Thailand	14%	China	10%
China	10%	India	10%	Japan	4%
Japan	9%	China	7%	Malaysia	2%

Source: UNCTAD (2012)

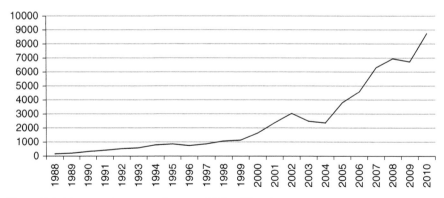

Figure 3.1 Myanmar's exports (current US$ millions)
Source: UNCTAD (2012)

energy and raw commodities—where the state retains extensive formal monopolies. Conversely, the secondary sector's growth was curtailed: Myanmar has not become a major centre of labour-intensive manufacturing for Western markets, unlike nearby former 'socialist' states like China, Vietnam, and Cambodia. This concentrated economic power in sectors dominated by the regime and its allies, as the following subsections illustrate.

GARMENTS

This was the sector worst hit by sanctions. The garments industry expanded rapidly in the late 1990s, its share of exports rising from 2.5 to 39.5 per cent from 1990 to 2000, peaking at US$582.8 million in 2001. Exploiting a lack of tariffs, 90 per cent went to the US and EU. In 2003 the US banned Myanmar garments imports and in 2005 the EU closed a regulatory loophole, curtailing imports further. By 2007 the sector had contracted dramatically, with exports reaching only US$282.7 million (Kudo, 2008: 998; U Myint, 2010: 33–4). The Garment Manufacturers' Association states that, from a peak of around 400 factories employing around 400,000 workers, the industry declined to about 100, employing 60,000, before recovering slightly to 120–30, employing around 100,000, thanks to Japanese demand (Zaw Win Min and Khine Khine Nwe, 2012).

Although Western sanctions ostensibly sought to harm state-owned enterprises and the government, the burden actually fell on the small-scale, private businesses comprising most of the industry. These factories operated on a 'cut, manufacture, and pack' model, whereby imported, pre-prepared fabric parts are assembled then exported. After deducting the cost of imported parts, manufacturers received only 6 to 10 per cent of the final retail price. After sanctions were imposed, this share was further cut. Coupled with fierce competition for the remaining market share, this bankrupted many small firms, while larger ones—often subsidiaries of foreign companies—survived. This concentrated the industry in the area where state-linked enterprises were most dominant: joint ventures with foreign partners (Kudo, 2008: 1009–12). The burden fell most heavily on the non-state-linked petit bourgeoisie and their workers. The government's loss was minimal because the sector had not even been paying export taxes before 2003. Pedersen (2008: 235–6) estimates it at five to ten million dollars. By contrast, annual gas export revenues reached US$2 billion by the mid-2000s.

TIMBER

Timber export embargoes have been far less devastating, but similarly curtailed the development of secondary sectors. The state formally exercises a monopoly over timber harvesting and export. Although in practice these tasks are subcontracted to favoured cronies, generating large profits for them, the government receives around US$300 million in annual revenues and timber is a key patronage resource, making it a tempting target (Woods, 2013). However, even targeted EU sanctions in 2007 did not dent Myanmar's log exports which, fuelled by insatiable Asian demand, grew from US$581.6 million to US$639.6 million from 2006 to 2010 (ITTO, 2012). The loss of EU markets largely affected small and medium-sized manufacturers exporting specialist products like handicrafts and flooring. The impact on state-owned and cronyist firms, which simply export logs, and on total government revenues, was 'negligible' (US Embassy, 2012b). Indeed, Myanmar logs and sawn timber still reached the EU via transhipment and secondary processing in Malaysia, Thailand, China, Laos, Vietnam, and Singapore (Milieudefensie, 2009). Again, therefore, the main burden fell on the fledgling manufacturing sector. The wood processing industry had begun expanding significantly around 2003, with around 150 factories operating at full capacity by 2006/7. But by 2009/10, under twenty remained at full capacity, around fifty at medium capacity, fifty at low capacity, and fifty had closed. The Myanmar Timber Merchants Association (MTMA) attributes this to sanctions and poor government policies (Barber Cho, 2012). Again, sanctions harmed non-state-linked businesses and curtailed the development of a secondary sector.

JADE AND GEMSTONES

EU and US sanctions on precious stones have had a similarly perverse effect. Again, the state exercises significant control over this sector, dispensing mining concessions to favoured cronies, often in joint ventures with the military-owned Myanmar Economic Holdings Ltd, and exporting precious stones through state-organized auctions. However, sanctions entirely failed to dent exports, which rose from US$150 million to US$300 million in the 2000s to US$1.5 billion by 2010–11, largely due to surging Chinese demand (Egreteau, 2011). Transhipment to the EU via Singapore and China is commonplace (US Embassy, 2008a). Again, the state and state-linked firms appeared unscathed, but in 2009 gem dealers complained that sanctions and declining demand had 'forced more than twenty jade and gem mines to close in the last six months', leaving 100,000 miners unemployed. Merchants said that sanctions were 'hurting the "little people" . . . including small traders and mineworkers' whilst having 'little effect on the regime' and its allies (US Embassy, 2009b).

Investment: Concentrating Development in Asian-Oriented Primary Sectors

Investment sanctions had similar consequences to trade embargoes. Their dampening effect on overall investment and economic growth has been relatively modest compared to the regime's own policies. To the extent that they made capital scarcer, this had two major consequences. First, Myanmar became more reliant on Asian investment and, since this was concentrated in primary, extractive sectors, so too was economic growth. However, since these sectors are dominated by the state and its allies, they have prospered, while the broader economy has struggled. Second, it boosted the power of domestic holders of capital which, in Myanmar's context, largely meant state entities and their allies.

Following SLORC's early pro-market reforms, foreign investment increased sharply in the late 1990s (see Figure 3.2). It was concentrated in sectors like oil and gas (33 per cent), manufacturing (20 per cent), hotels and tourism (15 per cent), real estate (14 per cent), and mining (7 per cent) (Steinberg, 2001: 153). Across this decade as a whole, Western investors figured heavily, mostly in hydrocarbons. Britain was the largest investor with US$1.5 billion pledged; the US ranked fourth with over US$200 billion, mostly in oil; and France was also a major investor (Liddell, 2001: 137–9). The main sanctions came in 1997, when the US banned new investments, and in 2004 and 2008, when the EU banned investments in state-owned enterprises and then the timber, gem-stones, and mining sectors. Although total investment stocks nonetheless continued to rise, the precise impact on foreign investment patterns is very difficult to ascertain. The only consistent data source is the ASEAN Secretariat, which depends on notoriously unreliable official government returns, and which does not disaggregate total flows by source after 2005. Insofar as these data are meaningful, they broadly mirror trade patterns, showing a shift away from Western sources to Asian ones, particularly China (see Table 3.3).

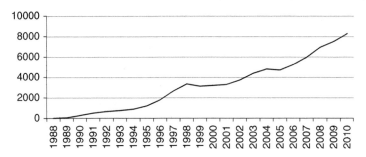

Figure 3.2 Myanmar's inward foreign direct investment stock (current US$ millions)
Source: UNCTAD (2012)

Table 3.3 Myanmar's main sources of new foreign direct investment

1995		2000		2004	
EU	56%	ASEAN	35%	China	46%
ASEAN	30%	EU	29%	EU	35%
USA	10%	USA	23%	ASEAN	4%
China	3%	China	2%	USA	0%

Source: ASEAN Secretariat (2006)

109

One could argue that sanctions slowed investment growth: had the 1995–8 trajectory continued, 2010 levels would have been reached around 2002. However, isolating the effects of sanctions from the government's own macro-economic policies (not to mention the 1997–8 Asian financial crisis) is virtually impossible. Despite some selective liberalization, the regime retained extensive control over the economy as a central component of its transition strategy. All foreign investment was subject to approval by the Myanmar Investment Commission, which sought to direct it into joint ventures and revenue-sharing agreements with firms owned by the state, the military, or crony capitalists. A more serious deterrent, perhaps, was the country's dual currency exchange rate. The official rate was fixed at six kyats to the US dollar, but the black market rate used by most of the private sector was far higher, peaking at 1,300 in 2007. Investing and remitting revenues at the official rate was obviously unprofitable, deterring many investors. Although low investment levels did constrain the development of both state-linked and private firms, economists generally attribute these to government policies, not sanctions (Tin Maung Maung Than, 2005: 372, 383–5; Myat Thein, 2004: 163, 197, 205, 210). This view is supported by pre-sanctions evidence: from 1988 to 1997, only one quarter of approved investment actually arrived because investors were deterred by the regulatory climate (Harn Yanghwe, 2000: 78).

If sanctions did marginally increase capital scarcity in Myanmar, their impact probably fell largely on private enterprises. In the 1990s, 39 per cent of FDI involved wholly owned foreign enterprises; 36 per cent, revenue-sharing ventures with the state; and 25 per cent, joint ventures, of which 63 per cent were with state-owned enterprises, 18 per cent with military-owned conglomerates, and 19 per cent with private sector businesses—often those favoured by the regime (Myat Thein, 2004: 256). Thus, as Aung San Suu Kyi argued, foreign investment was largely flowing to the regime and its supporters. However, thanks to their access to state power, these groups still retained the lion's share of post-sanctions FDI by partnering with Asian investors. The main groups squeezed out were the non-state-linked businesses that might have partnered with or serviced foreign-owned enterprises. Businessmen in fields like logistics and advertising thus complain of stagnating or declining business under sanctions (Moe Kyaw, 2012; Moe Myint, 2012). The overall effect, as with trade sanctions, was to reinforce the shift towards extractive industries servicing Asian investors and markets. Accordingly, two thirds of FDI became concentrated in Myanmar's resource-rich borderlands (TNI, 2011: 12). Conversely, the secondary and tertiary sectors received little investment, constraining employment.

To the extent that sanctions did increase the scarcity of capital, they also enhanced the power of those controlling what remained. In Myanmar, this meant the state apparatuses dispensing capital; well-capitalized enterprises of the military and regime cronies; and former smugglers and drugs barons. These latter groups were among the very few sources of domestic capital after the failure of the BSPP's development model and, as noted above, were consequently encouraged to launder their assets and invest in the national economy. They quickly became dominant in the private banking sector, and were consequently entrenched in the wider economy (Turnell, 2009: 265–70). This occurred before investment sanctions were imposed: as early as 1998, Lintner (1998: 179) observed that the 'current Myanmar Business Directory . . . reads like a who's who in the drug trade'. Yet, to the extent that sanctions increased capital scarcity, they reinforced the power of these regime-aligned groups. Because state-linked entities monopolized foreign investment, private business relied on domestic capital, absorbing 71 per cent of loans from private banks (Turnell, 2009: 274). Accordingly, large parts of the private sector effectively became dependent on regime cronies. Overall, then, investment sanctions arguably bolstered rather than changing Myanmar's economic power relations.

Grass-roots Disinvestment and Boycotts

Grass-roots disinvestment and boycott campaigns, modelled explicitly on the anti-apartheid movement's earlier efforts, produced similar effects to state-based sanctions.

DISINVESTMENT

From 1992 to 2000, fifty-six multinational companies withdrew from Myanmar due to disinvestment pressures. The impact was limited because, typically, it was those with little stake in Myanmar that left, whilst significant interests remained, notably oil companies such as Total and Unocal. Furthermore, some disinvestments were essentially fake. British American Tobacco, for example, simply transferred its subsidiary to a Singaporean–Myanmar joint venture which was licensed to continue production (Holiday, 2005: 333). In other cases, Asian firms stepped in: a Singaporean firm replaced Heineken; Malaysia's Petronas bought out Texaco (Johansson, 2000: 339). Alternatively, disinvestment benefited local regime-affiliated capitalists, who could acquire assets at fire-sale prices. For example, when Pepsi terminated its joint venture with regime crony Thein Tun, he acquired the plant, manufacturing a lemonade that proved more profitable (Prominent Myanmar Pro-Democracy Activist, 2012). To the extent disinvestment had any effect, it concentrated economic power in the hands of the regime's domestic and regional business partners.

TOURISM

Given Myanmar's limited economic relations with the West, the only significant boycott campaign was around tourism. Campaigners challenged 'Visit Myanmar Year' in 1996, when the regime failed to attract a hoped-for 500,000 visitors. Indeed, as late as 2011, Myanmar attracted only 816,193 tourists, over half of whom were cross-border day-trippers (mostly traders and visitors to casinos), yielding an income of just US$319 million (Ministry of Hotels and Tourism, 2011). The consequences were marginal for the government, significant for foreign investors, and very negative for small businesses and employment. Despite campaigners' claims that all tourism revenues benefited the regime, in fact the government only benefited directly in two ways. First, it required independent travellers to exchange US$300 (later US$200) for 'foreign exchange certificates' to be spent in Myanmar, generating a source of hard foreign currency. Secondly, it taxed property and profits at 5 per cent for wholly foreign hotels (comprising the majority) and about 10 per cent for the remainder. Even if Visit Myanmar Year had hit its target, anticipated tourism receipts were only US$150 million (Naw Angelene, 1996: 269–70; Chong et al., 1996: 277). Since the state would only receive a small share of this, the boycott was hardly a significant blow to government finances. The burden fell more heavily on foreign investors and their local partners—often major drugs barons like Lo Hsing Han, who partnered with Singaporean capital to build Yangon's Traders Hotel—who suffered significant losses. The construction industry—again, often dominated by regime cronies—also suffered as demand for new hotels slumped. However, the cronies simply changed their strategies, shifting from tourism into extractive industries. The main burden arguably fell on small businesses established to cater to a non-forthcoming tourism boom, such as tour companies, handicraft manufacturers, shops, smaller hotels and guest houses, and their employees. Their adaptation costs were far higher relative to their assets. Thus, like other sanctions, the tourism boycott reinforced the tilt towards the primary sector whilst constraining tertiary sector development.

The Dollar Ban

In 2003 the US banned the use of its dollar in any international banking transactions to and from Myanmar. Since Myanmar's economy is heavily dollarized due to the weak kyat, its major exports are typically priced and transacted in dollars, and since most government reserves were held in this currency, this was probably the most serious single sanction ever imposed. As the then-finance minister recalls, it made things 'very difficult ... we couldn't deal in the major currency we held ... we suffered a lot' (Abel, 2012). The ban could be evaded only with significant costs, but again these were most damaging for smaller, non-state-linked firms.

The dollar ban was evaded in various ways (US Embassy, 2003a). Some merchants began using euros, as did the government when, for example, auctioning gems. Others redirected their goods from Yangon's port across Myanmar's land borders where trade could be conducted in cash dollars. However, this constrained trade volumes and was only possible for around 60 per cent of imports and under one fifth of exports. More commonly, firms established proxy companies in Singapore through which to transact business, with accounts in Singaporean banks that could transact freely in dollars. Finally, firms also extensively used *hundi*, a transnational, black-market system of money-sending that is widely used for overseas remittances.

These sanction-busting measures involved significant costs, particularly for smaller firms. Transacting in euros added 1 or 2 per cent to overall costs, for businesses and government (Thiha Saw, 2012). Business leaders estimate that transacting via Singaporean proxies or brokers generally added 5 to 10 per cent in costs and time (Aung Than Oo, 2012; Tha Thun Oo, 2012). The growing use of *hundi* also reduced the state's access to foreign exchange since all overseas banking transactions had previously been routed through two state-run banks, enabling them to be taxed. However, this was more than compensated for by booming gas revenues. The US Embassy (2003a) reported that 'none of our contacts believes members of the SPDC are being materially hurt' and that any 'angst is being channelled into defiance and spin-stiffening'. For firms, the impact was keenest felt where profit rates were slim and consequently vulnerable to rising transactions costs. Larger firms, benefiting from economies of scale, were best placed to adapt, but smaller companies were forced to either discontinue trading or transact through larger ones (US Embassy, 2009e). Consequently, since most large businesses enjoyed good relations with the regime, the dollar ban most destructively affected smaller, private businesses without regime ties. The ban also hurt ordinary people: whilst evasive businesses enjoyed 'daily access to [banned financial] services', migrant workers remitting money via banks had transactions blocked, as did expatriates in Myanmar (U Myint, 2010: 40–3). Once more, sanctions mostly harmed those groups least able to adapt: those with fewest resources and connections to the regime.

Overseas Aid and Assistance

Restrictions on bilateral and multilateral loans and grants have had some impact. During the 1970s, the BSPP government became dependent on foreign assistance to finance investment and keep the economy afloat. By 1987 it was receiving US$500 million annually in aid and grants, and its total long-term debt was US$4.2 billion. After 1988, overseas assistance rapidly dried up, compelling SLORC to seek private foreign investment instead. Yet despite entering serious arrears with the World Bank and Asian Development Bank by the late 1990s, and mounting restrictions on IFI lending, the government still found foreign creditors, particularly Japan and Germany, and its long-term debt rose to US$6.3 billion by 2009 (Badgley, 1990: 211–12; UNCTAD, 2012). Without sanctions, perhaps the World Bank would have financed infrastructure investments like large-scale hydropower dams, as in nearby Laos. However, heavy Chinese, Thai, and Indian investment in dams, roads, ports, and pipelines has more than compensated for any loss. This carried consequences for the *nature* of development in the borderlands in particular, explored further in 'Sanctions' Impact on Coalitional Struggles'.

Meanwhile, post-1988 aid restrictions mostly harmed Myanmar's poor. Myanmar is an impoverished country: its average annual income of around US$1,500 places it just above the poorest sub-Saharan African states, and one quarter of its population lives on under US$1.25 a day (ADB, 2012: 3). Although aid levels recovered somewhat after 2001 to around US$120 million a year, this amounted to under US$3 per capita, an extremely low level by international standards. Although funding for international NGOs working in Myanmar doubled to US$30 million, this was just one tenth of the funds allocated to smaller countries like Nepal and Cambodia (Pedersen, 2008: 61). While SLORC/SPDC was frequently castigated for low spending on health, education, and welfare compared to the military, actually its spending levels were not significantly lower than those of neighbouring states. Myanmar's poor service levels are instead attributable to the fact that it received eight times less aid per capita than Vietnam, fifteen times less than Cambodia, nineteen time less than Laos, and fifty-seven times less than East Timor (Roberts, 2006: 17–19). Although the government nonetheless made progress towards its Millennium Development Goals (ADB, 2012: 6–9), sanctions clearly had negative consequences for Myanmar's poor.

Aid restrictions also constrained the development of alternative governance structures to the army. Donors deliberately bypassed the state, thereby failing to develop the civilian bureaucracy (Pedersen, 2006). Aid restrictions also constrained the development of Myanmar's fledgling NGOs, making it difficult for them to finance development projects. Even when funding was available, it was typically managed offshore, depriving NGOs of associated management fees and thereby their capacity to retain talented senior staff, who often moved to international NGOs. The dollar ban also hampered donations from abroad (Sai Sam Kham, 2012; Phone Win, 2012).

Targeted Sanctions: Visa Bans and Asset Freezes

Western 'smart' sanctions directed at regime leaders, senior officials, state-linked enterprise managers, USDA leaders, and their families apparently had very little impact. Myanmar elites have typically acquired all the financial, medical, and recreational services they need in Asia and the Middle East. Consequently, asset freezes in Western countries netted paltry sums: US$700,000 in the US by the mid-2000s, and just €70,000 in the EU by 2009 (Camroux and Egreteau, 2010: 279; James, 2005: 136). Western visa bans also impacted little on business, given Myanmar's highly Asia-oriented economy. One effect was to restrict elites' children from studying in Western universities, but this was at best a minor irritant. Several interviewees cited examples of elites' children being issued with new identities and passports, thereby evading the ban. Typically, therefore, the targets of 'smart' sanctions react by saying, 'it doesn't matter, because we don't have a linkage with them [the senders]...it doesn't affect us' (Abel, 2012). There is some evidence of cronies suffering inconvenience, particularly through restrictions on banking facilities in Singapore (US Embassy, 2008c). However, the effects were minor and could be circumvented by relocating proxy firms. The US Embassy was constantly adding cronies' new business ventures to the sanctions list, noting that they continued receiving lucrative deals from the regime. As one cable noted:

> sanctions may have complicated their lives, but...cronies continue to look for ways to circumvent US sanctions and expand their business empires...it remains business as usual...they can continue to funnel funds to Than Shwe and other top generals. In turn, the generals will continue to direct new business opportunities to the cronies, allowing the generals to profit personally while the Burmese sink into worse poverty. (US Embassy, 2008b)

Arms Embargoes

Western arms embargoes had the least impact of any sanction. Although the regime faced significant challenges in 1988, it received assistance from Singapore and Beijing to finance arms purchases. Subsequently Myanmar readily acquired weaponry from non-Western sources, particularly China and Russia, importing US$2.48 billion worth of armaments from 1989 to 2010 (World Bank, 2012). Myanmar did not need to develop a major domestic arms industry, but a 'network of private firms' was formed to assist the Ministry of Defence with procurement, with leading cronies like Tay Za said to be involved in mediating arms deals (Larkin, 2012: 45; Irrawaddy, 2008). The arms embargo's main effects were thus to increase the regime's dependence on China and draw leading businesses closer to the state.

Summary

The piecemeal sanctions imposed on Myanmar after 1988 had varying impacts, some quite severe, others negligible, but the military regime was generally able to evade them all. In the 1980s, limited Western sanctions affected South Africa because its economy depended heavily Western markets, reorienting to its hinterland was impractical, and East Asia's rise had just begun. Conversely, in the more variegated, post-Cold War international economic order, and given Myanmar's resource wealth and location amidst rapidly industrializing countries, Western sanctions had only limited traction. Nonetheless, sanctions did carry serious consequences. The economy endured heavy adjustment costs and, more importantly perhaps, was channelled down a particular development pathway, being profoundly shaped by demands for energy and commodities from neighbouring states. This concentrated growth in areas of state control, thereby enhancing the regime's power, while curtailing the potential development of labour-intensive manufacturing. The economic burden thus fell most heavily on sectors not linked to the regime, its patronage networks and its development strategy. We can now explore the political implications.

Sanctions' Impact on Coalitional Struggles

The Ruling SLORC/SPDC Coalition

Sanctions' limited economic consequences led many critics to argue they had no impact on the regime, or only counterproductive effects in intensifying SLORC/SPDC's xenophobic nationalism. Pedersen (2008: 161) maintains that the regime was unaffected because, since it extracts the resources it needs from the population, it would starve only when the population did. Taylor (2004: 35) similarly claims that SLORC/SPDC had the means to survive 'without outside help' and sanctions only stiffened the regime. Steinberg (2004: 49) presents the army as a 'state within a state' insulated from the wider economy and thus still able to provide crucial services to its dependents. Many of my interviewees from business, government, and non-NLD opposition parties likewise argued that sanctions had only hurt the people, not the regime and its allies. However, these judgements are based on artificial distinctions between the regime, the economy, and the wider populace. Although the regime's capacity to coerce subordinated groups was never seriously threatened, sanctions did undermine its ability to cultivate support for its transition strategy by weakening its performance legitimacy and constraining available resources. Although the regime's power bloc remained largely intact, it did not significantly broaden. Sanctions thus constrained the regime's transition to 'disciplined democracy'.

Sanctions clearly did not diminish SLORC/SPDC's capacity to finance the coercion of subordinate social groups. The regime faced danger in 1988, with widespread unrest and virtual state bankruptcy, and, less seriously, in the late

1990s, with persistent trade deficits and massive foreign exchange shortages. Yet the regime survived and, despite continued problems, by the mid-2000s the state's macroeconomic viability was better than ever. The army's size had more than doubled since 1988, extending its reach deep into the borderlands; persistent trade deficits were reversed by booming commodity exports; and foreign exchange reserves reached healthy levels (Steinberg, 2007: 230). As one senior government official states, 'sanctions did not paralyse us. We could continue...for a long time, even if Western countries did not lift sanctions. We could crack down on any domestic protests' (quoted in Kyaw Yin Hlaing, 2012: 204).

However, this coercive capacity was arguably maintained at the expense of cultivating broader popular legitimacy. To the extent that sanctions have constrained economic growth, they have limited government revenue, exacerbating persistent government budget deficits. The regime responded by printing money, transferring the cost onto the wider populace via high inflation, and by slashing social spending after 1997. The largely passive population adjusted to these costs; conversely, this strategy was unavailable to South Africa's rulers because the highly mobilized black population was demanding increased living standards. Nonetheless, there were political costs. Welfare improvements stalled, particularly in the borderlands, where most spending had been concentrated, and due to sanctions the cuts were not compensated for by foreign aid (Myat Thein, 2004: 147, 215, 220–4, 253). This clearly constrained SLORC/SPDC's efforts to pacify the borderlands and politically demobilize the wider population through improving social welfare. Similarly, since the late 1990s, regional army divisions have been forced to finance themselves locally, through predatory 'taxation', extortion of bribes, involvement in legal and illegal business activities, and forced labour for porterage and infrastructure construction. This deepened popular resentment towards the army, especially in the volatile borderlands. Thus, while Pedersen is correct that the army has survived by extracting resources from the populace, it is mistaken to suggest this has no political consequences.

The same applies to the general impact of sanctions in constraining and diverting economic growth. As explained above, SLORC/SPDC emphasized development as a means of 'consolidating' the masses behind its transition plans, seeking performance legitimacy similar to that enjoyed by other regional states. By hitting manufacturing, agricultural, and marine exports, sanctions concentrated growth in relatively low-employment extractive industries. This undermined the regime's efforts to prioritize economic development over political change. Although SLORC successfully tempted some activists to abandon politics for business in the early 1990s (Fink, 2007: 73), as growth became confined to sectors dominated by the state and its cronies, this strategy became less effective. Non-state-linked business leaders became increasingly disaffected with the regime's self-serving economic policies. Short-term survival strategies like the monetization of government deficits further undermined growth by constraining capital formation and foreign investment. Although many observers suggest that SLORC/SPDC did not care about the wider economy, this ignores the importance of economic development to the regime's transition strategy and its nationalist commitments. This is why regime officials frequently demanded that sanctions be lifted, arguing that they were undermining development and harming ordinary people (Pedersen, 2008: 206). Contrary to classical liberal expectations about sanctions, poor economic performance largely produced resentment rather than rebellion. However, the 2007 monks' protests were precipitated by falling living standards, and the regime's inability to respond with anything but force underscored its failure to win popular legitimacy.

The way sanctions helped constrict development to the primary sectors had particularly pernicious effects in the borderlands. The lack of other growth prospects apparently reinforced the military's dash to exploit natural resources like gemstones, timber, and hydropower. For instance, the MTMA argues that the aborted development of wood-processing industries spurred the government to intensify logging to meet its revenue targets (Barber Cho, 2012). This rapacious activity attracted growing popular resentment, spurring the development of environmentalist critiques and activism among ethnic minority youths, both in exile and in the borderlands (Simpson, 2013; Kiik, 2012). Moreover, the regime increasingly squeezed out major ceasefire groups like the Kachin Independence Organization (KIO) from the trade in timber and gemstones, capturing the rents for itself (Jones, 2014b: 10; Marshall and Min Zayar Oo, 2013; Woods, 2013). Myanmar's sanctions-enforced reliance on Thai and especially Chinese investors had similar consequences. Their projects often involve land grabs and forced displacement, with benefits accruing largely to investors, local ethnic minority elites, cronyist businessmen, and army commanders (TNI, 2011).

Whilst this rapacious natural resource exploitation has undoubtedly empowered the SPDC, helping it to survive sanctions, it also undermined the regime's own strategy for incorporating minority groups into the national order. In 2011 the KIO returned to armed struggle against the government, which the MTMA links directly to struggles over natural resources: 'we cannot get the peace agreement with the Kachins because of these natural resource [conflicts]. If we didn't have the[m] . . . we wouldn't have the rebellion' (Barber Cho, 2012). A development NGO leader concurs: 'a lot of conflicts are created over natural resources. Why? We don't have other economic opportunities. This is imposed by sanctions' (Phone Win, 2012). Similarly, a prominent Kachin peace mediator argues:

Because of sanctions . . . the government sided with the Chinese and opened more ways for illegal trading in our area. That gave benefit to the military government and also some . . . KIO [leaders] and [former] insurgent groups. But the people at the grassroots got no benefit at all . . . We don't get sustainable peace like this. It is more like an erosion that affects the peace process . . . People complain that, because of the ceasefire, because of the peace process, they lost . . . Sanctions are [supposed] to help the people at the grassroots . . . but it becomes reversed (Saboi Jum, 2012).

For SLORC/SPDC, pacifying the borderlands was seen as central to the transition to 'disciplined democracy'; as one general suggested, 'the mechanisms of democracy couldn't work because we had these insurgencies' (Abel, 2012). To the extent that sanctions reinforced a hyper-exploitative ceasefire capitalism in the borderlands, they therefore hampered this transition strategy.

Ultimately, however, despite these various constraints, the key power bloc underpinning military ruled remained intact, albeit narrow. The army did not experience factional strife sufficient to destabilize the regime. There was serious rivalry between factions headed by the SPDC's second- and third-ranked members, Maung Aye and Khin Nyunt, which eventually led to the latter's purge in 2004. However, this was not apparently linked to sanctions, except negatively. Khin Nyunt was a moderate reformist who cultivated closer relations with Western states, pursued reconciliation with the NLD, and issued the 2003 'roadmap to democracy'. Some argue that sanctions undermined him because they precluded any concrete benefits arising from cooperation with the West (Taylor, 2004: 30, 33, 34, 36). Others, however, suggest that his purge stemmed from a struggle over economic rents, and indeed he was imprisoned for corruption (Kyaw Yin Hlaing, 2012). In any case, the SPDC did not split, and the 'roadmap' survived the demise of its architect, suggesting considerable consensus over basic strategy. Similarly, despite low morale and desertions, the army remained loyal even when ordered to attack Buddhist monks in 2007. The purged bureaucracy also remained loyal, despite its ever-diminishing living standards.

Nor, unlike in South Africa, did Myanmar's bourgeoisie become a source of opposition or advocate political change. Instead, businesspeople collaborated with the regime or remained politically passive. This stemmed from Myanmar's particular political economy. Structurally, the bourgeoisie was divided between a minority of large-scale, cronyist interests and a large majority of small- and medium-sized businesses. The cronies had significant capital, power, and organizational strength, but little incentive to confront their patrons. The cronies and the regime were to some degree symbiotic, with the SPDC depending on business allies to provide services, operate extractive industries, and fund and execute state projects, including the construction of a new capital city. Ultimately, however, the government's control of licences, permits, concessions, contracts, and the judicial system gave it the upper hand (Jones, 2014b: 7–8). The US concluded in 2007 that even the cronies 'have no power to influence government leaders' but had to support the regime to secure their own prosperity (US Embassy, 2007a). The clear implication is that targeted sanctions on cronies were purely punitive and could not be expected to deliver political results.

Non-state-linked businesses had more reason to support reform in Myanmar, but as predominantly small-scale enterprises they were preoccupied with surviving and unable to mobilize politically. As one business leader recalls, 'we have been struggling for our survival . . . so, everyday, from morning to evening, we cannot tend to other issues' (Zaw Win Min and Khine Khine Nwe, 2012). The only collective organization for smaller businesses, the Federated Chambers of Commerce and Industry (FCCI), was less a bottom-up lobby group than a top-down control mechanism, with the government appointing all of its senior officers. Accordingly, many businesspeople felt unable to influence government policy and believed they would only face arrest if they spoke out (Tha Thun Oo, 2012). The FCCI's subsidiary groups also avoided 'politics', due to internal divisions and a desire to be seen as neutral when interacting with government (Barber Cho, 2012; Moe Kyaw, 2012). This partly reflected the fact that, given SLORC/SPDC's arbitrary control of many economic sectors and regulations, all businesses needed to cultivate good relations with the regime in order to prosper. For example, the MTMA feared that criticizing the regime could result in the government using its monopoly over timber to cut off the industry's supplies (Barber Cho, 2012). Insofar as sanctions concentrated economic growth and power in state-controlled sectors, they actually exacerbated this dependence on government goodwill and constrained the emergence of a more independent bourgeoisie capable of challenging the regime.

There is consequently scant evidence of business applying any political pressure as a result of sanctions. Several businesspeople interviewed said they had lobbied the government in response to sanctions, but in every case they had requested changes in economic regulations to alleviate the costs imposed, rather than political change. Their political lobbying was instead directed at Western states who were asked to lift sanctions (Zaw Win Min and Khine Khine Nwe, 2012; Aung Than Oo, 2012; Barber Cho, 2012; Thiha Saw, 2012). A few businesspeople raised political concerns informally with contacts inside the regime, but these were either rejected or not relayed to key decision-makers because even regime insiders feared the repercussions (Moe Myint, 2012). The businesspeople enjoying direct access to regime elites—the cronies—had no incentive to promote change, and there is no evidence of them having done so, despite their being personally targeted by sanctions. Instead they reportedly lobbied—often successfully—for additional business concessions to cover any losses (Moe Kyaw, 2012). Although cronies protested to Western embassies that they had been unfairly targeted, suggesting they suffered some loss and inconvenience, overall they arguably benefited from sanctions, which reinforced their dominance and the regime's reliance on them. As one business leader recalls, sanctions precluded 'proper competition from other, outside countries . . . sanctions gave them ten years to have a good share of the pie under the dictated economy, and to influence it as well' (Moe Kyaw, 2012).

Finally, as is common in late developing countries, Myanmar capitalists are not necessarily intrinsically liberal or pro-NLD. Indeed, some support the regime's basic philosophy. The vice-president of the Rice Industry Association, for example, argues that 'interest in democratisation is only the outsider's view. Local businessmen have a different perception . . . They prefer political and economic stability for the whole country' (Aung Than Oo, 2012). Even businesspeople more sympathetic to democracy are reluctant to back the NLD because they perceive it as economically illiterate and lacking any concrete alternatives to government policies (Wah Wah Tun, 2012). As one asks rhetorically, 'has she [Aung San Suu Kyi] even imported one tractor for a poor farmer to make his life a bit better? The NLD don't have any economic policies' (Moe Kyaw, 2012). Ultimately the regime could depend on considerable business support for its transition plans. Myanmar Egress, a business-organized NGO, bankrolled and trained many small opposition parties to participate in the 2010 elections, thereby lending it greater legitimacy, while around a hundred crony capitalists stood as candidates for the regime-backed Union Solidarity and Development Party (USDP) (Jones, 2014b: 8).

Other key social forces also stayed broadly within the power bloc sustaining military rule. Most critically, many ceasefire group leaders, whilst hardly enthusiastic about the regime, were nonetheless effectively co-opted into governing networks through inducements and coercion. As Callahan (2007b: 3–4) describes, they now form part of '"emerging political complexes" . . . flexible and adaptive networks that link state and other political authorities to domestic and foreign business concerns (some legal, others illegal), traditional indigenous leaders, religious authorities, overseas refugee and diaspora communities, political party leaders, and NGOs'. Sanctions did not prompt any group to return to rebellion, apart from possibly (indirectly) the KIO, and even this occurred after the transition from direct military rule was underway in 2009. Instead, many ethnic minority activists and leaders were hostile to sanctions, feeling they did not address minority issues, unduly prioritized democratization over urgent tasks of economic development and fuelled exploitative Asian investment projects (Seng Raw, 2001; Centre for Peace and Conflict Studies, 2010; Saboi Jum, 2012; Sai Sam Kham, 2012; Hla Saw, 2012). Again, with the partial exception of the KIO, anti-government sentiment did not revive the demobilized resistance groups or generate new forms of resistance that were politically significant. The divisions between ethnic minority and Bamar opposition groups were never transcended in Myanmar's repressive environment. Conversely, the alliance with the NLD withered as minority leaders realized that cooperating with the SPDC was the only way to embed their post-ceasefire gains. Whilst in the 1990s some ethnic minority groups had remained in rebellion and others boycotted the NC, when it resumed in 2003, all the ceasefire groups participated despite the NLD's boycott. And, despite again having their concerns ignored, ultimately they consented to the military-drafted constitution. Although some sympathetic protests occurred in the borderlands during the 2007 monks' protests, few minority groups declared their solidarity, and the ceasefires held (Zöllner, 2009: 68). Indeed, even as the monks were marching in Yangon, KIO leaders were attending pro-NC mass rallies, and they subsequently ordered their followers to vote 'yes' in the 2008 constitutional referendum (Sadan, 2009: 151, 153).

Finally, the Buddhist clerical establishment remained aligned with the military, though sanctions arguably helped provoke a rebellion among younger monks. The 2007 protests illustrated the sangha's deep internal divisions: while young, recently initiated monks led the demonstrations, the supreme council repeatedly instructed monks to abandon the protests (Zöllner, 2009: 39–40, 63–4, 67, 69, 71, 76–7). The protests were precipitated by the sudden withdrawal of government fuel subsidies, which further impoverished the urban population, upon whose donations monks rely. The government justified these cuts as necessary to address its budget deficit, which it blamed partly on sanctions (Zöllner, 2009: 28, 63). This may simply have been propaganda. Yet living standards were certainly declining; although the protestors blamed this on the government, it was arguably exacerbated by sanctions. Nonetheless, although the protests soon escalated into demands for the regime to step aside, since they did not trigger wider social revolt they could not secure this outcome. With the wider population remaining passive, the regime easily terminated the protests, dispersing monks to their home towns, brutalizing lay protestors, and restoring order within three days. As Zöllner (2009: 98–9, 101) observes, 'compared to 1988 . . . no mass movement developed and the amount of force employed as well as the number of physically affected people was low . . . [1988 was] a "popular uprising" aimed at a political transition . . . 2007, in contrast, was a "moral protest" which could not be converted into any tangible political changes'. Moreover, crucially, the protests occurred *after* the NC's conclusion; the military's transition plan was already being executed and continued unaffected. Its sluggish progress—with the constitutional referendum in 2008 and elections in 2010—does not even suggest that the 2007 protests accelerated its completion. Thus, even if sanctions played some role in generating the 2007 unrest, this did not generate political transformation.

To summarize: the impact of sanctions on the ruling coalition was negative but not disastrous. Contrary to claims that sanctions had no impact, constraints on economic development did hamper the regime's transition strategy, by limiting growth, intensifying predatory resource extraction, and thereby undermining the regime's legitimacy. Yet, despite various challenges, sanctions did not generate significant defections from the power bloc forged in the 1990s.

The Opposition Coalition

Although sanctions hindered the regime's transition strategy, they did not significantly assist the realization of the opposition's alternative. As described above, the NLD hoped that sanctions might discourage government repression, assist its moral struggle against the regime, and undermine the state's resources. While the latter was achieved, as described in the preceding subsection, this did not seriously undermine military domination. As for the other goals, while sanctions may have helped the NLD survive and reinforced its sense of moral superiority, they do not appear to have discouraged state repression. Moreover, external support apparently encouraged the pursuit of an unrealistic and moralistic strategy. Sanctions did not help broaden the opposition coalition but may actually have weakened it by provoking domestic opposition, precluding the emergence of potential opposition groups, compounding people's daily struggle for survival, and deepening the opposition's dependence on external backing.

Some NLD sources argue that external pressure, including sanctions, helped the NLD to survive government repression and continue its moral campaign. CEC member Han Tha Myint (2012) argues that 'without this help and support...our resistance and standing would be very hard for us [to maintain]. I doubt whether we could stand anymore...[Without it] the government would crush us very easily'. Pedersen (2008: 227) concurs that sanctions 'kept the NLD on life support'. However, the extent to which they actually restrained the regime is contestable. Chronologically, sanctions typically *followed* crackdowns on the opposition—notably in 1988–90, the late 1990s, 2003, and 2007—and were followed by further repression (Zaw Nay Aung et al., 2011: 10–13). Contrary to claims that sanctions preserved some political space, some non-NLD party leaders argue that 'whenever Western countries put forward pressure to the government, the government turned to oppress the people more' (Than Than Nu and Thu Wei, 2012).

If sanctions did encourage opposition forces to maintain their moral struggle, they arguably bolstered an unrealistic transition strategy that achieved little but deadlock. As noted earlier, the strategy of 'pressure and compromise' involved confronting the regime and issuing demands without mustering the resources and social mobilization necessary to compel the regime to comply. Although this rigid strategy partly stemmed from internal factors, Western sanctions apparently encouraged this deeply flawed approach. A former aide to Aung San Suu Kyi recalls that sanctions exacerbated the NLD's leader's 'stubborn and inflexible' posture of 'moral righteousness' (Prominent Myanmar Pro-Democracy Activist, 2012). CEC member Han Tha Myint concurs that the NLD 'sometimes' took a more confrontational stance than it would have without sanctions (Han Tha Myint, 2012). One former CEC member goes further, stating that 'only because of sanctions did we dare enough to make confrontation...and confrontation did not make any change' (Khin Maung Swe, 2012). Another recalls that sanctions were 'one of the reasons why the NLD chose that confrontational course...[yet] we haven't achieved anything, except that many of our colleagues were thrown into jail, or they lost their lives, and property, and everything' (Than Nyein, 2012). Insofar as sanctions reinforced this approach, rather than encouraging the NLD to pursue a compromise solution more commensurate to the opposition's actual power, they perpetuated a losing strategy. They arguably helped embolden the NLD's moralistic boycotts of the NC in the 1990s and 2000s, the 2008 referendum, and the 2010 elections. This certainly delayed the regime's transition strategy. General Khin Nyunt often argued that the transfer to a 'constitutional government' would 'happen a lot faster if negative elements inside the country would stop hindering the process', arguing that the Western policy of sanctions in support of these groups 'actually hinders Myanmar's path to democracy' (Asiaweek, 1999). Yet, since sanctions did little to help the opposition pursue a viable alternative, they merely prolonged the stalemate.

Sanctions may also have eroded the opposition coalition somewhat. As noted earlier, ethnic minority activists generally opposed sanctions as unhelpful in redressing their grievances. This only added to the issues dividing them from Bamar opponents of the regime. Furthermore, SLORC/SPDC used sanctions as part of their nationalist, anti-opposition campaigns. The military has long portrayed itself as a patriotic force defending Myanmar against 'internal and external destructionists', including the NLD and exiled oppositionists.

Taylor (2004: 38) argues 'this view is shared by others in Myanmar, who see these groups as allies of ethnic separatists'. SLORC/SPDC used the opposition's support for sanctions to reinforce their presentation as treacherous tools of foreign powers, apparently with some traction. Even former political prisoner Khin Zaw Win (2007: 286) denounces Myanmar's economic 'strangulation' as unpatriotic, arguing 'there can be no greater sacrilege or transgression than to actively advocate for punitive measures against one's own land and people'. All business leaders interviewed were firmly opposed to sanctions, too. The regime had some success in luring some NLD activists to abandon their political struggle for self-enrichment; one, Chit Khaing, even became one of Myanmar's leading crony capitalists (US Embassy, 2007c). Interviews of garment workers who lost their jobs and moved into prostitution also identified growing resentment of the 'sacrifices' imposed by sanctions on the people (Kyaw Yin Hlaing, 2004: 84). However, most opposition activists interviewed insisted that this nationalist anti-sanctions backlash was largely confined to the politically educated urban middle class and government supporters. In their view, it did not cost them significant support, with most people blaming economic problems on the regime. Yet even this perspective concedes that the impact of sanctions on the opposition coalition's size was moderately negative.

Sanctions also hampered the emergence of social forces which might have become opposition constituencies. Most importantly, by suppressing manufacturing they stymied the emergence of an organized working class. Despite trade unions being outlawed, garment workers began protesting for higher wages in 2005, staging sixty-one strikes in the first eight months of 2007 (US Embassy, 2006b, 2007b). This made garment workers by far the most militant segment of Myanmar's working class. All these protests occurred in private factories, because job security in state-owned factories was minimal; yet these private factories were decimated by sanctions, collapsing employment and dispersing many workers back into agriculture, abroad, or worse. As we have seen, the emergence of a black working class was pivotal for South Africa's transition. In neighbouring Cambodia, the rapid development of a garments industry from the mid-1990s generated a sizeable, militant working class which became a key constituency of the democratic opposition (Hughes, 2007). Generally, the absence or weakness of organized labour is associated with authoritarian or oligarchic domination in Southeast Asia (Deyo, 2006), and the importance of working-class mobilization for democratization has been recognized more widely (Rueschemeyer et al., 1992; Eley, 2002).

Similarly, in combination with government policies, sanctions hampered the emergence of capitalists independent of the state, and profoundly stunted the development of an urban middle class. One non-NLD opposition politician argues: 'in a society without a strong middle class ... democracy cannot prevail ... Because of economic sanctions, our economy went down to a zero level ... [so] how can democracy prevail? ... From that political economy point of view, we continually opposed sanctions' (Myo Nyunt, 2012). Contrary to this modernization theory perspective, we cannot be certain that any of the forces retarded by sanctions would necessarily have joined the opposition coalition. As chapter 1 argued, social forces are not intrinsically liberal or progressive, and middle classes are often 'contingent democrats' at best (Bellin, 2000). Nonetheless, by contributing to the stagnation of Myanmar's social development, sanctions constrained new possibilities from emerging.

Furthermore, insofar as sanctions exacerbated people's everyday struggle for survival by cutting aid and constraining employment and economic growth, they compounded the masses' political passivity. Sanctions senders apparently took a crude, classical liberal view of sanctions, expecting rising hardship to translate into political unrest. US diplomats, for example, suggested that 'as economic conditions continue to deteriorate, the workers have less to lose, raising the risk of a political backlash' (US Embassy, 2007b). In reality, as one ethnic minority politician argues:

> When the people became poorer and poorer, they became more apolitical... because they are only [focused] on their survival... [They] became poor [primarily] due to the false administration of the military regime, but due to sanctions they had to feel a double burden, and became even poorer... [The logic of sanctions] is very easy logic: when you become poorer, you have to fight the government. No: in actual life, this does not happen. When you become poorer, you become more fearful, and far away from politics—they became apolitical (Hla Saw, 2012).

This perspective was shared by many opposition interviewees. It is also borne out by the general absence of mass unrest after 1988, and the failure of the 2007 protests to attract widespread participation, even when they were triggered by a living standards crisis. An NLD CEC member suggests an inverse relationship between poverty and politicization, arguing that people 'are poor, so they are only thinking about... how to feed themselves. Most of them don't have time to think about politics. If they get richer, they will have time to think about politics and involvement in politics' (Han Tha Myint, 2012). Although the NLD would like to blame mass impoverishment entirely on regime policies, their claims that sanctions did not contribute to this situation are not credible.

Arguably, sanctions also had a psychologically demobilizing effect by encouraging people to rely on Western intervention to solve their problems. Opposition politician Myo Nyunt (2012) argues that they encouraged the belief that it is other people's responsibility to win democracy, with 'stupid politicians' even hoping for military intervention. Hopes and rumours of such intervention swirled around every political crisis since 1988; the saffron revolution was just the latest instance where an opposition too weak to topple the regime itself called for UN intervention (Zöllner, 2009: 61). The US Embassy (2003b) reported that 'many educated Burmese... are grasping at the idea of US military action as a tidy solution to intractable and complex political problems', noting that intervening was actually 'of questionable interest' to Washington. Fink's (2007: 3) anthropological study also observes that 'most Burmese hesitate to take action... [they] attempt to get on with their lives as best they can while indulging in the dream that perhaps one day the US or the UN will swoop in and remove the regime for them'. Although, as discussed above, there are many internal reasons for Myanmar's popular passivity, sanctions arguably reinforced this critical weakness, encouraging the populace to abrogate responsibility for their own liberation. A former NLD CEC member argues that 'sanctions...made some people think that sometime the international community might help us by making the activity against the authorities, giving us a wrong way of thinking...false hope' (Khin Maung Swe, 2012). Similarly, a progressive NGO leader argues that 'Western countries... exacerbat[ed] this situation where people are expecting a hero rather than acting themselves' (Sai Sam Kham, 2012).

Thus, while sanctions hampered the ruling coalition's transition strategy, they did not assist the opposition coalition to realize theirs. Sanctions may have encouraged the opposition to maintain its struggle, but also to pursue a strategy with little hope of success. Rather than expanding opposition forces, sanctions deepened tensions between them and constrained the emergence of new potential constituencies. By sustaining a hopeless struggle, foreign involvement encouraged over-reliance on ultimately illusory Western support. As Pedersen (2008: 228) comments, sanctions have 'not inspired people to join in the struggle for regime change...but perhaps rather to abdicate responsibility for their own situation'.

Conclusion

Given the radical imbalance of power between the ruling and opposition coalitions, which was at best modestly affected by sanctions, the ruling coalition ultimately succeeded in imposing its preferred political settlement. In 2003 the regime issued its seven-step 'roadmap' to 'disciplined democracy'; from 2004 to 2007 it reconvened the National Convention; in 2008 it staged a constitutional referendum; and in 2010 elections were held for a new government.

Nothing about this transition suggests that sanctions helped bring it about. It might be argued, for instance, that the roadmap was issued due to the sanctions imposed in 2003, following a crackdown on the NLD and the reincarceration of Aung San Suu Kyi. Even if this was true, the regime still took seven years to complete the roadmap, which hardly suggests that its hand was forced. Indeed, the contrary is true: having strengthened considerably against the democratic opposition and ethnic minority groups, it clearly felt confident to dictate the pace, form, and extent of the 'democratic' transition (Jones, 2014a). In the 1990s SLORC was forced to abandon the NC by the NLD boycott and ethnic minority demands. In the 2000s the NC proceeded despite another NLD boycott and with widespread ethnic minority participation. Notwithstanding ethnic minority reservations about the limited degree of regional autonomy on offer, in 2007 the NC approved a constitution virtually identical to the one SLORC had proposed in the 1990s. The 2008 referendum proceeded despite an NLD boycott campaign and over 100,000 deaths during Cyclone Nargis, which struck Myanmar just before voting commenced. In 2010 the opposition was badly fragmented: the NLD split over the question of participation, and forty parties contested the elections despite an NLD boycott. The USDA, converted into the USDP and led by ex-SPDC personnel, swept the board and formed the new government. Led by President Thein Sein, formerly the SPDC's third-ranking member, two thirds of the new cabinet were former military officers, while the military also occupied a quarter of parliamentary seats. Given the SPDC's tight control of this process, which ensured its preferred outcome and protected its interests, the idea that sanctions had somehow forced it to retreat from power is spurious.

Instead, it was the opposition that was forced to participate in a new political dispensation it had no hand in designing. After boycotting the polls, the NLD was increasingly marginalized as the new government pursued socio-economic reforms, attracting cautious praise from Western governments. After an opening was created by Thein Sein, the NLD participated in by-elections in 2012, resulting in the election of Aung San Suu Kyi and forty-two other NLD members to parliament. While the NLD is pursuing constitutional revisions ahead of the 2015 elections, with just 6 per cent of parliamentary seats it cannot achieve this without USDP and military support. Despite some liberalization, the opposition remains severely constrained, with ancien régime forces still 'holding the ring' (Jones, 2014b).

Another reason occasionally cited for Myanmar's transition is that the regime feared it had become too dependent on China. Since sanctions certainly exacerbated this dependence, it may seem plausible that they indirectly generated this outcome. However, this too is inaccurate. Myanmar's nationalist leaders, and the wider population, were certainly leery of China's growing influence. Crucially, however, the regime was prepared to tolerate this for two decades until it had achieved the conditions necessary to execute its transition strategy. As early as 2001, Steinberg (2001: 227–8) noted that 'much of the economy has moved into Chinese hands', with Chinese immigration 'changing the whole demographic balance in Northern Burma'. Yet it was a further decade before the military relinquished power. There is no evidence of any sudden escalation in Chinese influence that could explain this decision and, in any case, any explanation relying on short-term 'tipping points' entirely neglects the long-standing nature of the regime's efforts to secure 'disciplined democracy', which began in 1992. Again, the slow culmination of these plans does not suggest a sense of urgency to lessen Chinese influence. It instead reflects the state of Myanmar's social conflict: the regime's caution and its difficulty in corralling key social forces behind its transition strategy—a difficulty exacerbated by sanctions.

Finally, the fact that Thein Sein's government pursued the lifting of sanctions also does not indicate that they 'worked'. As shown above, sanctions did damage the economy and the military regime frequently argued they were harming the people; hence, it is unsurprising that Thein Sein sought their removal. But simply because sanctions inflicted economic pain does not mean they delivered political gain; in fact, Myanmar is a classic case of the opposite. Economic pain fell most heavily on social groups not aligned with the military regime. The political effects were, if anything, negative. Sanctions hampered and delayed the regime's planned transition to 'disciplined democracy', which is why the junta protested; but they did not significantly weaken the regime or its power bloc, nor did they enable the opposition to triumph instead: the net outcome was the settlement desired and designed by the military. Insofar as sanctions delayed this outcome, they only perpetuated a fruitless deadlock that prolonged military rule.

4

Iraq

Sanctioning Dictatorship

In August 1990, Iraq, led by Saddam Hussein's Ba'ath Party dictatorship, invaded and annexed Kuwait. Subsequently, UNSC Resolution (UNSCR) 661 imposed the most comprehensive sanctions ever devised, banning exports from, military sales to, and financial transactions with Iraq. This failed to force Iraq from Kuwait; it was instead defeated in a devastating military attack by a thirty-four-country coalition in February 1991. UNSCR 687, passed in April, imposed a peace settlement that maintained the embargo. Although later eased by the Oil For Food Programme (OFFP), by 1995 the embargo had cost Iraq US$85 billion in lost oil revenue; its GDP had plummeted from US$16.4 billion to US$3.5 billion, and its annual per capita income fell from US$969 to just US$171, below 1950s levels (Cordesman and Hashim, 1997: 140; UNCTAD, 2012). Casualty estimates, while contested, are high, ranging from 106,000 in one unpublished study to 1.5 million according to Iraqi government and NGOs sources, with UNICEF estimating 400,000–500,000 'excess deaths' among under-fives by 1998 (see Baram, 2000a: 185–206; Zurbrigg, 2007: 28–30).

Whether these devastating sanctions were 'successful' is also contested, partly because of disagreement over their goals. Ostensibly, UNSCR 687 demanded that Iraq accept Kuwait's sovereignty and borders; return Kuwaiti property and prisoners and pay war reparations; renounce terrorism; and verifiably destroy its arsenal of, and capacity to produce, weapons of mass destruction (WMD) and its long-range missiles. However, the resolution's inherent ambiguity left scope for minimalist and maximalist interpretations. Paragraph 22 stated that the embargo would end once Iraq's WMDs had been destroyed and reparations were being paid; this was the position of Iraq, France, and Russia. However, paragraph 21 stated that sanctions would be reviewed against Iraq's 'implementation of all relevant resolutions'. Since UNSCR 688 added demands for political liberalization and human rights improvements, insisting on paragraph 21, as the US and United Kingdom (UK) did, amounted to pursuing regime change (Graham-Brown, 1999: 58–60). Ample evidence suggests this goal was indeed sought. In 1991, President Bush stated the US would 'keep the pressure on Saddam until a new leadership comes to power', a position reiterated by other officials (Clawson, 1993: 9–10). In 1998, Congress passed the Iraq Liberation Act, directing the Central Intelligence Agency (CIA) to assist the Iraqi opposition in overthrowing Saddam. Similarly, President Clinton declared in 1997 that 'sanctions will be there until the end of time, or as long as [Saddam] lasts'. However, Clinton apparently saw sanctions as part of a strategy of 'dual containment' of Iran and Iraq, rather than an instrument to overthrow Saddam (Graham-Brown, 1999: 62–5). Gordon (2010: 190) persuasively argues that, while emphasis on regime change varied, Washington's 'consistent goal...was to keep Iraq from rearming' by keeping the state 'indefinitely' impoverished.

Given this disagreement, assessments of the embargo's 'success' vary. From the minimalist perspective, Herring (2002: 43) argues the outcome was 'Iraqi compliance, however grudging, with most of what has been demanded of it'. US Secretary of State Madeleine Albright infamously declared that 500,000 Iraqi children's deaths were 'worth it' because Saddam revealed his WMD and recognized Kuwait (CBS, 1996). The absence of WMD in Iraq after the 2003 invasion led some to reassess sanctions as being successful in disarming Saddam (Mazaheri, 2010). From the perspective that the goal was containment, a 1996 State Department review found sanctions an 'unqualified success' (Cockburn and Cockburn, 2000: 225). In 1998, a CIA official declared sanctions a 'demonstrable success' in containing Iraq, while in 2000 a Pentagon staffer crowed: 'Iraq is contained...It has a broken economy. It is an isolated state' (Cockburn and Cockburn, 2000: 138; Herring, 2002: 53). Lopez and Cortright (2004) also insist that 'sanctions worked' because they contained Iraq. However, most judgements are overwhelmingly negative. Typical is Tripp's (2007: 253, 257) argument that 'sanctions...had no appreciable effect on the power of Saddam Hussein's dictatorship...on the contrary, his hold had tightened'. Many observers imply that, consequently, even minimal goals were not met. Former CIA official Judith Yaphe (2003: 30) insists that not only had sanctions 'failed' to topple or modify the regime, 'nor have [they] modified Saddam's behaviour...or made him willing to forgo WMD'. Similarly, Dodge (2006: 456, 465–6) suggests that the 'failure of sanctions to coerce the Iraqi government...ultimately increased [Saddam's] power', enabling him 'to defy the institutions of the international community and resist... thirteen years of coercive diplomacy'.

Tracing the mechanisms by which sanctions impacted Iraq's economy, society, and polity demonstrates both how, and how far, they worked to secure various objectives. This chapter argues that sanctions did not merely strengthen Saddam; they significantly destabilized his regime, profoundly transforming state–society relations and the Ba'athist system of rule. However, in the absence of significant, politically organized societal opposition, this was insufficient to topple the regime, which stabilized considerably under the OFFP. Nonetheless, Saddam's transition strategy involved making significant concessions, particularly on WMD, but also on Kuwait and terrorism, in order to have sanctions lifted. Consequently, claims that he entirely and success-fully resisted coercive diplomacy are inaccurate. However, the US and UK were unwilling to recognize these concessions by lifting sanctions, because—given their failed attempts at regime change—doing so would violate their residual goal of containing Iraq. This committed them to perpetual sanctions, despite dwindling international support. As Iraq increasingly eroded the embargo, their plans unravelled, setting them on course for war.

The chapter has four sections. The first describes the main coalitions con-testing Iraqi state power. The second outlines the embargo's economic impact. The third and fourth sections analyse how this altered the size, composition, and strategy of Iraq's coalitions from 1991 to 1996 and from 1996 to 2003 respectively. The conclusion summarizes the embargo's outcomes and explores why identifiable 'successes' were not recognized as such.

Iraq's Coalitional Struggles

Iraq has suffered violence, intense social conflict, and authoritarian rule since gaining independence from Britain in 1932. The country's highly artificial postcolonial borders encompassed numerous tribes, several ethnic groups—predominantly Arabs, with a sizeable Kurdish population in the north, and other minorities—plus sharp religious divisions between Shiite Muslims, dom-inant in the south, and Sunni Muslims, dominant in the centre. Sunni elites dominated the state under Ottoman and British rule and this continued after independence. As Iraq slowly industrialized and urbanized, it was also drawn into regional and global political divisions, its population further polarizing between nationalism and pan-Arabism (which excluded non-Arab minorities and Shiites), and between conservative and radical ideologies. Since this diverse, fragmented society precluded any group's hegemony, Iraq's first four decades witnessed intense factional struggles over state power, short-lived governments, and frequent military coups. Whether under the Hashem-ite monarchy (1932–58) or the subsequent republic, coercion and military support were critical for the survival of every government, bolstered by the dispensation of development project contracts and sequestered land to clien-telist networks (Tripp, 2007: 105–85). This context of violence, patronage, and fragmentation shaped the coalitions in place by 1990.

Iraq's Ruling Coalition

The Arab Socialist Ba'ath Party seized power in a coup d'état in 1968. Its position was initially highly precarious and dependent on military support, forcing it to compromise with better organized forces, notably the Iraqi Communist Party (ICP). Contrary to rational-choice expectations of 'satisficing', the Ba'athists sought to neutralize their enemies by cultivating support 'on as wide a scale as possible' (Sluglett and Farouk-Sluglett, 2001: 228). It leant leftwards to co-opt the ICP and its supporters, buying it time to squelch Kurdish opposition; extended tight political control over the army; and courted support from both Shiites and Sunnis. This strategy was enabled by a massive influx of resources stemming from the nationalization of Iraq's oil sector just before the 1973 oil crisis. This financed unprecedented government patronage, which co-opted most social groups and divided the rest, consolidating Saddam Hussein's dictatorship. Coercion nonetheless remained important, and it perpetuated Shiite and Kurdish opposition. The 1980–8 Iran–Iraq War exacerbated this opposition and began unravelling the Ba'athists' nationalist–developmentalist coalition. The Kurdish north and the Shiite south finally rebelled following Iraq's defeat in 1991.

After its coup, the Ba'athists sought to incorporate all major societal forces into their ruling coalition. The party was initially brought to power by predominantly middle-class, urban cadres and army officers. However, the regime's core quickly shifted to Arab Sunni tribes in central and north-west Iraq, whose members were incorporated en masse into the party and state apparatus (Baram, 1986; Jabar, 2000). Gradually penetrating every domain, the party became an important mechanism for social control and patronage, swelling to 25,000 members and 1.5 million 'adherents' by 1980 (Sluglett and Farouk-Sluglett, 2001: 184–5). The ICP, Iraq's best-organized party and the Ba'athists' most serious rival, was cajoled and coerced into joining a National Patriotic Front in 1973, which adopted a nationalist-socialist platform of nationalization and state-led development. Arab Shiite support was also courted through land reform, patronage for industry, oil nationalization, and Shiites' inclusion in the party leadership (Baram, 1986).

After the regime stabilized on this remarkably broad base, it moved to neutralize, co-opt, or suppress alternative power centres. The army was purged and Ba'athified, with non-Ba'athist activity outlawed within the military. Units directly controlled by the presidency and party—the Republican Guard (RG), special forces, and the Popular Militia—were established to deter coup attempts, and overlapping intelligence agencies were created to detect any anti-regime activity. The regime was thereby 'coup-proofed' and the army converted from an autonomous, pivotal force into a loyal support base (Tripp, 2007: 187–9, 206–7). The bureaucracy was similarly subordinated to the party, while a new constitution placed the cabinet under the authority of its Revolutionary Command Council (RCC). This essentially merged the state into the Ba'ath Party which, after Saddam became president in 1979, was also purged of remaining dissenters.

The Ba'athists also suppressed rival political forces. With ICP backing, the state crushed a Kurdish separatist insurgency in 1974, splitting the resistance, co-opting the Patriotic Union of Kurdistan (PUK) and many local chiefs into a Baghdad-centred patronage network, and diluting the Kurdish population through Arab resettlement (Tripp, 2007: 203–6). The Ba'athists then moved against the ICP, taking over its mass organizations and intensifying state harassment, peaking in a brutal 1979 crackdown that drove the ICP's surviving members into quasi-exile in the Kurdish north (Sluglett and Farouk-Sluglett, 2001: 186–9). Southern Shiite revivalism remained the final challenge. It was contained by banning some religious groups, incorporating some Shiites into government and patronage networks, and emphasizing the regime's Islamic credentials (Sluglett and Farouk-Sluglett, 2001: 198–9; Tripp, 2007: 208–9). The Ba'athists thus subordinated, divided, and disorganized most rival forces, depriving its opponents of any organizational vehicle. As Makiya (1998: 275) observed: 'all forms of organisation not directly controlled by the party have been wiped out. The public is atomised and broken up ... [leaving it] profoundly apolitical.'

This strategy was enabled by booming oil revenues, which financed the coercion and patronage necessary to maintain an unprecedentedly broad and state-dependent support base. Thanks to nationalization, government oil revenues increased from US$575 million to US$26 billion from 1972 to 1980 (Marr, 2004: 161). This enabled a vast expansion in the state's economic functions. By 1977, 80 per cent of output and 89 per cent of trade were state controlled (Marr, 2004: 163). While 40 per cent of government spending was on security, the oil boom also financed tax cuts and massive expenditure on consumer subsidies and welfare (Tripp, 2007: 206). Consequent rising employment and living standards won 'wide acceptance of the regime in many quarters' (Sluglett and Farouk-Sluglett, 2001: 173). Per capita income more than tripled from 1973 to 1976, generating a loyal, urban middle class including over half the population, and expanding the working class (Alkazaz, 1993: 216; Marr, 2004: 167). By the late 1970s, 20 to 25 per cent of Iraqis were directly or indirectly state employed, with further fifth in the security forces (Marr, 2004: 166; Makiya, 1998: 38). Development spending, dispensed through the Ba'ath Party and favoured tribes, generated loyal networks of 'kinship capitalism'. This strengthened the Sunni-dominated 'class-clan' at the regime's core, but also incorporated Kurdish and Shiite elites into a burgeoning millionaire class (Jabar, 2003a: 174–5, 2003b: 125). The traditional Shiite bourgeoisie either acquiesced or were deported to Iran, destroying autonomous centres of business power (Chaudry, 1991: 21). The government also eliminated the powerful landlord class, nationalizing their land and leasing it to peasants.

The Ba'athists thereby crafted 'a system of dependent support through selective use of economic powers' (Tripp, 2007: 198). Loyalty became a rational act, particularly when the alternative was imprisonment or worse. Coupled with their political demobilization, Iraqis were transformed into 'sycophants of the... social welfare state' (Natali, 2010: 25). The material benefits they received were accompanied by popular ideologies of Iraqi nationalism, Arab 'socialism', and anti-imperialism. Tired of constant unrest, most Iraqis apparently welcomed authoritarian stability (Makiya, 1998).

However, by the time sanctions were imposed, this solid ruling coalition had been severely damaged by the devastating 1980–8 Iran–Iraq War. Costing an estimated US$452.6 billion, the war brought about 'the end of development': after double-digit growth in the 1970s, the economy shrank, never recovering to 1980 levels (Alnasrawi, 1994: 100–2). Government spending fell by a third, and the state became dependent on Arab and Western loans, totalling US$80 billion by 1988 (Alkazaz, 1993: 223; Rohde, 2010: 109). Social and development spending was slashed and imports halved. Inflation reached 369 per cent by 1988, halving incomes and destroying the middle-class prosperity central to the regime's legitimacy (Alnasrawi, 1994: 95, 123; Marr, 2004: 203, 208). In 1987, the regime initiated crash structural adjustment, privatizing non-strategic sectors, returning all land and swathes of industry and commerce to landlords and favoured business elites, and smashing Iraq's remaining trade unions. The regime thus largely abandoned its earlier support base among workers and consumers, cultivating support from burgeoning rural and urban capitalists (Ishow, 1993; Chaudry, 1991). Black marketeering, smuggling, theft, and corruption became rife. Structural adjustment merely exacerbated the economic crisis, with GDP shrinking a further 9 per cent in 1988–9 and demobilized soldiers rioting in the streets (Alnasrawi, 1994: 114; Davis, 2005: 229). In desperation, the regime retreated to military Keynesianism, fuelling the military-industrial complex and eventually annexing Kuwait's oilfields to 'solve' its crisis (Chaudry, 1991).

Iraq's subsequent military defeat caused the regime's authority to implode. At least half of Iraq's routed army deserted, many fleeing to their southern hometowns and spurring widespread Shiite uprisings (Marr, 2004: 241). The Kurds also rebelled. Iranian assistance had enabled them to resume their insurrection in 1979, but Saddam had crushed it using massive violence and chemical weapons in 1987, killing over 100,000 Kurds. In 1990, the Kurdish parties seized control of northern Iraq, with even chiefs allied to Baghdad joining the revolt. Only the regime's core 'class-clan' held firm: the Sunni centre remained calm and its representatives in the RG loyal, enabling their deployment against the rebels. The Shiites—disorganized, leaderless, and divided by sectarian ideology—were swiftly suppressed, followed by the weakly armed Kurds (al-Jabbar, 1994). However, a Western no-fly zone effectively terminated Baghdad's rule over the north, leaving it under local Kurdish control. This symbolized Iraq's dramatic reversal in geopolitical fortunes, its invasion of Kuwait having turned virtually every regional state against it, including the Arab League. Although the regime restored order elsewhere in Iraq, its once broad coalition was in tatters, reduced to its Sunni Arab core, the elite parts of the bureaucracy and security apparatuses, and a slender class of state-linked business elites.

The regime's subsequent political strategy changed over time, and in response to sanctions, so it is explored in depth later ('The Impact of Sanctions on Iraqi Social Conflict: 1990–6'). Initially the regime promised reform, offered its opponents negotiations, and courted public support by retreating to traditional, state-based development to repair war damage. However, sanctions rendered this unsustainable beyond 1992, forcing the regime back into crisis-driven austerity to ensure its short-term survival, limiting its patronage to key supporters and deepening its alliances with tribal and criminal–business elites. Nonetheless, contrary to accounts emphasizing Saddam's 'defiance', one consistent aspect of Saddam's strategy after mid-1991 was compliance with core UN demands, insofar as this did not threaten regime security, so as to terminate the embargo as quickly as possible. This continued even after resource flows increased under the OFFP, though growing recognition that the US and UK would never lift sanctions also led the regime to intensify other efforts to fragment the embargo.

The Opposition Coalition

Reflecting decades of regime repression, co-optation, and divide and rule, the Iraqi opposition was extremely fragmented and weak when sanctions were imposed, with at least seventy different opposition groups in exile (Francke, 1994: 153). The Iran–Iraq War isolated them from their main population bases and destroyed their organizational structures; consequently, while the regime was in crisis after the Gulf War, so were they. The intifada caught them entirely by surprise, rendering them unable to lead (al-Jabbar, 1994: 98–106). Moreover, crucially, the destruction of the left and other secular democratic alternatives left no movement capable of unifying Iraq's disparate ethnic and religious communities around a common, universalist platform. The opposition instead comprised five rather incompatible strands: the frequently warring Kurdish parties, the Kurdish Democratic Party (KDP) and the PUK; Shiite Islamists, notably the Da'wa Party and the Supreme Assembly of the Islamic Revolution in Iraq (SAIRI); the rump ICP; a few liberal democratic nationalists; and the disgruntled ex-Ba'athists of the Iraqi National Accord (INA). Although the first four strands eventually combined as the Iraqi National Congress (INC), they remained weak and fractious, with incompatible aspirations.

The INC formed in 1992 after lengthy wrangling, and in 1993 became based in northern Iraq, sheltered by the Western no-fly zone. Its most powerful component was the Kurdish parties. The KDP, led by Mas'ud al-Barzani, dominated the Kurdish north and west, while Jalal Talabani's smaller PUK ruled most of the south and east. Combined, they fielded about 80,000 militiamen by 2003 (Stansfield, 2003: 136). Their main goal was regional autonomy from Baghdad, which was opposed by many nationalists and communists. Among Shiite Islamists, SAIRI was the best organized and most popular. Inspired and financed by Iran, it had 3,000–4,000 guerrillas, some of whom had aided the intifada (Baram, 1998: 52–3). However, Iraq's Shiites were heavily divided along class lines and its clerical elite was too weak to unite it around an Islamist identity; consequently, SAIRI's appeal was always constrained (Jabar, 2003c). Its divisive sectarianism played into Saddam's warnings of inter-communal strife if his regime fell. The once mighty ICP now numbered just a few hundred cadres, with virtually no links inside Iraq. Having abandoned communism for social democracy, they favoured a non-sectarian, multi-ethnic Iraqi polity. However, this alienated the Kurds and Islamists. Finally, a small group of liberal democratic nationalists around the financier Ahmed Chalabi assumed leadership of the INC as the party most acceptable in Washington, upon whose patronage and protection the INC ultimately depended. Liberalism was an extremely thin reed in Iraq, since most liberal anti-Ba'athists had simply emigrated. Over 500,000 intellectuals and professionals left during the 1980s, bringing the total emigré population to two million (Tripp, 2007: 218; Francke, 1994: 153). Chalabi thus had no real constituency within Iraq, while his arrogance and CIA ties frequently alienated his INC allies.

The INC lacked a coherent transition strategy. 'The opposition groups [were] not united on what constitute[d] possible or desirable methods for achieving change' and none 'publicly declared a programme of action designed to bring [it] about' (Francke, 1994: 175). The Kurds and democrats favoured a vague 'collaborative effort' between the people and military. Islamists favoured guerrilla tactics and a popular uprising, but their unpopularity beyond the south, and the lack of a southern no-fly zone, made this difficult. The ICP emphasized popular mobilization, but also had no means to achieve it (Francke, 1994: 175). Initially, the INC apparently hoped that establishing a rival 'government' on Iraqi soil would sap the regime's strength and legitimacy by encouraging military and bureaucratic defections, avoiding the need for civil war (Cordesman and Hashim, 1997: 65–6).

Ultimately, though, the INC relied heavily on Western intervention to remove Saddam for them. Chalabi urged the West to deploy human rights monitors to 'deter the regime from committing further human rights abuses' and to 'implement' UNSC resolutions on regime change, 'to bring about democratic political change ... by the removal of Saddam Hussein' (Chalabi, 1994: 228–30). Initially, the INC also supported sanctions, though they were extremely vague on how they were meant to support their transition strategy. Chalabi (1994: 229) argued that, combined with OFFP aid delivered by the UN, sanctions would make people 'realise that their livelihood is independent of Saddam Hussein, then it is a short step to conclude that his removal from power is possible'. Francke (1995: 15) suggests that the INC saw sanctions as a means to weaken the regime's coercive apparatus; deepen military, Ba'athist, and popular discontent that would 'target the Saddam regime'; and buy time for the opposition to connect with internal dissidents and, most importantly, for Western action against the regime. From this perspective, sanctions were supposed to 'work' through the resource deprivation and political fracture mechanisms. This was not far from the 'naive' view embraced by Western commentators, who also expected sanctions to work by provoking popular discontent (Dodge, 2010: 84–5, 87). For example, the *New York Times* reported the US government's view that, 'by making life uncomfortable for the Iraqi people, [sanctions] would eventually encourage them to remove President Saddam Hussein from power' (Lewis, 1991).

A final opposition group, not involved in the INC, was the INA. These disgruntled, exiled Ba'athists sought to replace Iraq's leadership but leave much of the regime intact. The INA consequently opposed the INC as traitors and rejected Western intervention. Its transition strategy instead involved encouraging a military coup (Francke, 1994: 162–3). Despite its authoritarian orientation, it attracted US support because a coup seemed more likely and less destabilizing than a mass uprising and full democratization. The Middle East director of the US National Security Council, for example, declared that 'our policy is to get rid of Saddam, not his regime' (Arnove, 2000: 11). Saudi Arabia bankrolled the INA for similar reasons.

Having thus identified the main forces contesting Iraqi state power, we can explore sanctions' economic impact, then how this affected coalitional struggles.

The Economic Impact of Sanctions on Iraq

UN sanctions fell into two phases: before and after the OFFP (see Table 4.1). In phase one, coupled with extensive war damage, sanctions comprehensively crippled the Iraqi economy;[1] in phase two, the OFFP enabled a modest revival.

---

[1] Distinguishing the effects of the Iran–Iraq and Gulf wars from those of sanctions is impossible. The estimated reconstruction costs of each war reached US$63 billion and US$200 billion

Table 4.1 Main sanctions imposed on Iraq

Date	Measure
August 1990	Comprehensive UN embargo on trade and financial transactions with Iraq, excepting imports for humanitarian purposes. Overseas assets frozen.
April 1995	UNSCR 986 establishes the OFFP, a 'temporary measure to provide for the humanitarian needs of the Iraqi people' until Iraq complied with UNSCRs. All imports required UNSC approval.
December 1996	UN–Iraq Memorandum of Understanding allows the OFFP to begin. Iraq allowed to export US$2 billion of oil every six months. Revenues, deposited in a UN escrow account, are allocated thus: 59% for humanitarian imports for central and southern Iraq; 13% for imports for the Kurdish region; 25% for war reparations; and 3% for UN administrative costs and weapons inspections.
February 1998	UNSCR 1175 lifts ceiling on Iraqi oil exports to US$5.26 billion every six months.
June 1998	UNSCR 1175 permits Iraq to import US$300 million of oil industry spares, raised to $600m in May 2000.
December 1999	UNSCR 1284 removes ceiling on Iraqi oil exports.
May 2002	UNSCR 1409 loosens import restrictions, limiting UNSC scrutiny to a specific Goods Review List.
2003	Sanctions mostly lifted following US invasion of Iraq.

Phase One: 1990–6

Iraq's rentier economy relied entirely upon government oil revenues being recycled into other sectors through state-owned enterprises, government consumption, contracts, subsidies, and import purchases. Consequently, embargoing Iraqi exports—of which oil comprised 96 per cent (Mahdi, 1998: 45)—had a tremendous multiplier effect. Government income collapsed from US$522 million to US$74 million from 1991 to 1994, destroying its capacity to finance economic activity and imports. Government spending fell from US$2.1 billion to US$514 million from 1991 to 1995, sustained only by printing money, which generated hyperinflation (Duelfer, 2004: ch. 2, 15). Iraq depended on imports for 80 per cent of its capital goods and inputs, many consumer goods, and over US$2 billion of food annually (Al-Kudayri, 2002: 212). Even if their purchase could somehow be financed without oil exports, excepting food, these items were embargoed. Massive shortages ensued, exacerbating inflation and shrinking industrial output by 80 per cent by 1992 (Al-Kudayri, 2002: 212). Iraq's GDP contracted sharply; food prices soared by 1,500–2,000 per cent during 1991 (Alnasrawi, 1994: 123); and real incomes plummeted (see Figure 4.1).

respectively (Rohde, 2010: 45; Alnasrawi, 1994: 95). However, in the six months between the imposition of sanctions and Operation Desert Storm, the Iraqi government estimated its losses at US$18.1–25.1 billion in decreased exports and production, increased production costs, and delayed development projects, suggesting that sanctions seriously worsened Iraq's economic crisis (Alnasrawi, 1994: 119).

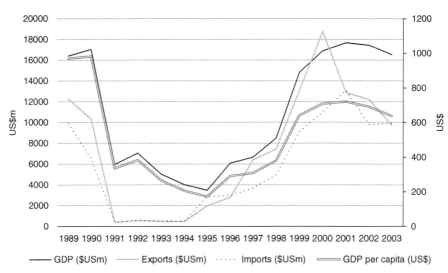

Figure 4.1 Iraqi economic indicators (current US$ millions)
Source: UNCTAD (2012)

Unsurprisingly, the distributional costs of sanctions were widespread, with uneven effects akin to radical structural adjustment. Those with foreign currency, productive assets, skills, land, political connections, and competitive businesses not reliant on imports fared better than others (Boone et al., 1997: 21–4). Access to oil for smuggling was particularly lucrative, benefiting a thin sliver of politico-business elites in the centre and north, discussed further later ('The Impact of Sanctions on Iraqi Social Conflict: 1990–6'). With food imports curtailed, domestic agriculture also expanded, benefiting landlords and stimulating de-urbanization, with the proportion of Iraqis engaged in agriculture increasing from 13 to 40 per cent during the 1990s (Cockburn and Cockburn, 2000: 125–6; Marr, 2004: 295). However, agriculture also severely lacked inputs and equipment, constraining yields and profits (Cordesman and Hashim, 1997: 140–2). In industry, the largely uncompetitive state sector fared terribly, with government funding constricted to oil, cement, chemicals, and textiles (Marr, 2004: 295). Conversely, sanctions spurred 'the revival of the private sector' in areas catering to the sanctioned population, like commerce, foodstuffs, and basic goods, but other sectors collapsed (Gazdar and Hussain, 2002: 55–6).

Unemployment soared to an unprecedented 40 to 70 per cent (Rohde, 2010: 68; Zurbrigg, 2007: 10). Hyperinflation devastated salaried workers, and the middle classes spawned by Ba'thist developmentalism were swiftly impoverished. The state sector preserved employment over wages, and the private sector vice versa. Public sector employees thus lost 62 per cent of their income, while skilled private sector workers lost 17 per cent, and unskilled ones 43 per cent (Gazdar and Hussain, 2002: 43, 46). Only leading officials and business-men experienced real-terms increases in income (Alnasrawi, 1994: 165). By the mid-1990s a state employee's median income was just US$5 per month (Moore and Parker, 2007: 2). By 1999 an estimated two million people had emigrated, draining the country's educated and technical elite (Griffin, 2000).

Phase Two: 1996–2003

The OFFP permitted only a modest economic recovery from this catastrophe. As Figure 4.1 shows, oil exports rose sharply from 1996, exceeding 1990 levels by 2000. However, they remained constrained by UNSC-imposed export ceil-ings, and by inadequate supplies of equipment and spare parts. Consequently, by 2003, from a possible income of US$220 billion, Iraq made only US$64 billion (Zurbrigg, 2007: 47, 17). This financed rising imports, but with a considerable lag because the Iraqi government received only 53 per cent of the proceeds and the US and UK repeatedly placed 'holds' on 'dual use' items (i.e. any 'related' to WMD, however implausibly, including even stationery). Consequently, despite submitting import contracts worth US$46.8 billion to the UNSC by December 2002, Iraq had received only US$24.8 billion worth of goods (UNOIPOFF, 2002). This was just US$0.29 per person per day, one quarter of the sum allocated to each UN mine-sniffing dog (Zurbrigg, 2007: 15, 22). The OFFP stabilized the Iraqi dinar, halting hyperinflation and thus easing the pressure on living standards. However, while unemployment fell to 28 per cent (Duelfer, 2004: ch. 2, 213), per capita income remained below 1990 levels. The Kurds benefited disproportionately from the OFFP, since their allocation was 22 per cent higher per capita than the rest of Iraq. Moreover, they uniquely received 10 per cent of their allocation in cash, which financed smuggled imports and local employment, stimulating the wider economy. They also endured fewer 'holds' (Azam and Saadi-Sedik, 2004: 360–2; Garfield, 2000: 50–1; UNOIPOFF, 2002).

The distribution of OFFP revenues is discussed later ('Iraq's Coalitional Strug-gles under the OFFP') as part of the ruling coalition's strategy, but can be summarized briefly here. After years of market chaos, the OFFP substantially restored the state's economic power. Since the government controlled most oil exports, it also bought and distributed imports. Although some imports were actually misdirected, the regime formally allocated 51.6 per cent to food and its handling; 8.8 per cent to agriculture; 8.5 per cent to health; 6.3 per cent to oil spares; 7.3 per cent to electricity; 6.2 per cent to housing; 4.6 per cent to water and sanitation; 4.5 per cent to communications and transportation; and 2.1 per cent to education (UNOIPOFF, 2002). This partly revived the devastated public sector and particular industries. A modest recovery in transportation, power, chemicals, and pharmaceuticals was underway by 2002, mostly among state-owned enterprises; conversely, 85 per cent of private factories had closed and only 115 (semi-)private firms remained listed on the Baghdad stock exchange (Braude, 2003: 107–15). However, the *informal* private economy apparently dominated, since only 40 per cent of workers were state-employed by 2003 (Duelfer, 2004: ch. 2, 213). Finally, renewed food imports, whilst decreasing consumer prices, seriously undermined Iraqi agriculture.

By 2003 Iraq's economy had recovered to around 1990 levels, though incomes were still lower. However, since the Iraqi economy was experiencing deep structural crisis in 1990, the OFFP was clearly no bonanza. As Gordon (2010: 126) argues, even combined with illicit trade, the OFFP 'could not have significantly restored an economy reeling from US$200 billion in [war] damage... and a loss of GDP... of US$40 billion a year'. Nonetheless, sanctions were gradually easing and Iraq was steadily reintegrating into the global economy. We can now examine how this affected Iraqi social conflict.

The Impact of Sanctions on Iraqi Social Conflict: 1990–6

Phase one of sanctions had dramatic consequences for all sides in Iraq. The ruling coalition was profoundly damaged. The threat posed by sanctions to the regime's social base and political survival was quickly realized, generating major concessions to UN demands. Sanctions also aborted an initial strategy of state-led reconstruction, forcing the regime into austerity measures in order to survive. With its social base, coercive capacities, and economic control crumbling, the regime had to reconstruct itself atop corrupt networks of smugglers, businessmen, and tribal leaders. Struggles for increasingly scarce resources intensified, escalating unrest within key support groups and creating serious intra-regime conflict, spurring further concessions to international pressure. However, the opposition could not exploit this disarray. The INA's plots failed miserably due to the regime's prior coup-proofing, and even impeded disarmament. Sanctions also exacerbated the INC's internal divisions. The Kurdish parties' sanctions busting generated severe KDP–PUK conflict, pushing the KDP into de facto alliance with Saddam. Consequently, when the INC launched a major military operation in 1995, it fragmented, and the impoverished Iraqi population remained passive. These internal divisions also permitted Saddam to 'invade' the north in 1996, neutralizing the INC.

Regime Responses, 1990–2

The Ba'athist regime's initial strategy involved making important concessions internationally, while offering superficial reforms and reconstruction spending domestically.

The dominant view in the literature is that the regime simply did not care about the embargo's impact on the populace, because it did 'not depend on popular support to stay in power' (Byman et al., 1998: 134). Saddam's successful defiance is attributed, in Weberian fashion, to the 'autonomy built up by the Ba'athist regime over 35 years of rule' (Dodge, 2006: 466). However, this overstates the regime's separation from society, overlooking the 'class-clan' and 'kinship capitalism' at its heart, its quest for a broad support base, and its increasing destabilization as economic growth collapsed and social conflict intensified, even before sanctions. It also wrongly assumes that the regime was indifferent about sanctions' impact on the population, despite the possibility of a repeat of the 1991 uprising and the threat to its residual nationalist-'socialist' legitimacy. Actually, sanctions were so devastating that, had Saddam not prioritized their removal, his own survival would have been unlikely.

The regime quickly realized that sanctions were immensely damaging and their termination was essential to avoid social and political collapse. Saddam told his inner circle: 'we do not accept that our people will die of hunger... like Somalia... our clear objective... is the lifting of sanctions' (CRRC, nd-j). He was increasingly alarmed at the government's dwindling ability to feed the population, fearing 'an uprising' (CRRC, nd-n). The regime, he concluded, must 'prove to our people... that we tried everything possible' to end the embargo, otherwise 'the country will eat itself' (CRRC, 1994d). 'The only thing that can satisfy our citizens is to lift the sanctions,' Saddam insisted (CRRC, 1994e). His inner circle agreed. Vice-President Taha, for instance, warned that 'very few' people remained loyal to the regime, insisting: 'we have to stop this disaster immediately, because the sanctions are killing us. We have to boost the morale of our people and stop the negative results of sanctions' (CRRC, 1991b).

Accordingly, the regime's initial strategy combined short-term measures to stabilize Iraqi society with concessions to end the embargo. In March 1991 the government accepted all UN resolutions and the RCC rescinded all laws on Kuwait's annexation, pledging to pay reparations and return Kuwaiti plunder (Marr, 2004: 239). In mid-1991 it also destroyed most of its WMD (discussed in detail later). Domestically, Saddam appointed a technocratic prime minister, announced political reforms, courted tribal sheikhs, amnestied intifada rebels, and offered talks with opposition parties (Jabar, 1997: 28). Although these moves yielded few lasting results, it bought the regime time to stabilize, luring some oppositionists, including the Kurdish parties, into negotiations.

Economically, the government cannibalized its reserves of food, gold, consumer goods, and machinery to finance short-term consumption, predominantly via the private sector, concentrating scarce resources on reconstruction and food.[2] Saddam argued these measures, directed explicitly at 'the poor', were essential to 'prove the [regime's] ability to lead' (CRRC, nd-k). A costly reconstruction campaign sought to repair war damage, boost popular morale, and restore government services. This apparently revived some infrastructural and industrial capacity but, given massive shortages of necessary supplies, it also exacerbated inflation and thereby the collapse of living standards (Mahdi, 1998: 50). The main beneficiaries were the state-dependent business elites who received many of the reconstruction contracts (Cockburn and Cockburn, 2000: 121, 126). To prevent unrest, the regime also instituted food rationing, distributing food reserves and around US$1 billion of imports financed by liquidating state assets (Clawson, 1993: 36–8). Rations were distributed for a nominal fee (US$0.12) and initially covered around two thirds of daily requirements (Graham-Brown, 1999: 168). Given hyperinflation, rations increased recipients' effective earnings by 5–122 per cent in 1991 (varying by income), rising to 120–1,390 per cent by 1993 (Alnasrawi, 1994: 90–2; Clawson, 1993: 48). However, again, regime-linked corporate suppliers and distributors gained disproportionately, being permitted to engage in widespread smuggling and dominate the domestic market in exchange for securing steady food supplies, which further tightened 'the symbiosis of the government and the private sector' (Gazdar and Hussain, 2002: 58; see also Graham-Brown, 1999: 168–70; Cockburn and Cockburn, 2000: 125; Sakai, 2001: 32; Natali, 2010: 50). The regime's initial response to sanctions was thus shaped by its historical class bases among consumers and the state-fostered business class.

The regime also made crucial concessions on WMD to end the embargo. Saddam's inner circle, overwhelmingly drawn from the RCC, was somewhat divided on this issue. The 'doves'—notably Foreign Minister Tariq Aziz and Oil Minister Amer Mohammed Rashid—favoured compliance 'to get rid of sanctions', as Tariq put it (CRRC, 1995f). These long-serving Ba'athist apparatchiks always recognized that the UN's demands were both 'political' (regime change) and 'technical' (disarmament, etc.), and promoted cooperation on the basis that full 'technical' compliance would suffice to get sanctions lifted (CRRC, nd-i, 1995d). They also argued that WMD were now useless since their deployment would provoke massive retaliation from Israel or the US (CRRC, nd-i). They were opposed by the 'hawks'—notably, Vice-President Izzat Ibrahim, Defence Minister Ali Hasan (Saddam's cousin), and the Minister of Military Industrialization, Hussein Kamil (Saddam's son-in-law). Vehement nationalists and members of the regime's Sunni core, they warned that the WMD inspectors—the UN Special Commission (UNSCOM)—would pursue

---

[2] This included the absorption or export of around US$500 million of Kuwaiti plunder (Clawson, 1993: 30). Sanctions thereby vitiated the achievement of one of their ostensible goals.

'sabotage activities', and compared the OFFP to 'colonisation' (CRRC, nd-n, nd-f). They suggested that Iraq could resist because sanctions would strengthen Iraq's unity and self-reliance, weakening the embargo over time (CRRC, nd-h). Most fundamentally, they did not believe that technical cooperation would end sanctions. As Izzat remarked, 'nothing is acceptable for America, except our removal . . . The US will not allow the Security Council to pass a resolution that will lift the boycott' (CRRC, nd-h). The hawk/dove division was therefore a tactical one over which policy was likeliest to end the embargo.

Given his concern to lift sanctions to forestall societal upheaval, Saddam was swayed by the doves. Despite popular views of Ba'athist Iraq as a one-man autocracy, Iraq's archives consistently show Saddam being remarkably collegial, neutrally chairing meetings of subordinates, often not voicing his opinion until the end, if at all. While Saddam often expressed similar suspicions to Izzat (CRRC, 1991a), and initially appeared to side with the 'hawks' by concealing Iraq's WMD, after mid-1991, with sanctions biting hard, he consistently sided with the 'doves'. He firmly dismissed Ali Hasan's suggestions of rallying Iraqis to attack UNSCOM (CRRC, 1994e), and supported accepting the OFFP to restore access to vital resources (CRRC, 1995h).

Accordingly, in July 1991 Saddam ordered Hussein Kamil to destroy Iraq's WMD stocks and programmes, and a MIC-based National Monitoring Directorate (NMD) was established to promote compliance with UN demands (Duelfer, 2004: ch. 1, 46). The Iraq Survey Group (ISG) found that Iraq terminated its nuclear programme and destroyed its entire chemical arsenal in 1991, with 'no credible indications' of any subsequent attempt to rebuild them (ISG, 2004: 9, 11). Iraq's biological arsenal was destroyed entirely during 1991–2. The regime sought to protect related infrastructure and expertise, generating suspicion that it planned to restore its arsenal. Actually, these moves apparently sought to defend Iraq's development by protecting its heavy industry, which was tightly connected to military production.[3] American investigators found 'a complete absence of discussion or even interest in biological weapons at presidential level', and even related experimentation was abandoned in 1995 (ISG, 2004: 14). All remaining sites were destroyed in 1996, and Iraq's crippled industrial base would, in any case, have vitiated any attempt to restart a biological weapons programme (ISG, 2004: 14–15). Iraq's long-range missiles were also destroyed in 1991. Iraq later smuggled in missile components, and its scientists designed missiles with a prohibited range, but these never progressed beyond blueprints, and both parts and plans were destroyed (ISG, 2004:

---

[3] Saddam frequently lauded scientists and advanced technology as central to Iraqi development (e.g. CRRC, 1977–8, nd-h, 1995a). Saddam believed that UNSCOM sought to deprive Iraq of modern technology (Duelfer, 2004: ch. 1, 63).

7–8; Katzman, 2003: 7). Thus, Iraq was entirely disarmed of WMD and their delivery systems by the mid-1990s, as recognized by UNSCOM inspectors, US Congressional reports, and some scholars (e.g. Ritter, 2005; Katzman, 2003; Cordesman and Hashim, 1997: ch. 17).

Crucially, however, the regime opted to disarm unilaterally, fearing the army would suffer 'psychological losses' if foreigners publicly destroyed Iraq's WMD (CRRC, nd-d). This rendered absolute verification of Iraq's disarmament virtually impossible. UNSCOM was left chasing documentary evidence of the extent of Iraq's WMD programmes and the destruction of all related materials. Often, proof was simply non-existent, enabling the US and Britain to maintain the embargo (Ritter, 2005: 39–41, 93).

Regime Responses, 1992–6

In this period sanctions accelerated the disintegration of the regime's social base and, consequently, the state's capacity to control Iraq's society and economy. To avert collapse, Saddam had to adopt a new strategy involving massive economic and political capitulations to private forces, notably the rural and mercantile bourgeoisie. This brought the regime some relief, but also generated new destructive dynamics as key support groups struggled, increasingly violently, for diminishing resources.

By 1992 the regime's once broad social base, already shaken by war and rebellion, was disintegrating. At the leadership level, the RCC had shrivelled, becoming dominated by Sunni loyalists, and no longer reflected the diversity of Iraqi society (Marr, 2004: 292). Ba'ath Party membership almost halved after the intifada, its mass organizations losing their power and appeal (Rohde, 2010: 63–4). Vice-President Izzat reported that the reconstruction drive had failed to restore the party's membership and morale, warning Saddam that 'sanctions are killing us' (CRRC, 1991b). With the state struggling to pay its employees, the bureaucracy shrank to under 17 per cent of the workforce, the lowest level since the 1970s, and officials were forced into corruption and moonlighting to survive (Marr, 2004: 294). Tariq warned Saddam that 'Iraq is collapsing', with government departments 'disintegrating' and 'corruption and bribery . . . out of control' (CRRC, 1991b). The military, already weakened by war and mass defections, shrank by two thirds, to just 375,000 by 2000 (Cordesman, 2000: 42, 47). Despite claims that the military remained formidable, in reality soldiers' living standards declined so radically that, by 1994, the Ba'ath Party reported that 244,666 men had deserted (CRRC, 1994b). The regime also conceded that it had 'lost' Iraq's middle classes, as they were wiped out by sanctions (Rohde, 2010: 64).

This loss of resources and societal support profoundly eroded the regime's regulatory capacity, severely constraining its strategic options. In 1992, as reconstruction faltered, the government attempted to institute a 'siege economy', imposing trade and price controls and even executing forty-two price-gouging merchants (Cordesman and Hashim, 1997: 42, 141–2). However, contrary to views of a regime maintaining or even increasing its robust, authoritarian control under sanctions, these interventions had little effect, merely pushing economic activity into the black market. Officials reported that they had lost control of trade to smugglers, destroying their ability to manage the economy (CRRC, 1992b, 1994a). Indeed, the state's share of GDP had collapsed from 55.3 to 13.6 per cent from 1989 to 1992 (Mahdi, 1998: 53). Saddam complained that 'the grip of the police is not what it used to be... [because of] the sanctions', noting that 'no one complies' with government price controls or tax demands, and that RCC decrees had 'no effect in practice' because even the courts declined to implement them (CRRC, 1993c, 1994c, 1996b). Ba'ath Party reports likewise showed that the brutal punishments specified for deserters were applied in only 0.1 per cent of cases (CRRC, 1994b). Saddam lamented: 'I don't think our state is regulated' (CRRC, 1993a).

The regime was therefore forced to revive the 'neoliberal' policies attempted in the late 1980s. This involved concentrating resources on key supporters and a renewed socio-political shift away from consumers and employees towards business and landed elites, the embargo's main beneficiaries.

In May 1994 Saddam became prime minister, initiating a pro-market 'stabilization programme'. The government abandoned its commitment to centralized financial management, directing individual ministries to raise their own funds and permitting them to open overseas accounts to facilitate smuggling (Duelfer, 2004: ch. 2, 46). It stopped printing money, imposed new taxes and service charges, cut subsidies, privatized assets, and deregulated private enterprise (Baram, 1998: 65–72). Far from manipulatively cultivating state dependency, as many suggest in relation to rationing, Saddam explained that this programme was intended to encourage 'reliance on individual and family abilities to face the blockade' (CRRC, 1994g). Rations were cut by 33 to 50 per cent and their recipients limited to 3.5 million state employees and their families. By 1995 rations provided only 1,000 calories per day and covered just two weeks per month (Cordesman and Hashim, 1997: 140–2). Private overseas remittances, estimated at US$1.2 billion annually, became vital to families' survival (Hiro, 2002: 13).

The regime's few remaining resources were concentrated among key support groups. Baram (2000a: 206–10) found that loyal areas were typically better shielded from the embargo's humanitarian effects than those participating in the intifada. While the army was slashed, with even the elite RG more than halved (Rohde, 2010: 55), spending was concentrated in the 15,000-strong Special Republican Guard (SRG), created in 1988 as the regime's ultimate protector. For everyday security, the regime relied increasingly on cheap but poorly trained militias like Fedayeen Saddam, controlled by Saddam's son Uday. A small, ID2,000 pay rise was targeted at 1.7 million military veterans and their families (CRRC, 1994g). State assets were sold cheaply to security officers, veterans, Ba'athist officials, and other designated 'friends of the president', based on their rank and service. As Sassoon (2012) demonstrates, distributing rewards based on time served was a long-standing practice, and made continued loyalty to the regime a rational act in the straitened circumstances of sanctions. Overall, these privileges were restricted to about 3.5 million Iraqis, 17 per cent of the population (Alnasrawi, 2001: 110–11).

Austerity measures and capitulations to market forces were accompanied by political concessions to groups benefiting from sanctions, aimed at bolstering the regime's societal support. Sanctions-induced food shortages significantly boosted the position of Iraq's tribal sheikhs, to whom agricultural land had been re-privatized in the 1980s. Landowners now received high prices for their crops, land grants, and input subsidies (Ahmad, 2002; Mahdi, 1998: 57–8; Graham-Brown, 1999: 197, 204). Even Kurdish landowners were drawn into supplying the government (Graham-Brown, 1999: 166). With party and state apparatuses withering, the regime was forced to recognize this economic shift politically by accelerating the outsourcing of governmental authority and responsibilities to tribal leaders, a process begun in the late 1980s. Under this 'neo-tribalist' policy, sheikhs were: appointed to lead local governments instead of Ba'athist officials; incorporated into the National Assembly and security forces en masse; given direct access to Saddam; permitted to maintain armed retinues; and given free reign over the peasantry, with their traditional legal powers and autonomy being restored (Baram, 1997; Dawisha, 1999). Even impoverished urban Iraqis were forced to recreate tribal arrangements to survive. By 1995 'the village had conquered the city . . . transforming the capital and the regime's social base' (Baram, 1997: 21).

Another group of beneficiaries was the sanctions-busting mercantile elite. Since the regime had fostered much of this elite, and had adopted pro-business policies in the late 1980s, these merchants initially enjoyed wide latitude and bonanza profits. Yet, as living standards collapsed, Saddam complained that sanctions were 'benefiting the wealthy class', which could 'lead to a feeling of inequality and a resentment and an uprising' (CRRC, nd-n). Yet, reflecting the state's collapsing control, Tariq reported that smugglers had 'surpassed the capacity of the Interior [Ministry]' to regulate. Even government security forces were illegally smuggling goods without permission (Schenker, 2003: 45–6). Tariq argued: 'we need to take over' (CRRC, 1992b).

Consequently, the regime used its tried-and-tested, carrot-and-stick methods to establish new partnerships with the nouveaux riches. Its 1994 economic deregulation platform made extensive concessions to them. Moreover, a 1992 ban on luxury imports was never enforced; banking was substantially privatized and deregulated; private sector groups were permitted to acquire and manage state enterprises; private merchants continued importing and distributing food; the government declined to tax its private contractors or trade with Jordan; and the hawala system was legalized (Graham-Brown, 1999: 164–70; Baram, 1998: 128; Duelfer, 2004: ch. 2, 255). However, despite abandoning much economic regulation, the regime nonetheless sought to create a 'limited access order' (North et al., 2007), coercively constraining lucrative opportunities to those loyal to Saddam. It moved to grab the best smuggling routes for itself and its immediate allies while extracting loyalty and bribes from other *Qitat al-Hisar* ('cats of the embargo', or 'fat cats'). As one 'fat cat' explained, purchasing the support of high-ranking patrons became essential to avoid extortion by lower-ranked officials. In exchange for bribes and political support, the cats received 'autonomy in the black market'. Another businessman explained the rules: 'if you have money, you can do anything you want. Just don't say bad things about Saddam or compete with his family' (Braude, 2003: 117–21). Iraq's peculiar political economy afforded the regime greater success than in Myanmar, where a similar strategy was pursued (see chapter 3). Given Iraq's development around oil, non-oil export smuggling was 'marginal', yielding only tens of millions of dollars annually (Mahdi, 1998: 46). Since the government owned and operated Iraq's oilfields, it thus had huge leverage over export smuggling. The overwhelming concentration of Iraq's trade at just five of around 500 possible border-crossing points also made it amenable to regime control, because the state's dwindling capacities could be focused here (Duelfer, 2004: 137). Infrequent public executions of price-gouging merchants simply helped to keep the rest in line.

With this new settlement, the regime's own networks became more dominant in smuggling, thereby extensively criminalizing state apparatuses. The leading networks were established by Hussein Kamil and Uday Hussein. Hussein Kamil's MIC became a key hub, establishing several oil-smuggling front companies, mostly exporting to Turkey. The proceeds were used to finance smuggled imports, which MIC distributed via allied companies, and to dispense contracts to firms, with larger awards determined by Saddam, his sons, the head of the Iraqi Security Services, and Vice-President Taha (Duelfer, 2004: 72–4; Cordesman and Hashim, 1997: 143). Uday also established front companies for oil smuggling to Turkey and barge-based smuggling operations with Iran, along with import rackets in consumer goods like cigarettes (CIJ, 2002: 44–5). Smuggling by Uday's Fedayeen Saddam was reportedly 'rampant' (CRRC, 1998a). In 1993 control over diesel smuggling was handed from the state oil company to these various regime-linked interests (CIJ, 2002: 29). Private companies were also extensively used for illicit imports and financial transfers, with regime-aligned businessmen receiving the most lucrative opportunities (Duelfer, 2004:

69, 72, 88–91). In this period, most sanctions busting occurred through official government-to-government trade protocols, particularly with Jordan and Turkey. Estimates of its annual value range from US$300 million to US$1 billion (Clawson, 1993: 49–50; Duelfer, 2004: ch. 2, 20; CIJ, 2002: 9). While paltry compared with pre-sanctions trade, this nonetheless generated some revenue to distribute to regime supporters and avert collapse.

This settlement between the regime and 'fat cats' helps explain why the Iraqi bourgeoisie remained largely loyal to Saddam. As explained earlier, the independent, Shiite bourgeoisie had been steadily eliminated, while the nouveaux riches were largely fostered by and reliant upon state patronage, making Iraqi capitalists unlikely anti-regime activists. Moreover, many thrived under sanctions. A UN Food and Agriculture Organization survey noted that, amidst widespread humanitarian suffering, 7 to 9 per cent of Iraqis were 'doing very well through trade and access to other attractive means of making money' (Graham-Brown, 1999: 184). Indeed, Ali Hasan told Saddam that businessmen were 'having good times under the sanctions' and 'none ... want sanctions to be lifted' (CRRC, 1994e).

One particularly crucial alliance fostered by sanctions busting was that between Baghdad and the KDP. Most oil smuggled to Turkey went by road through KDP-controlled territory. To facilitate this, KDP leader Mas'ud Barzani's front company, Asia World, was cut into the trade, and 'taxes' were paid to the KDP 'government'. By 1996 this route yielded an estimated US$596 million annually. About 17 per cent went to the Iraqi government and firms, 9 per cent to the KDP administration, and 18 per cent to KDP-linked companies (CIJ, 2002: 34). This income enabled Kurdish merchants to smuggle food and consumer goods, which were then transhipped to Iraq via state-linked business networks. The Kurds had little choice but to participate, since they faced both UN sanctions and an Iraqi government 'embargo' after 1990, leaving the Kurdish administration dependent on smuggling for around 80 per cent of its income (Natali, 2010: 45). However, given its politically mediated nature, 'most of the [smuggling] revenues benefited individuals tied to the KDP or PUK, private companies linked to the state, and privileged entrepreneurs', fostering 'an emergent quasi-private sector dependent on Baghdad' (Natali, 2010: 50, 48). Thus, the KDP, the opposition's strongest force, effectively became allied with Saddam. As discussed later ('Sanctions and the Iraqi Opposition, 1990–6'), this seriously damaged the opposition coalition.

The regime's shrivelling resources and shifting social base occasioned changes in its legitimating ideologies, too. As even paper and ink became scarce, the regime's once rich cultural output shrivelled, offering little more than a personality cult of Saddam (Davis, 2005). As it was forced to dismantle the residual welfare-developmentalist state, the Ba'ath Party also had to abandon the nationalist-socialist ideology that had accompanied it, retreating to declaratory anti-Zionism and anti-imperialism (Cordesman and Hashim, 1997: 15), and the promotion of particularist identities that legitimized the regime's enforced reliance on local elites. Government leaders feted Arab tribal culture, re-emphasizing their once suppressed tribal affiliations (Baram, 1997; Dawisha, 1999). Secularism was jettisoned for religiosity. To bolster its Sunni core, the regime encouraged fear of Shiites and of religious strife should the regime falter. The population 'retreat[ed] into particular clans and sects' to seek comfort from their suffering (Rahim, 1994: 191). 'Economic sanctions [thus] fuelled sectarianism' (Yousif, 2010: 360). This, too, undermined the opposition coalition, as discussed later ('Sanctions and the Iraqi Opposition, 1990–6').

Although this new strategy helped prevent the regime's collapse, it also generated new sources of resistance and disorder. The brutal suppression of the intifada, rising sectarianism, and collapsing state services fuelled a widespread Shiite revivalist movement in the south. Ayatollah Mohammed Sadiq al-Sadr's welfare work gained him extensive support among the urban poor, as well as mercantile and tribal leaders excluded from Saddam's patronage network, creating a new anti-regime force (Jabar, 2003a: 170–1; Abdullah, 2006: 85–6). The government also remained embroiled in counter-insurgency warfare in the southern marshes, where SAIRI guerrillas operated.

Neo-tribalism came at an even heavier cost. Tribal sheikhs exploited their restored powers, engaging in banditry and tribal warfare. By 1991 the General Security Directorate reported that competition for state patronage had already generated thirty-five inter- and intra-tribal conflicts, some violent, and growing friction between tribes and party-state officials, making the tribes a 'liability' for public order (CRRC, 1991–2). Even some sheikhs complained to Saddam that party state officials appeared powerless to control this violence (CRRC, 1992c). Military and Ba'athist leaders deeply resented this loss of authority, urging the government to downgrade the sheikhs' powers (CRRC, 1991–2, 1992a). Coupled with the use of militias like the Fedayeen Saddam to settle private scores (Sassoon, 2012: 150), these developments led many Iraqis to lament that their once-robust state had degenerated into 'uncontrolled tribal and gang warfare' (Davis, 2005: 239).

Most importantly, neo-tribalism increased the regime's vulnerability to tribally based military coups. Because key tribes were directly incorporated into state apparatuses, so were tribal dissatisfactions. Accordingly, what might begin as an inter-tribal struggle for power and resources 'under the present regime' could more easily morph into an anti-regime struggle (Sakai, 2003: 157, my emphasis). This risk increased as sanctions destroyed incomes, including within the military units employing many tribesmen. By 1995 even the most 'basic needs' of soldiers, such as uniforms and shoes, could not be provided (CRRC, nd-g). Accordingly, from 1993 to 1996 at least five coups were attempted, two involving the RG and one even the SRG. Most originated within formerly loyal clans, including segments of Saddam's own al-Bu Nasir tribe, which saw him as no longer able to provide for them (Baram, 1998: 48–51; Cordesman and Hashim, 1997: 20–56). As Cordesman and Hashim (1997: 56) note, these were 'clan-oriented struggles... [to gain or] preserve power by getting rid of a man... perceived as the reason that sanctions continued'. An informant on the 1994 plot reported that the conspirators were motivated by the 'collapsing economic situation and the worsening social conditions'; they 'did not accept what has befallen Iraq because of Saddam Hussein. [He] and his family are living in luxury whereas the Iraqi people are living in misery and hardship.' After overthrowing him, they planned to 'normalis[e] relations with all countries' (CRRC, 1994–8). Saddam's fear that sanctions would prompt uprisings was clearly justified.

These internal rebellions arguably pushed Saddam into increasingly desperate measures to end the embargo. Throughout 1994 the regime insisted that it had complied with UN resolutions, issuing a 'full, final, and complete' declaration on biological weapons and demanding that sanctions end (Duelfer, 2004: 46–7). With the UNSC resisting any change, in September 1994 Saddam decided to re-invade Kuwait, hoping this might break the international 'conspiracy' to 'starve Iraq', or at least 'prove to our people... that we have tried everything possible' (CRRC, 1994d). Baram (1998: 148) argues that this gambit reflected the regime's 'fear of domestic unrest' amidst the aforementioned tribal rebellions and coup attempts. However, Staff General Ra'ad Majid al-Hamdani (2003: 173) warned Saddam that the army now lacked 'the combat capabilities to permit a second invasion... [due to] the economic, military and political embargo'. Saddam relented: troops massed on the border in October, but did not invade. The gambit failed miserably, drawing US military retaliation and a condemnatory UNSC resolution. Saddam backed down, directing the National Assembly to formally recognize Kuwait's borders and sovereignty in November 1994 (Katzman, 2003: 9). Thus, although sanctions provoked counterproductive behaviour, contrary to their stated goals, they also weakened Iraq's capacity to follow through. Arguably, coupled with military pressure, they indirectly produced compliance.

Perhaps most importantly, the regime's degeneration into criminal business networks created severe internal rifts, including within Saddam's own family. With responsibility for fundraising outsourced to individual ministries, and income sources suddenly contracting to limited smuggling opportunities, fierce '"turf" wars [emerged] over control of this parallel economy' (Graham-Brown, 1999: 171). The principal protagonists were regime insiders from Saddam's al-Bu Nasir tribe: Hussein Kamil, Uday and Qusay Hussein (Saddam's sons), and Barzan al-Tikriti (Saddam's brother-in-law). Partly reflecting neo-tribalism, this intra-clan rivalry had initially emerged via marriage alliance politics in the 1980s (Jabar, 1997: 24–5). However, it was now severely exacerbated by rivalry for

scarce resources. Around 1993 Uday began contesting Hussein Kamil's dominance in smuggling, particularly with Iran, publicly attacking him through his
media outlets (CIJ, 2002: 68). In 1994 Uday exploited Hussein Kamil's convales-
cence following brain surgery to take over several MIC networks (Cordesman and
Hashim, 1997: 25). Upon Hussein Kamil's return, he also clashed with Qusay's
cronies in MIC and the Transport Ministry. When Hussein Kamil reported one
of them to Saddam for corruption, Qusay apparently directed the state security
apparatuses to investigate his brother-in-law (CRRC, 1996a). Hussein Kamil thus
fled to Jordan on 7 August 1995 with his brother—the co-commander of the
Special Security Office and head of the Tribal Chiefs' Bureau—and other relatives,
including two of Saddam's daughters. From Amman he launched a Council for
National Salvation dedicated to overthrowing Saddam.

Saddam rightly observed that this outcome reflected 'the creation of
empires in the Ba'ath party' (CRRC, 1995e). Because ministries were instructed
to raise revenue independently, each was struggling over diminishing economic opportunities and forging criminal business alliances. As the Iraqi
Intelligence Service (IIS) reported, Hussein Kamil had established a network
of 'officials and ... shady characters' which became 'untouchable by the law'
(CRRC, 1995g). Saddam acknowledged that he had been empowered to 'us[e]
the state for his personal and private interest' by claiming to act on the
president's personal authority (CRRC, nd-e, m). This was possible, his advisors
explained, because Saddam's inaccessibility allowed various 'empires' to act
without oversight (CRRC, 1995b). Saddam linked all this directly to the 'difficulties' created by the embargo. While smuggling was necessary, he said,
some officials took 'advantage of ... sanctions ... [they] started to rely on the
financial bases and on what these capitalistic bases entailed ... [creating] an
overlap between the official and personal' (CRRC, 1995j).

Hussein Kamil's defection was a serious blow, provoking panic and purges
in Baghdad. Recognizing that that the Ba'ath Party had become 'a tool or stair
for his relatives so they can sneak into authority', Saddam dismissed several
close family members from their governmental posts, including Uday and
Ali Hasan (CRRC, nd-m; Baram, 1998: 10–11). The bureaucracy and military
were purged of those linked to Hussein Kamil, while MIC was partially dismantled and reassigned to other departments (Cordesman and Hashim, 1997:
26–8; Graham-Brown, 1999: 159–60).

The defection also generated further international concessions. In Jordan
Hussein Kamil discussed Iraq's WMD with Western officials. While rightly
insisting that 'nothing remained' of Iraq's arsenal and that UNSCOM had
been 'very effective', he revealed that WMD-related documents had been
dispersed to MIC employees' homes, suggesting that UNSCOM would need
to launch 'a new war of searches' (UNSCOM/IAEA, 1995). These revelations
seriously damaged Baghdad's efforts to satisfy the UNSC and lift the embargo.

Yet Hussein Kamil's defection also removed a leading 'hawk' from Saddam's inner circle. Through 1995 Saddam's advisors had debated whether to accept the OFFP, increasingly agreeing that the UN might never lift sanctions, whatever Iraq did. The hawks, particularly Hussein Kamil, argued that UNSCOM's 'insignificant, silly questions', designed to account for all WMD-related materials and documents, merely aimed to perpetuate sanctions. Since further disclosures would only assist this strategy, they advocated defiance. Despite their growing scepticism, the doves maintained that technical compliance could still end the embargo. They lamented the careless, unilateral disposal of WMD in 1991, arguing that 'we are responsible' for the deadlock (CRRC, 1995c). Hussein Kamil's defection removed the hawks' leading representative, while Ali Hasan's subsequent ouster deducted another. Tariq and other doves exploited this to promote intensified cooperation with UNSCOM, arguing that Hussein Kamil had pursued confrontation only as part of a plot to provoke Western military attacks (CRRC, 1995e, g).

Consequently, the regime became more cooperative, 'bending over backwards' as UNSCOM's chief inspector put it (Ritter, 2005: 110). To pre-empt Hussein Kamil's revelations, the government blamed him for Iraq's troubles with UNSCOM, announcing the discovery of many WMD-related documents at his farm and handing them over. The government also expanded the NMD's presence to every ministry and company to enforce compliance with UN demands. Saddam repeatedly ordered his ministers not to engage in any activity that could undermine compliance, while MIC officials and scientists were instructed to surrender any WMD-related documents on pain of death (Duelfer, 2004: 47, 49). Finally, as the Iraqi dinar further collapsed during 1995, Baghdad began negotiating the OFFP's terms with the UN.

By the mid-1990s, then, sanctions had significantly transformed the Iraqi state and regime. Having virtually bankrupted the state, sanctions compelled an enormous shift from the regime's traditional strategy of state-led welfarist developmentalism, and its social base among consumers. Through ad hoc, crisis-driven measures, the regime's base shifted to the few groups benefiting from sanctions, previously dominant under the Iraqi monarchy: landlords and business elites. Despite some counterproductive effects, these changes fulfilled several official goals of sanctions, particularly on WMD. Moreover, they significantly destabilized the regime, even in its heartlands. Why were opposition forces unable to exploit this disarray to oust the regime?

Sanctions and the Iraqi Opposition, 1990–6

Although sanctions weakened the regime, they also weakened the opposition. The INC benefited from the regime's disintegration and was able to launch a military raid from the north in 1995. However, the popular uprising it sought to provoke never occurred, partly because of sanctions' impacts on the masses. Moreover, the INC was fatally undermined by the KDP's alliance with Baghdad, which allowed Saddam to penetrate the north and render the INC defunct by 1996.

The opposition coalition grew modestly as the regime's based shrivelled under sanctions. The IIS reported that rising poverty had made citizens vulnerable to external subversion and encouraged educated Iraqis to emigrate, with many becoming opposition supporters (CRRC, 2001d). The INA was founded by Ba'athist defectors (Hiro, 2002: 78), and by 1995 the INC had also attracted around 3,000 defectors, including former head of military intelligence General Wafiq al-Samarra'i. He led an INC military raid into Iraq in March 1995, precipitating the collapse of several Iraqi brigades (Marr, 2004: 271). However, despite revealing Iraq's military weakness, the incursion did not spark the popular Shiite uprising in the south, or the coup in Baghdad, that the INC had intended (Baram, 1998: 56–8). Why?

A large part of the answer is that sanctions exacerbated the opposition's pre-existing divisions and disarray. First, sanctions themselves proved divisive. The opposition initially supported sanctions for want of a better alternative. However, reacting to Iraqis' terrible suffering, the ICP split from this consensus, pursuing the lifting of sanctions as a 'patriotic duty' and arguing that 'a starving population has neither the will not the strength to rebel' (Francke, 1995: 16). Following internal divisions, SAIRI also called for sanctions to target the regime, not the people (Al-Bayati, 2011: 24). The INA remained anti-sanctions and competed violently with the INC for US backing, bombing its headquarters in 1995 in a botched attempt to assassinate Ahmed Chalabi (Cockburn and Cockburn, 2000: 213–14).

More importantly, sanctions severely intensified intra-Kurdish rivalry. Under Western protection, the north held elections for a local administration in May 1992. The vote was evenly split between the PUK and KDP, producing an uneasy power-sharing arrangement. However, while the KDP was incorporated into the Iraqi regime's sanctions-busting networks thanks to its control of the Turkish border, the PUK was not, and its control of the Iranian border yielded far less income. The PUK demanded a share of KDP revenues, precipitating an intensifying struggle for resources and power that paralysed and divided the local administration. By 1994 Kurdish militias were clashing, with INC mediation barely keeping the peace. The weaker PUK sought Iranian support, receiving some money, weapons, and training (Baram, 1998: 53). The KDP turned to its allies in Baghdad. Writing to Saddam, Mas'ud renounced the INC's 'mercenaries', claiming to 'love and appreciate your Excellency'. Saddam intensified the 'secret relationship' by sending arms, arguing, 'it's in our interest to settle this battle' for the KDP, given the PUK's Iranian connections (CRRC, nd-a). This escalated the conflict.

This intra-opposition division undermined the INC's March 1995 offensive and fatally weakened the INC. The CIA helped plan the operation, but the US withdrew its air support on INA advice that the manoeuvre would provoke massive Iraqi retaliation. The KDP also withdrew, seizing the opportunity to grab PUK-held territory (Hiro, 2002: 81). SAIRI also demurred, considering the plan risky and ill-conceived (Al-Bayati, 2011: 64–5). Given this uninspiring performance, the Iraqi population's passive reaction is perhaps unsurprising. Worse still, in 1996 KDP–PUK conflict escalated again. The PUK sought Iranian military assistance, prompting the KDP to invite Baghdad to intervene. With support from 30,000 Iraqi soldiers, the KDP overwhelmed the PUK. This army also attacked the INC headquarters, seizing documents and arresting many members, exposing all of its ongoing plots (Tripp, 2007: 256–8, 266). This was a major boost to the regime: it had ousted the main opposition organization from Iraqi soil and reasserted power over the north. For the KDP, the INC was 'extinct'; the CIA agreed it was 'defunct', ending its funding in 1997 and shifting its patronage to the INA (Cockburn and Cockburn, 2000: 278–9).

However, while effective in sabotaging INC activities, the INA proved no more successful in ousting Saddam, due to its reliance on coup plots. The INA was assisted by CIA operatives within UNSCOM, who contacted conspirators inside Iraq and installed monitoring devices to intercept communications and locate Saddam to facilitate his assassination (Hiro, 2002: 82–3, 101–2, 105–7; Ritter, 2005: 163–4). From Amman the INA successfully recruited a network from the regime's inner core, including the SRG, RG, and the General Security Service (Cockburn and Cockburn, 2000: 228). However, like the other coup plots discussed earlier, they were ultimately thwarted by the state's strategic selectivity. Saddam had 'coup proofed' his regime by the 1970s, with the state's coercive apparatuses constantly spying on one another. This structure, while weakened by sanctions, was nonetheless maintained through prioritized resource allocation. Consequently, despite vast increases in the number of coup plots under sanctions, they were all detected and defused well before their fruition. The INA plot was no different: Iraqi intelligence penetrated it in early 1996. Chalabi warned the CIA of this, but his counsel was dismissed as sour grapes. In June 1996 the government rounded up the conspirators, purging over 800 officers and dissolving the SRG's third battalion (Cockburn and Cockburn, 2000: 226–9). Although the regime was doubtless rattled, the plot had failed. It was the last significant threat that Saddam faced.

The other half of the explanation for the opposition's failure relates to the Iraqi masses. Explanations for the absence of popular opposition usually highlight the pervasive fear generated by Iraq's security forces (Makiya, 1998), and/or the rationing system, which many authors claim was 'manipulated' to extract loyalty (e.g. Graham-Brown, 1999: 169; Salman, 2000: 87; Mazaheri, 2010: 258). However, the frequent implication that the regime essentially threatened to starve anyone who rebelled is unsustainable.[4] Only areas not under government control did not receive rations: the north, and the southern marshes. Elsewhere international NGO inspections found 'identical' rations were distributed via an 'exemplary', 'comprehensive and equitable' system (Clawson, 1993: 40; Gazdar and Hussain, 2002: 57). During the OFFP the UN found no evidence of misuse or hoarding of humanitarian supplies (Herring, 2002: 49–51). 'Manipulation' apparently involved only *additional* perks for key support groups (Baram, 2000a: 210). Nor was rationing unprecedented: consumer subsidies were used by *all* post-independence Iraqi governments to maintain popular support (Gazdar and Hussain, 2002: 63). As discussed earlier, Saddam saw rationing as essential to avoid an 'uprising'. Rather than involving a simplistic 'bread-for-loyalty' exchange, the system's main effect was that 'Iraqis tend[ed] to see any disruption of the political system as a threat to their own livelihood', incentivising 'passivity' (Baram, 1998: 67). As an RG report warned: 'any disruption of the ration card system will lead to chaos' (CRRC, 2001c).

Moreover, given sanctions-induced cuts in rations, the population *never* depended entirely upon them; indeed, as noted, Saddam actively encouraged self-reliance. By 1992 rations provided only 37 per cent of pre-sanctions calorific intake, less than required for survival. To survive, Iraqis had to supplement rations with market-based activities beyond state control (Moore and Parker, 2007: 2). This daily struggle for subsistence was time-consuming and depoliticizing, as in Myanmar (see chapter 3). As one Iraqi intellectual scoffed when 'foreigners urge us to overthrow Saddam Hussein ... You are looking at a people whose energy is drained simply looking for the next meal' (Makiya, 1998: xviii). The UN's humanitarian coordinator concurred that even Iraqis concerned with governance were now 'preoccupied with survival at its most basic level' (Halliday, 1999: 36). One man told reporters: 'we're like animals. We can only think of food and drink ... they have taken away our dreams' (van der Gaag and Arbuthnot, 2000: 159). Thus the daily struggle in Iraq's extremely harsh market conditions, rather than straightforward state dependency, destroyed opportunities for resistance.

Importantly, however, the embargoed population was already suffering from decades of depoliticization and atomization. As described earlier, the Ba'athist regime had eliminated or absorbed all independent civic and political groups and cultivated widespread economic dependency, leaving no collective organizations able to mobilize and sustain political resistance. The unlikelihood of hardship generating resistance in this context had

---

[4] Alternatively, Oeschlin (2014: 25) argues that authoritarian regimes subjected to sanctions deliberately 'decrease the supply of public goods' to make citizens' revolts 'most costly', claiming specifically that the Iraqi regime pursued a deliberate 'strategy to make the middle class struggle'.

already been demonstrated by the limited response to collapsing living standards during the 1980s; sanctions only exacerbated Iraqis' existing tendency to adapt themselves to hardship. Thus, while workers suffered grievously under the embargo, the ICP's destruction left them without alternative political representation, while their trade unions had first been absorbed into the Ba'ath Party then smashed in the 1980s. Consequently, unlike in South Africa, there was no organized working class able to promote regime change. The common suggestion that the embargo's destruction of Iraq's middle classes was particularly deleterious for chances of democratization (e.g. Mazaheri, 2010: 264; Yousif, 2010: 361) is also a naive perspective that ignores their origins and trajectory. Iraq's urban middle classes were never 'liberal'; they had always supported authoritarian rule. The Ba'athists had also decimated the independent Shiite bourgeoisie, fostering a state-dependent class of businessmen and urban professionals. As regime creatures, lacking any independent organizations, these groups were unlikely to promote democratic change. They could not initiate a coup themselves, and lacked the numbers or inclination for rebellion. At best they were a latent support base for a coup that would leave the basic regime intact (Clawson, 1993: 47).

Sanctions undoubtedly exacerbated this pre-existing atomization and depoliticization. First, as discussed earlier, a starving population had neither the will nor the capacity to rebel. Secondly, widespread suffering arguably helped the regime to discredit opposition groups, because they were associated with Western policies. Anecdotal evidence suggests that the regime successfully presented sanctions as a Western conspiracy to starve Iraq, generating a nationalist backlash domestically and in other Arab countries (Cordesman and Hashim, 1997: 15, 109, 153–5; Doyle, 2000; Cockburn and Cockburn, 2000: 118, 139; Hiro, 2002: 17; Halliday, 1999: 36; Ritter, 2005: 1). The government 'used [the opposition's] outside support to tarnish the opposition's image and brand it as treasonous, beholden to foreign masters bent on the destruction of the country' (Bengio, 2000: 94; see also Kubba, 1994). The CIA quickly concluded that the INC 'lacks credibility inside Iraq...Many deride the organization's...close ties to the West' (CIA, 1993: 24). The IIS reported that their support for sanctions was 'enough to send the Iraqi opposition to the history bin' (CRRC, 2001d).

Thirdly, sanctions caused rapid social decay, fostering particularist identities that further retarded collective action. The Ba'ath Party command lamented the embargo's 'great psychological effect', reporting massive rises in family breakdown, mental illness, criminality and atomization (CRRC, 1999b). As state control collapsed, rising crime and insecurity led to the disintegration of local communities, declining sociability, and a retreat into nuclear families (Al-Ali, 2000: 75, 78; Halliday, 1999). The destruction of state welfare and the regime's embrace of neo-tribalism and sectarianism accelerated society's degeneration into ethnic and religious groups (Makiya, 1998: xxx–xxxi, 104, 106; Marr, 2004: 297; al-Jabbar, 1994: 115). This actually assisted the regime's strategy, since its 'perspective [was] adopted even by those seeking to overthrow it' (Al-Khafaji, 1994: 28): even opposition leaders began emphasizing their tribal affiliations (Sakai, 2003: 159). Rising particularism, especially sectarianism, destroyed any remote possibility of a universalist platform emerging to unite and mobilize Iraq's disparate communities, and enabled the Ba'ath Party to posture as uniquely capable of preserving Iraq's national integrity and domestic order. Similarly, despite the clear dangers of neo-tribalism, tribal fragmentation enabled divide and rule: if one tribe rebelled or plotted a coup, forces from another could be deployed against it. Their fragmentary identities precluded them unifying into a force capable of toppling the leadership (Baram, 1998: 25–31).

Thus, while sanctions did not originally create the opposition's deep divisions or Iraqi society's disorganization and demobilization, they clearly exacerbated them. In spurring intra-Kurdish division, sanctions severely fragmented the opposition coalition and boosted the regime. Saddam's ideological strategy also multiplied the atomizing effects of the widespread poverty inflicted on Iraqis, decreasing the likelihood of resistance.

Iraq's Coalitional Struggles under the OFFP

Under the OFFP Iraq's escalating social conflict eased substantially, enabling a shift in regime strategies. The limited restoration of oil revenues partially reinvigorated the state's economic role and patronage powers, enhancing the regime's power relative to the social forces upon which it had become dependent. The regime could retreat somewhat to earlier strategies of rule, increasing the Ba'ath Party's role and producing modest, state-led development. The regime thereby stabilized. The Iraqi opposition, meanwhile, was in profound disarray, becoming reliant on US military intervention. The association between the opposition, the US, and UNSCOM gradually undermined and terminated Iraq's cooperation in 1998. While never returning to WMD, the regime shifted to manipulating the OFFP to erode sanctions. By around 2000 Iraq was on the verge of international rehabilitation, threatening the US–UK goal of containment, let alone regime change.

Regime Responses to the OFFP

The OFFP generated a modest economic revival, with GDP recovering to pre-sanctions levels by the early 2000s. Although the resources this generated for the regime should not be exaggerated, the OFFP partially restored the state's economic role and thus the regime's support base. It also substantially re-empowered the state vis-à-vis landlords and private smugglers, permitting a partial retreat from neo-tribalism and revival of the Ba'ath party's role.

The OFFP substantially altered the power relations between the state and Iraq's quasi-private sector. In negotiations with the UN, Baghdad insisted on administering the imports purchased with oil export revenues, so as to retain control of Iraq's economic development and prevent the UN directing resources to anti-government 'conspirators' (CRRC, nd-b, 1995h). Although this delayed the start of OFFP imports to December 1996, crucially it ensured that the state's economic role, substantially destroyed by sanctions, would revive. The government's dominant role in trade was gradually restored. Initially only food and medical imports were allowed, but later oil spares and other equipment necessary to restore public services were permitted. Accordingly the state's allocation of resources to industry, construction, and welfare services increased, partially revitalizing the public sector. Conversely, the relative economic power of Iraq's quasi-private sector actors declined. With the state importing food, food smuggling waned. Merchants shifted into vehicles, machinery, and luxuries, still benefiting from regime protection rackets (Sakai, 2001: 32), while other regime-linked firms again received government contracts. Iraq's landlords fared much worse: as 80 to 100 per cent of basic staples were now imported, prices collapsed, terminating the agricultural mini-boom (Duelfer, 2004: ch. 2, 207). This destroyed agricultural profitability in many areas, particularly the north, increasing reliance on government handouts (Natali, 2010: 61–3). The surviving landlords became dependent on state patronage, as government subsidies provided up to 80 per cent of agricultural inputs (Gordon, 2010: 131).

Although the state received no oil revenue directly, its budgetary position nonetheless improved. OFFP imports freed up about US$1 billion that the regime had been sourcing elsewhere (Baram, 1998: 73). The regime also corrupted the OFFP. It exploited its authority to allocate export contracts by selling some oil at below-market prices in exchange for kickbacks, and its power to select importers by inserting artificial 'service charges' into contracts, with collusive firms paying the excess to the government. These manoeuvres yielded around US$229 million and US$1.5 billion respectively by 2003, about 16 per cent of the regime's illicit income under sanctions. While meagre compared to the US$8 billion raised through oil smuggling, this nonetheless enabled greater discretionary spending (Duelfer, 2004: ch. 2, 19). From 1994 to 2001 official government revenue increased from US$94 million to US$668 million, while spending grew from US$514 million to US$1.1 billion from 1995 to 2001 (Duelfer, 2004: ch. 2, 15). The regime also redirected about US$1.9 billion of OFFP imports to agencies ineligible to receive them, like the military (Volcker et al., 2005: 294).

The regime distributed these additional resources to its traditional constituencies, marking a partial revival of earlier ruling strategies. Consumers received significant relief. From 1997 the Trade Ministry sold imported commodities at below-market rates, deflating prices for the first time (Graham-Brown, 1999: 166). The calories supplied by government rations also increased by 50 per cent, though by 2002 they still provided only two thirds of families' monthly requirements (Mazaheri, 2010: 258; Zurbrigg, 2007: 18). Social services modestly improved. Schools became marginally better resourced, and housing and water supplies improved (Gordon, 2010: 131–2). The annual health budget rose to around US$354 million, still just US$0.04 per person daily. These meagre improvements arrested, but could not reverse, the nutrition and public health disaster that had already killed 5 to 10 per cent of Iraqis (Zurbrigg, 2007: 19, 44, 41). The relief provided nonetheless deepened the population's dependence on the state.

The Ba'athists' traditional bases in the bureaucracy, military, and state-linked industries were also favoured. Within the bureaucracy, influence shifted back from pro-privatization technocrats to moderately reformist, but basically statist, Ba'athist apparatchiks under Vice-President Taha's Higher Economic Committee (Sakai, 2001: 32–4). The Ministry of Planning was re-established and, in 2001, new five- and ten-year economic plans signalled renewed attempts at state-led development (Duelfer, 2004: ch. 2, 201). This was spearheaded through MIC, whose budget grew from US$7.8 million to US$350 million from 1996 to 2002, supplementing around US$365 million in smuggling revenues (Duelfer, 2004: ch. 2, 66, 71). These resources were used to revive sectors like transportation, electricity, chemicals, and pharmaceuticals, with beneficiaries concentrated in state-linked enterprises (Braude, 2003: 107–15). Reviving construction also benefited traditional constituencies in cement production and contracting (Gordon, 2010: 131). State employment recovered to around 40 per cent of the workforce, though 28 per cent of Iraqis remained unemployed by 2003 (Duelfer, 2004: ch. 2, 213). The regime also funnelled resources to the military. The formal military budget remained low—just US$124.7 million by 2002, with around 40 per cent devoted to the RG and SRG. However, this was supplemented with smuggled goods and around US$1.4 billion of diverted OFFP imports, mostly vehicles, machinery, and conventional weaponry (Volcker et al., 2005: 294; Duelfer, 2004: ch. 2, 63, 69, 79–80, 267–89). This apparently improved army morale substantially, with one senior general describing the OFFP as a 'kiss of life' (al-Hamdani, 2003: 178).

New resources and opportunities also strengthened the regime's dominance over Iraqi capitalists. Increased patronage deepened businesses' reliance on regime largesse. MIC, state-owned enterprises, and the IIS all used private firms to procure imports, directing the most lucrative deals to government allies or joint ventures. Contracts to lift oil were similarly dispensed, and illicit OFFP kickbacks were also routed through private front companies, which took a cut (Volcker et al., 2005: 260, 265, 270–1, 288–9, 302–8; Duelfer, 2004: ch. 2, 69, 72, 84, 88–91). Smuggling networks were also reordered, with those led by the disgraced Hussein Kamil and Uday Hussein being absorbed by Qusay Hussein's intelligence services. Qusay did not use the proceeds merely to enrich his own coterie, which had earlier generated severe instability. Instead, he funnelled them to the SRG, RG, and intelligence agencies, thereby strengthening the state's coercive apparatuses (Duelfer, 2004: 63–5; CIJ, 2002: 31, 42, 51, 61, 65). The criminalization of state institutions thus continued apace, but in a less politically threatening manner. Alongside MIC and the oil ministry, numerous other ministries continued smuggling; the central bank and state-owned banks ran illicit networks of foreign bank accounts; Iraq's diplomatic service transported cash and facilitated overseas bribery (discussed later in this section); and the IIS was used for sanctions-busting procurement missions (Duelfer, 2004: ch. 2, 4–5, 46).

Renewed resource flows thus enabled the regime to repair its traditional social base and retreat from the coalitional shifts undertaken earlier. The key beneficiaries were state-based and state-linked entities dominated by the Sunni 'class-clan'. As Hiro (2002: 16) observes, the 'new category of middlemen' generated by OFFP contracting often had 'blood ties to influential . . . clans in central and southern Iraq', and, like smuggling elites, they became 'enthusiastic backers of the Ba'athist regime'. Renewed patronage—however meagre compared to the pre-sanctions era—apparently curbed the scarcity-induced tribal conflicts and coup attempts that had earlier plagued the regime. In February 1996 Kamil and his fellow defectors, having sought clemency, were officially pardoned, then killed upon returning to Iraq. Thereafter, apart from the aforementioned failed INA conspiracy, the only recorded coup plot was a half-baked scheme by the exiled General Najid al-Salihi, who claimed support from only sixty to seventy officers and which relied upon non-forthcoming US aerial bombing (Al-Bayati, 2011: 107). Saddam was also able to moderate his dangerously narrow reliance on his kinsmen, tilting away from Tikritis towards long-serving Ba'athist cadres and technocrats (Baram, 1998: 32–44). The relative decline of Iraq's tribal bourgeoisie also allowed Saddam to temper neo-tribalism. Although tribal representation in the national assembly increased (Sakai, 2003: 158–9), the Ba'ath Party's role was strengthened to counterbalance the sheikhs. Despite its post-Gulf War disarray, the party was never entirely marginalized; indeed, it became more important as formal state institutions withered. As its resources increased under the OFFP, so did its membership. The party played important roles in mediating between the state and tribes; distributing food and welfare assistance; implementing Saddam's faith campaign; recruiting militiamen; securing high turnouts for the 1995 'referendum' on Saddam's presidency and the 1996 parliamentary elections; and mobilizing large crowds for national demonstrations (Sassoon, 2012: 40–1, 78–81, 86, 187), including a 500,000-strong anti-sanctions 'jihad' in May 1998 (Hiro, 2002: 69).

The regime–KDP alliance also strengthened under the OFFP, with power shifting in Baghdad's favour. As noted earlier, the Kurdish north benefited from a disproportionate share of OFFP revenues, plus cash transfers, with local expenditure reaching US$613.7 million and OFFP imports US$1.1 billion by December 2002 (UNOIPOFF, 2002). These resources were routed not through the local administration but the UN and contractors linked to the Kurdish parties, bolstering the latter's patronage powers and reducing their economic rivalry (Natali, 2010: 53–71). Nonetheless, the KDP continued collaborating in Baghdad's oil-smuggling racket, preventing Kurdish reconciliation or a KDP return to the INC. Meanwhile, renewed legal exports lessened the regime's dependency on the KDP. It shifted much oil smuggling to Syria, which became Iraq's primary illicit income source from 2000 to 2003, with Turkey falling into second place. This increased the regime's share of total oil rents, reducing the KDP's relative power, and reallocated smuggling routes from Uday's to Qusay's front companies, thereby bolstering the state's coercive and intelligence apparatuses (CIJ, 2002: 17, 40, 42). Baghdad's 1996 'invasion' of the north also enhanced its control. By 2001 Iraqi intelligence had thoroughly penetrated the region, including both main Kurdish parties, and was funding their smaller rivals to sow further division, though Saddam still prioritized relations with the KDP (CRRC, 2001a). In a 2002 visit to Saddam, Barzani's nephew reported that the KDP 'discuss[ed] any important issues' with the IIS director and requested 'orders' from Saddam, describing the party as 'soldiers under your command' (CRRC, 2002).

The WMD component of the regime's strategy also evolved, though more in response to Western policy than the OFFP. Following Hussein Kamil's defection, reasonably good cooperation with UNSCOM ensued from 1995 to 1998, resulting in the destruction of the last facilities that could conceivably be used to produce biological weapons in 1996 (Duelfer, 2004: 47, 49). Since no WMD remained, UNSCOM now focused on finding definitive documentary evidence of the earlier destruction of the weapons and related material, and on discovering the 'concealment mechanism' used to evade disarmament before July 1991. Hussein Kamil's revelations had indicated SRG involvement in this, leading UNSCOM to insist on inspecting them, and later Qusay's Special Security Office, the organization devoted to Saddam's personal security (Ritter, 2005: 258). As a senior inspector notes, given that UNSCOM was known to be penetrated by CIA agents pursuing the US goal of regime change, these demands presented a 'genuine national security risk' (Ritter, 2005: 155). Although 'hawks' never regained their ascendancy in Saddam's inner circle,

Qusay's understandable determination to shield the Special Security Office—and, by extension, his father—became a serious impediment to cooperation. It fuelled UNSCOM suspicion that the regime was hiding something, exacerbated by the discovery of VX nerve gas residue in 1997. However, as the ISG later found, notwithstanding the smuggling of missile parts, the regime's 'deceptive' activities were generally counter-intelligence measures to protect Saddam (Duelfer, 2004: ch. 1, 52–3, 64). Conversely, Iraqi suspicion seemed well justified by UNSCOM's involvement in intelligence gathering to facilitate the mid-1996 CIA/INA coup plot (Ritter, 2005: 151–6, 167–9, 172–4, 227, 242, 245, 261). The CIA also persuaded UNSCOM to perform intrusive inspections around Tikrit, which deepened Iraqi suspicions and caused cooperation to be suspended in June 1997 (Ritter, 2005: 194–202, 227–8, 231).

Cooperation was terminated altogether in August 1998. A cache of WMD-related documents discovered at an air force base in July soured relations. For UNSCOM, the US, and the UK, it proved the regime's intent to conceal and rebuild its WMD programme. However, the Iraqi defence minister was actually furious that the documents had not been destroyed, blaming bureaucratic incompetence, and the military redoubled its compliance efforts to avoid further 'procrastination' over sanctions (CRRC, 1998c, b). The final breakdown followed US efforts to have UNSCOM precipitate a crisis to justify US bombing intended to satisfy domestic American opinion, and by US pressure to prevent UNSCOM from gathering evidence that might allow the UNSC to finally certify Iraq's compliance (Ritter, 2005: 269–77, 287–8). Having long been sceptical that 'technical' compliance was possible, Saddam finally saw that Iraq's 'choice' was to 'have sanctions with inspectors or sanctions without inspectors'; he chose the latter (Duelfer, 2004: ch. 1, 61).

The regime's strategy for ending the embargo now shifted to intensifying sanctions busting so as to render the embargo meaningless, which the OFFP certainly facilitated. Sanctions busting became more overt and widespread, with other Arab states (excluding Saudi Arabia and Kuwait) gradually re-engaging with Iraq for economic reasons while opposing sanctions on humanitarian grounds. By 2000 regular international flights and trade fairs resumed, and by 2002 Iraq had signed eleven free trade agreements with Arab states and had been readmitted to the Arab League (Hiro, 2002: 150; CIJ, 2002: 54–5). Oil deals were signed with Chinese, British, Russian, French, Dutch, Spanish, Indian, and Algerian firms in anticipation of sanctions being lifted (Katzman and Blanchard, 2005: 25). The regime also selectively dispensed oil-lifting permits to foreign entities to encourage them to lobby against the embargo. British and American oil firms were initially targeted, followed by French and Russian business and political figures, creating a transnational patronage network worth US$130 million, which even included the head of the OFFP, Benon Sevan (Alahmad, 2007: 589–91; Duelfer, 2004: ch. 2, 31–4).

Despite US and British insistence on maintaining the embargo, mounting demands for change gradually eroded it (see Table 4.1). In 2000 China announced its opposition to sanctions, and seventy US Congressmen petitioned President Clinton to end them (Duelfer, 2004: ch. 2, 55; Baram, 2000b: 9). In 2001 US–UK proposals for 'smart' sanctions to tighten regional enforcement were defeated by commercially-motivated Russian and Middle Eastern resistance, with Moscow instead forcing through a reduction in reparations (Duelfer, 2004: ch. 2, 55; Alkadiri, 2001: 31). To maintain sanctions, London and Washington were forced to weaken them: UNSCR 1409, passed in May 2002, permitted unlimited oil exports and confined import 'holds' to a specific Goods Review List. As Tripp (2007: 268) states, 'Iraq was poised on the verge of international rehabilitation . . . ma[king] a mockery of UN sanctions'.

Despite this strategy's success, the regime never abandoned its commitment to WMD disarmament, believing itself compliant to the very end. The doves remained ascendant, and they saw no reason to jeopardize 'technical' compliance. The NMD continued destroying documents and programmes violating UN resolutions. Despite the partial restoration of MIC's military-industrial complex, its minister banned any activity that might jeopardize the lifting of sanctions. And Saddam continued to check that no secret programmes existed (Duelfer, 2004: 53, 57, 59). After 9/11 Baghdad unsuccessfully tried to re-engage the US and UNMOVIC, UNSCOM's successor. As the US began threatening war in 2002, Saddam was initially bemused, asking 'what can they discover, when we have nothing?' However, in December, following UNSCR 1441, Saddam ordered officials to 'cooperate completely' with UNMOVIC (Duelfer, 2004: ch. 1, 61–2). He was prepared to restart inspections because 'Iraq didn't manufacture WMD . . . we are confident that we can clarify these facts' (CRRC, 2002). Taha and Tariq, tasked with implementing UNSCR 1441, also pursued full cooperation, with Taha even making concessions without Saddam's authorization (Duelfer, 2004: ch. 1, 72, 16). Iraq issued another full declaration; destroyed all disputed missiles; opened all sites to inspection; forced scientists, MIC officials, and RG officers to sign affidavits denying possession of WMD under pain of severe punishment; and had the national assembly outlaw WMD (Duelfer, 2004: ch. 1, 62–3). Even as Washington moved to invade, Saddam was convinced that Iraq was compliant and that President Bush was bluffing. Iraq's director of military intelligence reported that Saddam did not believe the US would invade, asking, 'why would they come here when they don't need anything from Iraq? They have already fulfilled the[ir] goals' (Duelfer, 2004: 66). Likewise, Saddam told Barzani's nephew that the US would 'avoid coming to Iraq', since Baghdad was not involved in 9/11 and had no WMD, Washington lacked international support, and US forces were already engaged in Afghanistan. 'In our assessment, the Americans will not strike, or maybe they will only strike military targets. They will not take an action to change the regime,' he stated (CRRC, 2002).

The regime's strategy under the OFFP thus exhibited changes and continuity. Modest resource increases enabled a retreat from short-term survival strategies and capitulations to private forces, and a constrained return to state-led reconstruction and neo-patrimonialism. This stabilized and partially reconstituted the regime's traditional support base, enabling it to balance forces off against one another. In contrast to the spiralling unrest and disintegration beforehand, 'after 1996, the state of the Iraqi economy no longer threatened Saddam's hold on power' (Duelfer, 2004: ch. 2, 9). In fact, by 2003 the regime had *surplus* resources. Only US$6.48 billion of the US$8 billion in illicit trade revenues had been spent. Iraq's overseas assets were estimated at US$2 billion. Iraq's domestic banks—93 per cent of which were state-owned—held US$2.24 billion in deposits, while the Central Bank held US$1 billion plus four tonnes of gold and MIC had reserves of US$300 million (Duelfer, 2004: ch. 2, 25–8, 39–41, 47–8, 51, 251). A regime under serious societal challenge would have desperately expended this money. Saddam's careful dispensation of OFFP resources apparently sufficed to satiate powerful social forces, while weaker groups had adapted themselves to hardship. Notwithstanding this, the WMD-related aspects of the regime's strategy displayed greater continuity. Although the doves' quest for technical compliance was thwarted by the US and UK, the hawks never recovered their lost influence, and disarmament thus continued alongside intensified sanctions busting.

The Opposition under the OFFP

While the ruling coalition stabilized, opposition forces weakened further. Internally, although sanctions and Saddam's ruling strategy stimulated an anti-regime Shiite challenge in the south, its sectarian nature limited its appeal, making it easy to decapitate. Externally, the INC was essentially defunct after 1996, merely lobbying Washington for military intervention. Islamists were more active, but still at non-threatening levels and they also depended on American intervention. Crucially, neither Washington nor Iraqi opposition groups could formulate any strategy to oust the regime.

After the INC's ouster from northern Iraq and internal coup threats ended with the influx of OFFP resources, the regime's main internal challenge was Shiite revivalism spurred by sanctions-induced poverty and the state's religious turn. The regime saw the movement, clustered around anti-government clerics independently providing welfare and security for local communities, as a growing security threat. Consequently, it assassinated leading cleric Ayatollah Sadiq al-Sadr in 1999, sparking weeks of unrest. However, this was limited to the Shiite south, underscoring the inherent limitations of particularist movements. Al-Sadr's Shiite fervour made him entirely unacceptable to the regime's Sunni core, while his fierce anti-Western posture also alienated him from external supporters of regime change (Abdullah, 2006: 85–6).

Outside Iraq, anti-regime forces fared no better. Although Hussein Kamil's defection provoked considerable regime panic, he proved unable to rally support or assume leadership of the exiled opposition due to mutual distrust and ideological incompatibility. Dejected, Hussein Kamil and his coterie sued for a pardon, returning to Iraq with his coterie in February 1996, only to be murdered by their relatives. The INC never recovered from its 1996 defeat, losing its base, many members, and the KDP—which thwarted attempts to restore INC bases in Kurdistan in 1998–9 by refusing to guarantee their security (CRRC, 1999a). Chalabi was thus reduced to lobbying US Republicans for aid and intervention. This generated the 1998 Iraq Liberation Act, which allocated US$97 million to train and fund opposition forces. However, this *weakened* the INC because it prompted SAIRI, fearing undue Western influence, to defect and form a rival 'group of four' with the PUK, KDP, and INA (Al-Bayati, 2011: 131). Because SAIRI was the INC's only remaining significant force, this defection thwarted US plans to train INC cadres to 'invade' Iraq and provoke responses that might trigger US intervention (Hiro, 2002: 88–92). SAIRI's alternative proposals, however, also consistently relied on US air power creating a southern 'safe haven' where anti-regime forces could regroup and develop—a scheme repeatedly rejected by US diplomats (Al-Bayati, 2011: 42, 60, 101–2). Consequently only US$5 million of Congressional funding was ever disbursed (Katzman, 2003: 13). The CIA focused on the INA but, as we have seen, the regime's coup-proofing thwarted its schemes. Furthermore, in 1997 the INA lost its base in Amman following an economically driven Iraqi–Jordanian rapprochement (Baram, 1998: 130). By cleverly manipulating the OFFP, Saddam substantially neutralized yet another threat.

The opposition's fundamental problem remained its inability to formulate a coherent strategy to unite even the regime's external opponents, let alone mobilize support within Iraq. While Chalabi never articulated a clear strategy, nor did the Americans or any other group. The memoirs of SAIRI's London representative repeatedly underscore this lack of basic leadership. He lamented the absence of a clear strategy following the intifada. In 1995 he told the British: 'we needed an action plan for the opposition and operational leadership inside Iraq'. In 1998 Chalabi was eventually persuaded of the need for 'agreement on a complete project and a military plan to topple the regime'. Yet, in successive discussions, Chalabi repeatedly asked 'what could be done to activate the Iraqi opposition . . . [only] at the end of the meeting'. The opposition consequently looked for US direction—which was also not forthcoming. In September 1999 the PUK's Jalal Talabani again 'asked the question we all wanted answered: did the US have a strategy to topple Saddam?' US Assistant Secretary of State Martin Indyk demurred: 'we need your help...We've been asking [you] for a plan for years and we haven't gotten it' (Al-Bayati, 2011: 69, 97, 86, 119, 122). No one was apparently willing to take responsibility, merely shunting the crucial issue back and forth. As the IIS reported, the INC 'couldn't achieve anything'; even 'uniting itself efficiently' was impossible since most oppositionists 'do not consider [Chalabi] as an acceptable leader' (CRRC, 2001b).

The opposition's declining efficacy thus posed little threat to the regime; inter-coalitional struggle actually declined under the OFFP. It is virtually impossible to identify how OFFP benefited the opposition in any way. Chalabi opposed it, rightly arguing that it would only strengthen the regime (Al-Bayati, 2011: 76). But this left him supporting an embargo that was starving hundreds of thousands of Iraqis to death, while offering no constructive alternative—a position that was divisive and damaging within the INC, let alone inside Iraq.

Conclusion

UN sanctions profoundly shaped Iraq's intra- and inter-coalitional struggles and strategies, yielding many of their ostensible goals.

In the first phase, they had immense impact. The Ba'athist regime lost the resources necessary to maintain its traditional coalition. Key support groups, state agencies, and the state's regulatory capacities crumbled. The regime was forced into alliances with empowered social groups, particularly 'fat cats' and the tribal bourgeoisie, and to abandon its secular, welfarist developmentalism for austerity, market mechanisms, neo-tribalism, self-reliance, and sectarian religiosity. Increasing competition for declining resources sparked growing unrest, defections, rebellions, coup plots, and internal struggles. This invalidates claims that sanctions had no effect, merely strengthened Saddam's grip, or even left the 'same' regime in power, since the regime clearly transformed in important ways. Nonetheless, opposition forces failed to exploit this disarray. These already fragmented groups lacked a coherent strategy to rally a divided, disorganized population. Sanctions produced some defections to the opposition, but also enforced a depoliticizing focus on subsistence and a divisive retreat into particularist identities. The embargo's most damaging effect for opposition forces was its role in exacerbating KDP–PUK conflict and driving the KDP into alliance with Baghdad which, in turn, led to the INC's defeat in 1996.

Under the OFFP, additional resources enabled the regime to amend its transition strategy and strengthen its position. The state regained its role in resource allocation, enabling a perilously narrow support base to be broadened through a constrained revival of state-led development. A rather modest economic recovery apparently sufficed to restore powerful core groups' faith in Saddam; consequently, after 1996 the regime faced no further threats from those actually capable of destabilizing it. The decline of opposition groups only continued under the OFFP. Bereft of resources, supporters, and ideas, they became increasingly dependent on the US to effect regime change.

Because the regime's strategy consistently prioritized the lifting of sanctions, Iraq made many concessions to satisfy the senders' ostensible goals, negating claims that Saddam was able to simply resist coercive diplomacy for thirteen years. To recap, the goals specified in UNSCR 687 and 688 were: acceptance of Kuwait's sovereignty and borders; the return of Kuwaiti plunder and foreign prisoners and the payment of reparations; the renunciation of terrorism; improvements in human rights and political liberalization; and disarmament. Let us address these in turn.

First, Iraq accepted Kuwait's borders and sovereignty in November 1994. This chapter has showed that sanctions, coupled with military coercion, indirectly secured this outcome.

Second, although Kuwaiti goods and prisoners were not fully returned, reparations were initiated. Although sanctions drove Iraq to absorb much Kuwaiti plunder, a 'substantial amount' was returned in 2000, and items like Kuwait's national archives were returned from 2002, though only as war loomed. Similarly, 608 of 628 MIA cases were outstanding by 2000, with Iraq boycotting cooperation from 1998 to 2002 (Katzman, 2003: 9–10). However, sanctions forced Saddam to accept the OFFP, and 25 to 30 per cent of revenues from this went to Kuwait as reparations. By March 2003 US$18 billion had been paid, about 41 per cent of Kuwait's UN-approved claims (Zurbrigg, 2007: 35; Katzman, 2003: 10). Thus, despite uneven cooperation, this goal was being substantially achieved.

Third, whether Saddam renounced terrorism is debatable. The US kept Iraq on its list of terrorist-sponsoring states for harbouring the Abu Nidal Organization and the Palestinian Liberation Front, and paying US$25,000 to families of 'martyred' Palestinians, including suicide bombers (Katzman, 2003: 8). However, while sanctions might have increased Iraq's incentives to use 'unconventional warfare', its terrorist activities apparently ended in the early 1990s. From 1991–3 the US accused Iraq of thirty-nine terrorist attacks; thereafter, no such incidents were recorded (Cordesman and Hashim, 1997: 286–9; Hiro, 2002: 190–1). The IIS assessed these early operations as amateurish failures, with bombs often detonating prematurely, killing their operatives, since, 'because of the embargo, [we] lack devices and substances needed for the manufacturing process' (CRRC, 1992–4). There was no return to state-sponsored terrorism under the OFFP, and no Iraqi link to 9/11 or al-Qaida.

Thus, sanctions arguably forced Iraq to abandon its terrorist operations, notwithstanding its relations with some minor groups, reflecting a token ideological commitment to Palestinian liberation.

Fourth, Iraq clearly failed to enhance human rights and political liberalization. This is unsurprising, since these goals were tantamount to demanding regime change. Superficial political liberalization was only briefly entertained in 1991 and, although the regime's coalitional base and ruling strategy changed substantially, its brutal and authoritarian character did not. The Polity data register no change from 1990 to 2003 (INSCR, 2012), while from 1998 to 2003 Freedom House (2014) consistently rated Iraq 'not free', with the worst possible scores for freedom, civil liberties, and political rights. The regime was widely accused of mistreating the Marsh Arabs, and torturing its enemies (Katzman, 2003: 3–4, 7–8). However, in the absence of a stronger domestic opposition, sanctions could not support significant change from outside the regime, while the OFFP dampened pressures from inside. Given this context, the embargo substantially worsened Iraqis' human rights, since it grievously violated the socio-economic rights that the Ba'athists had previously delivered upon, notwithstanding their curtailment of civil–political rights.

Fifth, sanctions succeeded in securing the destruction of Iraq's WMD and delivery systems. A consistent element of Saddam's strategy from mid-1991 was to comply with UN disarmament demands in order to terminate the embargo. Even when cooperation with UNSCOM was suspended, there was no attempt to revive WMD-related programmes; instead, destruction efforts continued.

Why, then, did Western governments not recognize Iraq's successful disarmament? The usual answer is that Iraq's deceptive behaviour misled Western intelligence agencies into believing that WMD still existed. Scholars and practitioners have argued that, merely to *appear* to be retaining WMD, Saddam was willing to pay US$25 billion annually in lost oil exports (Graham-Brown, 1999: 87), either to maintain the support of the military or his inner circle (Baram, 1998: 46, 49; Ritter, 2005: 5), or to deter Iran, Israel, and internal enemies (Duelfer, 2004: ch. 1, 23–34). These arguments are highly implausible.

This chapter shows that Saddam consistently sought to demonstrate Iraqi compliance to terminate the embargo. Because he did not portray an ambiguous image, privately or publicly, the claim that he pretended to retain WMD to maintain military or elite support is nonsensical. Orders to destroy WMD were circulated among even mid- and junior-level military officers as early as 1991, making it inconceivable that the military was unaware of disarmament (CRRC, 1987–95, 1998c). Similarly, Saddam repeatedly told his inner circle and cabinet that no WMD-related material remained: 'They have destroyed everything!' he exclaimed in 1993; and even UNSCOM had recognized that

'Iraq implemented ninety-five per cent of the resolutions' (CRRC, 1993b; see also CRRC, 1995d, 1995i). Saddam's advisors made similar remarks (CRRC, nd-c, 1995i). Internal Ba'ath Party documents also noted that due to its 'complete cooperation . . . Iraq has no WMD' (CRRC, 2003). The regime regularly broadcast its compliance, to national and international audiences. In 1997, for instance, Saddam publicly declared: 'Iraq has complied with and implemented all relevant resolutions . . . There is absolutely nothing else' (Cockburn and Cockburn, 2000: 271). Consequently, in his view, '*any* regular citizen is wondering [why sanctions persist] . . . we destroyed the weapons . . . we destroyed the factories . . . we did everything they asked for' (CRRC, 1994f, my emphasis).

Given these public declarations, the claim that Iraq bluffed about WMD to deter external enemies is also dubious. The doves' position, which apparently swayed Saddam, was that WMD were useless against Israel and Kuwait given their protection by the US (CRRC, nd-i). The argument is more plausible in relation to Iran, but the evidence is also weak. The ISG makes the strongest argument, but it is based on selective and over-interpreted comments by Saddam and regime officials (Duelfer, 2004: ch. 1, 29, 44, 49, 51). For instance, it cites Saddam telling an American interrogator that 'the threat from Iran was the major factor as to why he did not allow the return of the weapons inspectors' and that he would 'have done was what necessary' to defend Iraq from Iran (FBI, 2004: 1–2). This is hardly definitive proof. In fact, the full transcript shows that Saddam was insisting that his public speeches were aimed at 'demonstrating Iraqi compliance' and that 'Iraq did not have WMD' (FBI, 2004: 1–2). The regime undoubtedly feared Iran: it supported SAIRI and the PUK and was supposedly pursuing nuclear weapons while Iraq had disarmed. However, what Saddam feared was not that UNSCOM would expose Iraq's disarmament to Iran, but that its operatives 'would have directly identified to the Iranians where to inflict maximum damage to Iraq' (FBI, 2004: 2). One of Saddam's close advisors similarly stated, in private: 'we did not stop them [inspecting sites] because we are hiding something, rather because we fear for our security and our sovereignty from the spies' (CRRC, nd-l). This was hardly baseless paranoia. Iraqi intelligence knew that UNSCOM was penetrated by the CIA, had provided intelligence for INA coup plots, and had collaborated with Israeli intelligence, Israel being another WMD-possessing state which, had previously attacked Iraq.[5] There is simply no concrete evidence,

---

[5] Israeli intelligence fed (often false) intelligence to UNSCOM, significantly shaping its activities, notably the focus on the Special Security Office, while UNSCOM became 'the best source of high-quality intelligence that Israel had ever had'. The CIA feared Israel was using this to ' "plan an F-16 strike" into Iraq' (Ritter, 2005: 145, 127; see 91–136, 144–6, 180–9, 198–9, 226–8, 237–9, 252, 267, 276).

including in the available Iraqi archives, of any intention to deceive any external power about Iraqi capabilities. Instead, Saddam apparently wanted the UN to properly fulfil UNSCR 687 paragraph 14, which sought 'in the Middle East a zone free from WMD and all missiles for their delivery' (Duelfer, 2004: 51). That is, if Iraq had to disarm, so should Israel and Iran, so as to ensure Iraqi security. This probably explains Saddam's claim to have wanted a 'security agreement with the US to protect [Iraq] from threats in the region' (FBI, 2004: 3).

A more persuasive interpretation of the West's failure to recognize Iraq's disarmament, which also better reflects ample evidence that the intelligence was fixed around rather than driving the decision to invade Iraq, is that the US and UK governments were less concerned with Iraq's *current* capabilities than its potential *future* ones. By 1996 'UNSCOM no longer had a viable case regarding substantive non-compliance' (Ritter, 2005: 186). Western intelligence agencies had no solid contradictory evidence either. CIA leads to UNSCOM were persistently faulty. After 1995 the CIA had no sources in Iraq and, after UNSCOM's withdrawal in 1998, no indirect information either. All that remained was 'imaginative speculation' based around 'worst-case scenario[s]' (Gordon, 2010: 195). Given the lack of solid intelligence to prove that Iraq retained WMD, this speculation increasingly focused on the notion that Saddam would rebuild WMD *after* the embargo ended. For the US and UK, mitigating this risk required either regime change or Iraq's *permanent* containment through sanctions. In the CIA's view, sanctions would not achieve regime change, but they did 'limit Iraqi capability to pursue policies that menace US interests'; if the embargo ended, 'Saddam would accelerate efforts to rebuild…WMD' (CIA, 1993: 31). By the late 1990s CIA officials were speculating that Iraq could develop intercontinental ballistic missiles within fifteen years. Hawkish think tanks formed an echo chamber, warning (completely incorrectly) that Iraq could reconstitute its chemical and biological weapons programmes within months, and suggesting that its 'lack of cooperation' indicated its intention 'to reconstitute its pre-Gulf War [WMD] capacity as rapidly as possible once sanctions are lifted' (Cordesman, 2000: 82, 85–6, 90). That Iraq's *post*-embargo capabilities were the real concern is also suggested by the ISG's post hoc insistence that 'extensive, yet fragmentary and circumstantial' evidence suggests that 'Saddam pursued a strategy to maintain a capability to return to WMD after sanctions' (Duelfer, 2004: ch. 1, 59).[6]

Consequently, as prospects for regime change dwindled after 1996, maintaining sanctions became more important for the US and UK. Accordingly, Washington backed inspections only insofar as they perpetuated the embargo,

---

[6] These dubious claims are also based on a handful of over-interpreted quotations. There is no firm evidence, including in the available Iraqi archives.

withdrawing support 'whenever [UNSCOM was] close to a breakthrough on Iraq's final status' (Ritter, 2005: 290; see 170, 182, 255, 267, 288). The US and UK were also intransigent in using 'holds', blocking efforts to rehabilitate the Iraqi economy, and resisting reform of the sanctions regime (Gordon, 2010: chs 3–4, 6). Similarly, as evidence of disarmament mounted, they moved the goalposts, shifting the emphasis to human rights in 1997/8 to prolong the embargo (Tripp, 2007: 253).

However, by around 2000 containment was disintegrating. Iraq was gradually eroding the embargo and international support for its maintenance, leaving London and Washington increasingly isolated on the UNSC. To maintain sanctions, they were forced to accept their progressive dilution, which only undermined their efficacy. Consequently, regime change increasingly seemed the only means to maintain 'dual containment'. Endorsing the ISG's dubious judgements, British Prime Minister Tony Blair (2010: ch. 13) argued that, without intervention,

> sanctions would have been dropped; and it would have been impossibly hard to reapply pressure to a regime that would have been 'cleared'. Saddam would then have had the intent [to rebuild WMD]; the knowhow; and, with a rising oil price, enormous purchasing power ... Saddam would have re-emerged stronger, a competitor to Iran both in respect of WMD and in support of terrorism.

Fear that weakening sanctions were undermining containment was increasingly apparent in the US Congress, too (Gordon, 2010: 168–70). US policymakers believed that the embargo was 'eroding' and since 'without sanctions Iraq has no reason to fear or abide by UN resolutions ... Saddam would pursue WMD' (Yaphe, 2003: 30–3). US President Bush (2010: ch. 8) argued that without the 2003 invasion, 'sanctions, already falling apart, would have crumbled. Saddam still had the infrastructure and know-how to make WMD.' This risked 'a nuclear arms race between Iraq and Iran'.

This perspective has contradictory implications for assessing the efficacy of sanctions in securing the implicit—yet arguably primary—goal of 'dual containment'. Logically, the claim that 'if sanctions were lifted, Saddam would rearm' implicitly accepts that sanctions *had* disarmed and thereby contained Iraq. It was the erosion of sanctions that undermined this goal. Nonetheless, that they were eroding also undermines claims that the embargo was 'successful' because it contained Saddam. The root problem was that the US and UK could not brook any economic rehabilitation that might help revive Iraqi military power, because they believed that Saddam would *always* threaten their interests in the Middle East whenever he had the resources to do so. Consequently, Saddam could never satisfy the sanctioners: however weakened Iraq became, the US and UK would not risk its *future* revival so long as Saddam remained in power. With their regime change efforts failing miserably, they were thus left defending a *permanent* embargo to 'keep Saddam in his box', as Bush (2010: ch. 8) put it. When this became unsustainable, they faced total defeat; since they were unwilling to accept this, their options narrowed to war. The primary goals driving and sustaining the embargo, coupled with the regime's sanctions-busting strategies, were therefore critical in paving the road to war in 2003—and the catastrophe that followed.

Conclusion

This book has developed and deployed a new analytical framework for understanding how international economic sanctions work—or do not work—to transform target societies and states. Rather than focusing on sanctions instruments themselves, it has put target states and their internal social, economic, and political dynamics centre stage. The socio-political forces struggling for power and control over resources within these states are the 'raw material' upon and through which sanctions act. Starting our analysis there is not only theoretically sound; it also helps to temper unrealistic estimations of external powers' capacity to manipulate politics in other states. In each case study, outcomes were fundamentally determined by the historical evolution of socio-political conflict, which was sometimes shaped, but never entirely remoulded, by international economic statecraft. Sanctions could not generate powerful political oppositions where none previously existed; nor, despite sometimes inflicting massive economic damage, could they shatter ruling coalitions where they were not already in decay. These findings echo studies of other forms of foreign intervention that highlight their inability to overwhelm local conditions, even when enormous coercive and economic resources are deployed directly on the ground (Jones, 2010; Hameiri 2010).

Drawing general conclusions from a small number of quite disparate cases is always difficult. What follows are necessarily tentative thoughts, positing hypotheses for future research to explore. Nonetheless, the cases investigated carry weight far beyond their number, because they are so symbolically important for policymakers' and campaigners' arguments about the utility and operation of sanctions. Comparing their outcomes is consequently useful to highlight the limitations of sanctions and to illustrate how the primacy of local power relations undermines simplistic reasoning about them: the analogical claim that, for example, because sanctions 'worked' in South Africa, they will work elsewhere, or that because comprehensive sanctions 'failed' in Iraq, targeted sanctions are preferable. Comparing these pivotal cases also helps shed critical light on why sanctions remain appealing to policymakers, despite their widely varying outcomes, and thus on the normative dimensions of their use. Although these normative issues have not been a central concern of this book, they remain central in determining whether or how sanctions should be used.

Sanctions and Ruling Coalitions

In each case study, the impact of sanctions on ruling coalitions was heavily conditioned by the degree of *autonomy* experienced by significant social forces, particularly vis-à-vis the state.

South Africa differed substantially from Myanmar and Iraq, for example, in that the bourgeoisie and middle class enjoyed greater relative autonomy from state power. In South Africa, because it had developed and acquired primacy under imperialism, and because the Afrikaner nationalist government did not expropriate it after 1948, Anglophone capital was always independent of direct state control. Afrikaner capital initially relied heavily upon state sponsorship, but was outgrowing its incubator by the late 1970s, its interests harmonizing more with the Anglophone conglomerates. This afforded organized business independent resources and room for political manoeuvre in the 1980s when its interests diverged from those of the apartheid regime, allowing it to gradually desert the ruling coalition and pursue an alternative dispensation. Conversely, the Iraqi and Myanmar states had expropriated their relatively independent national bourgeoisies in the 1960s and 1970s. In Iraq, a class of fat-cat contractors instead emerged, heavily dependent on state contracts and patronage. Myanmar's tycoons were likewise government creatures. The state's extensive economic role permitted widespread control over businesses of any significant size, while smaller business owners were too fragmented to offer resistance. Similarly, in both states, limited middle-class employment was fundamentally dependent on state spending. Thus Iraq's and Myanmar's middle classes were simply too weak and state dependent to move against these regimes, and largely remained within their ruling coalitions.

Importantly, this remained true even when sanctions inflicted extreme economic costs. The Iraq embargo devastated the urban middle class, and profoundly hurt the interests of Iraq's 'class-clan', leading some formerly loyal tribal leaders to perceive Saddam Hussein as a liability, rather than a useful patron. Yet, given their historical reliance on political intervention to secure socio-economic benefits, these groups apparently remained unable to imagine life without an authoritarian patron. Consequently they merely backed coup plots that would have removed Saddam but left the basic regime intact. The degree of political change that could be reasonably anticipated by harming these groups was thus intrinsically limited. Moreover, since the state's strategic selectivity was primed precisely against plots of this kind, their efforts were doomed to failure.

Furthermore, rather than distancing these groups from state power, sanctions tended to draw business and government officials closer together unless pre-existing dynamics were already dividing them. The South African regime's evasion of the oil and arms embargoes fostered a significant military-industrial complex, tying big business to the state. Iraq's oil smuggling networks corralled the mercantile elite into Saddam's protection racket, even recruiting parts of the Kurdish opposition. And in Myanmar, sanctions only increased the tycoons' reliance on government patronage and concentrated power in the hands of those closest to the regime. In South Africa it was only when big business interests from both white communities had begun chafing against government dirigisme that they rejected further sanctions-busting collaboration, instead advocating reform and deregulation. This was the result not of sanctions but of three decades of rapid economic development that fundamentally altered their interests.

Finally, trying to fragment a ruling coalition can generate unforeseen and counterproductive outcomes. In 1980s South Africa sanctions did sharpen divisions between conservative and reformist whites, as many advocates had hoped. Fortunately, by the late 1980s, conservative forces were too weak to triumph in the struggle over how to respond to sanctions; had they not been, Afrikaners might well have 'retreated into the *laager*', as opponents of sanctions cautioned (Hanlon and Omond, 1987: 63).[1] This risk was greater in previous decades, since reformists were much weaker and fewer in number. Sanctions only divided the ruling bloc in a progressive direction because the intervening years of socio-economic development had changed the balance of forces, underscoring the historical contingency of sanctions outcomes. Where reformist forces are absent or weak within the ruling coalition, sanctions can easily undermine them. In Iraq, for instance, the continuation of the embargo into the mid-1990s, despite the regime's disarmament, weakened the regime doves, strengthening the hawks' case for confronting the UN by invading Kuwait. This dangerous internal backlash was only curtailed by Kamal Hussein's defection, which was merely an unintended and unforeseen by-product of sanctions. Similarly, some suggest that reformers within Myanmar's military junta were undermined by the persistence of Western sanctions despite the concessions they had offered (Taylor, 2004), though this was impossible to verify.

---

[1] The *laager* was a mobile fortification of wagons used by early Dutch colonists.

Sanctions and Opposition Forces

The SCA framework suggested three basic channels through which sanctions might affect opposition forces. First, sanctions could help break up the ruling coalition and prompt defections to the opposition. Second, they could alter the basic social structure, reducing or destroying some social groups while generating new ones, which could transform political possibilities for both the ruling and opposition coalitions. Third, sanctions might not alter the composition of coalitions, but they could help opposition groups realize their strategy to seize state power. Overall, our findings suggest that sanctions are more destructive than productive. Whilst they sometimes assisted in fragmenting ruling blocs, they were less effective in generating new societal bases of resistance. Without exception, even the severest sanctions could *not* manufacture opposition where none previously existed. We did not tend to see previously passive 'innocent bystanders' mobilized by welfare losses (cf. Major and McGann, 2005). In the absence of a pre-existing, strong, well-organized opposition, defections from the ruling bloc were not politically productive and ruling coalitions survived through redistributing costs and benefits. Moreover, where oppositions were weak and fragmented, sanctions typically exacerbated this, rather than assisting them to develop and realize coherent transition strategies. These findings gel with recent research on democratization that finds that 'without effective domestic... organisations and a democratic focus leading to a more favourable balance of power, it is hard to imagine how any amount of external assistance will make much difference' (Stoner et al., 2013).

Sanctions produced defections from ruling coalitions in two cases: South Africa and Iraq. In South Africa white big business elites gradually distanced themselves from apartheid and sought rapprochement with the ANC and UDF. However, this only occurred in the 1980s, when opposition forces were sufficiently robust to disrupt the apartheid regime's survival strategy. In the 1960s and 1970s the regime was able to violently suppress the weaker opposition and obtain sufficient resources to engage in sanctions busting that strengthened the ruling coalition. In the 1980s, however, the intensity of black resistance could be quelled only through massive coercion and social spending, which could not be financed simultaneously with large-scale sanctions busting. It was only when rising social conflict generated this inescapable trade-off that white capitalists began defecting. The importance of a well-organized, relatively attractive, and united opposition was further underscored by the Iraq case. Here the sheer severity of sanctions did generate significant defections from the ruling coalition, as formerly loyal tribes rebelled and Saddam's inner circle fragmented. Yet, due to the Iraqi opposition's intense ideological divisions and political disorganization, very few defectors joined their ranks. Instead they launched individual revolts, enabling Saddam's 'divide-and-rule' strategy to save his regime. SCA's emphasis on the state's strategic selectivity further helps explain why these revolts failed, given the regime's previous 'coup-proofing' measures. These findings suggest that defections from ruling coalitions are unlikely to be politically productive in the absence of a strong pre-existing opposition. This accords with studies of 'pacted' transitions from authoritarianism, which underscore the importance of rising societal oppositions in tempting regime 'soft-liners' to negotiate an alternative dispensation (O'Donnell and Schmitter, 1986).

While the SCA framework's expectation that sanctions might change the composition of societies was borne out, in practice this rarely benefited opposition coalitions. The only clear instance where it did was in relation to the South African oil embargo, which spurred domestic coal production, thereby expanding the number and power of mineworkers, who became a key element in the anti-apartheid alliance. This entirely unforeseen and unplanned outcome was arguably unique to South Africa's peculiar political economy, making it non-generalizable. Moreover, even this was offset by the simultaneous generation of an extensive military-industrial complex that bolstered the ruling coalition for two decades.

In our other cases, the emergence or decline of social forces only weakened the opposition. In Myanmar the crony capitalists partly produced by sanctions were firmly pro-government. Growing rural poverty and the destruction of Myanmar's incipient working class did nothing to enhance opposition mobilization, only deepening depoliticization and passive cooperation with the regime. A similar dynamic occurred in Iraq, where the transformation of urban working and middle classes into an impoverished urban and rural underclass merely intensified state dependency and locked much of the population into a depoliticizing struggle for daily subsistence. The new criminal-mercantile elite generated by sanctions busting initially destabilized the Iraqi regime, though never through any political action, let alone by joining the opposition. Ultimately, moreover, this elite was co-opted into stable, regime-dominated networks. Worse yet, this included the KDP's emergent mercantile leadership, further undermining the Iraqi opposition. Thus, absent strong socio-political contestation, the clear tendency was for social groups to prioritize their survival or prosperity over political change, even when this involved pacts with previously despised regimes.

The direct political effects of sanctions on opposition coalitions were also frequently counterproductive. The Myanmar case illustrated how sanctions could provide moral support and encouragement to an opposition, keeping it on 'life support'. However, this was counterbalanced by some middle-class defections from the opposition and the retarded development of organized labour and independent business elites which might have served as opposition bases. Moreover, sanctions apparently encouraged the NLD to maintain an unrealistic transition strategy based on boycotting the incumbent regime's reconciliation attempts and demanding an immediate transfer of power based on the 1990 election results. While perhaps encouraging feelings of moral righteousness for both the NLD and its Western backers, the reinforcement of this strategy had no discernible political effect beyond delaying a transition dictated by the military. It is difficult to see how this served the people of Myanmar well.

Furthermore, sanctions were divisive for opposition groups in every case studied. This reflects the fact that social conflicts are not confined to inter-coalitional contestation but also involve struggles for leadership, authority, and loyalty within coalitions. Where oppositions were already weak and fragmented, sanctions exacerbated these weaknesses. The NLD experienced defections and a growing rift with ethnic minority leaders frustrated by the effects of sanctions and the narrow focus of NLD and Western policy. The fractious INC was also further divided by sanctions, with groups like the ICP opposing the embargo and the KDP defecting to the regime. The ANC and UDF also faced an anti-sanctions backlash from non-white regime collaborators and groups aligned to Inkatha. The ANC/UDF were uniquely successful in maintaining their opposition coalition under the pressure of sanctions, preventing the self-interest of some black workers and emergent middle-class elements taking priority over the political struggle. However, this involved not only decades of grass-roots politicization of the non-white masses, but also considerable 'black-on-black violence' as the ANC and Inkatha (backed by the apartheid regime) struggled for supremacy, which killed 10,000–20,000 people (Kaufman, 2012). While liberals condemned this, it may simply have been necessary to maintain the ANC-led coalition and prevent a viable, 'moderate' third force from emerging under the strain of economic crisis and sanctions to collaborate with the apartheid regime.

The cases also provide interesting insights into the importance of organized labour in generating democratic transitions (Eley, 2002). What ultimately dug the grave of South African apartheid was not sanctions, but rather the inexorably increasing dependence of the white-owned economy on an increasingly organized and militant black working class. The irresolvable contradiction between this economic dependence and the political disenfranchisement of non-whites was sustainable only so long as blacks remained disorganized and depoliticized. However, the education and unionization required by capitalist industrialization by the 1970s undermined this quiescence, laying the basis for a resistance that could not be crushed without creating an economic crisis. Since the regime was unwilling to do this, COSATU was able to become the backbone of the internal anti-apartheid struggle, surviving even when the civic resistance of the UDF was quelled. Working-class agency was thus critical in shaping the practical effects of sanctions in the 1980s.

This contrasts starkly with our other cases. In Iraq the independent working class had been forcibly demobilized by the Ba'athists' destruction of the ICP and the capture of its associated organizations in the 1970s. Furthermore, unlike in South Africa, the dominance of state-led development in oil-rich Iraq left workers ultimately dependent on government largesse. Consequently the Iraqi working class had no organizational capacity to rebel against Saddam, no matter how impoverished they became under sanctions. In Myanmar the failure of 'socialist' development meant virtually no working class had even emerged, while its nascent organizations were crushed in the 1970s. Sanctions only worsened the situation by preventing the class's revival. To expect workers in Iraq or Myanmar to play any significant role in regime change was thus fanciful at best.

A similar argument applies to other cases where South Africa is invoked to justify sanctions, notably Palestine. Here the key political economy relations are practically the opposite of those in South Africa. Although Israeli businesses depended on Palestinian labour from the 1960s to 1980s, a deliberate strategy to reduce this reliance after 1987 has now left Palestinian workers dependent on Israel to provide them with jobs and livelihoods. Moreover, since the Palestinian 'leadership' has entirely neglected the mobilization of workers into resistance organizations, Palestinian workers lack an organized labour movement and are even compelled to construct Israeli settlements on their own land. The idea that sanctioning the Israeli economy will 'work' as it did in South Africa is consequently nonsensical (Jones, forthcoming). The most detrimental effect would likely be on Palestinians themselves, who lack the organizational capacity to rebel, let alone the leverage over economic activity exploited by COSATU.

Arguably the Palestinian case instead underscores the profound difficulty of organizing workers in today's neoliberal, globalized economy. Historically, trade unions were able to play a pivotal role in democratization because the national scale of economic production enabled them to organize national strike actions and national political parties to assert their interests. Since the late 1970s global production and capitalist power have been reconfigured on a transnational scale. This has considerably weakened the power of organized labour, which is still largely organized along national lines and can therefore be bullied or bypassed by alliances between transnationally mobile businesses and state elites competing for investment. Much of the capitalist world experienced violent struggles over this reconfiguration in the 1980s, which organized labour decisively lost. This trajectory underscores the historical uniqueness of the South African case. There, capitalist elites, locked (partly by sanctions) into a national pattern of development, could not escape their dependence on local organized labour, giving the latter significant leverage. But this no longer holds in most cases, including South Africa itself, where local conglomerates exploited the end of apartheid to globalize their operations, shifting their headquarters overseas. Analytically this reinforces the case for historically situated analysis rather than transhistorical assumptions about the behaviour of social groups or the effects of sanctions instruments. Politically, it raises the question of how or even whether politically progressive and transformatory coalitions can be built under conditions of neoliberal capitalism. Certainly the relative decline of forces like trade unions means that prospective sanctioners cannot reasonably assume that there are ready agents for democratic change in many societies, just waiting to be activated by sanctions.

Overall these findings clearly reinforce Galtung's (1967) dismissal of the 'naïve theory' of sanctions, which simplistically expects embargoes to stimulate popular discontent that will compel governments to change course. Notably the best organized and most strategically adept opposition force considered in this book, the ANC, never expected or wanted sanctions to serve this function. They denied that sanctions were intended or required to stir black unrest; indeed, they recognized that growing unemployment was divisive. The ANC/UDF coalition was only able to withstand this division and the potentially demobilizing effects of rising poverty due to its unusually robust organization across multiple sites of struggle, particularly the trade unions. Where this organization was weak or absent, ruling forces found it far easier to simply shift the burden of sanctions onto subaltern groups by, for example, printing money to finance government expenditure, transferring the cost to the wider population through high inflation. These findings challenge explanations of social unrest based on 'relative deprivation' (Gurr, 1970), which have been deployed in both classic and more recent sanctions scholarship (e.g. Baldwin, 1985: 200–1; Escribà-Folch, 2012). As the Myanmar case showed, the misguided notion that just one more turn of the sanctions screw will push impoverished citizens into rebellion clearly remains attractive in important Western policy circles. Particularly where existing opposition forces are weak and/or disorganized, this is simply nonsense.

Summing up, this study demonstrates that local socio-political dynamics overwhelmingly determine the outcomes of sanctions episodes. Of particular importance are the composition, size, and interests of key social forces, and the balance of power between them. Where a society has multiple clusters of authority, resources, and power, rather than a single group enjoying a monopoly, and where key groups enjoy relative autonomy from state power and the capacity for collective action, sanctions may stand some chance of changing domestic political trajectories. In the absence of these conditions, their leverage will be extremely limited.

Targeted Sanctions: Not So 'Smart'?

Rejecting the 'naïve theory' of classical liberalism does not imply any endorsement of 'inverted liberalism' and therefore targeted sanctions. Simply because many opposition forces are ineffective does not necessarily mean that *all* citizens of non-liberal states are passive, vulnerable 'victims'. Nor does it imply that their passive cooperation is unimportant for the maintenance of state power in countries with authoritarian regimes.

Indeed, the SCA framework's insistence that state power is founded upon such routinized cooperation and thus on the maintenance of coalitions of key socio-political groups was clearly borne out by the case studies. Many white businessmen in South Africa, particularly Anglophones, claimed to be powerless to change the apartheid government's policies, but in fact their growing civil disobedience and refusal to continue supporting sanctions busting were critical in eroding the regime's capacity to resist democratic change. The UDF's capacity to render the townships ungovernable and paralyse state institutions, and the black unions' ability to disrupt the economy, were even more important in constraining state power and the efficacy of the apartheid regime's strategy of rule. In Iraq, Saddam's primary motivation for dismantling his WMD arsenal in order to end the embargo was to avoid popular rebellion. Similarly Myanmar's military regime founded the 23-million-strong USDA, promoting patronage-based development to court popular acquiescence or at least passive cooperation. Thus even brutal dictatorships with highly disorganized oppositions require a degree of societal consent and cooperation to remain in power.

Because inverted liberalism does not recognize this social basis to state power, its associated policy of targeted sanctions rests on misguided assumptions. This was clearly demonstrated in the Myanmar case, the most significant 'test bed' for smart sanctions to date. Targeted sanctions could often have no effect because the presumed vulnerability—e.g. a desire to use services in or travel to Western countries—was non-existent. But more importantly, their targets, particularly among business elites, lacked any real capacity to influence government policy. Moreover, their very *targeted* nature made them even easier to evade than sectoral embargoes. Travel sanctions directed only at named individuals can be readily evaded by anyone able to secure a passport in an alternative name, and 'smart' sanctions are generally aimed precisely at such individuals. Similarly a company targeted by sanctions can readily establish proxies, particularly in the opaque business environments found in countries likely to be targeted by sanctions. The dollar embargo created far greater problems for Myanmar's crony capitalists than company-based restrictions, because it encompassed the entire economy, making it tougher to evade.

The Myanmar case also undermines the idea that targeted sanctions can necessarily avoid the problem of 'collateral damage'. As noted earlier, this is central to the appeal of 'smart' sanctions, which seek to punish those 'responsible' for policies whilst avoiding harming innocent 'victims'. Yet, rather like so-called 'smart' bombs, this precision is arguably more of a fantasy than reality. In Myanmar's case Western officials simply tore pages out of the Yangon business directory and added the listed companies to their sanctions lists.[2] Consequently, firms were sanctioned whose owners were among Myanmar's few 'clean' big businessmen and among the even fewer willing to speak to Western diplomats, prompting the embarrassed US Embassy (2009d) to relent.[3] It may be tempting to recommend technical solutions for such problems, like gathering better data. However, those countries most likely to be subjected to sanctions are precisely those where good data is hard to acquire. There is a reason why Western officials resort to such crude methods.

More importantly, though, even in the unlikely event that absolutely precise targeting became feasible, 'smart' sanctions would still frequently inflict collateral damage due to the strategic response of targets and third parties. Because targeted sanctions are easier to evade, their costs can be more easily shifted onto others, directly or indirectly. When Myanmar's crony companies suffered, they merely lobbied their military patrons for extra concessions, maintaining their profit levels at the expense of other social groups. For example, car import licences, a favourite mode of patronage used to assuage discontent, allowed cronies to charge US$20,000 for twenty-year-old used cars—an exorbitant rent extracted from the urban middle classes (Ardeth Maung Thawnghmung, 2011: 651).[4] When cronies' tourism businesses flopped due to Western boycott campaigns and targeted sanctions, they moved into extractive industries, pillaging Myanmar's natural resources and displacing ethnic minority populations. These findings reinforce studies of Angola and Zimbabwe, where sanctions targeted at named individuals inflicted extensive collateral damage to wider population groups, by restricting public services provided by targeted elites or prompting investor flight and economic crisis (Eriksson, 2011: esp. 156, 210, 214–16, 219–21). The cases in this study show that such cost-shifting is only impeded when opposition

---

[2] The businessman who produces Myanmar's leading business directory recognized that this was happening when a clear correlation emerged between his product and the sanctions lists (Moe Kyaw, 2012). A senior British Foreign and Commonwealth Office (FCO) official acknowledged that this 'Yellow Pages problem' was generic to targeted sanctions (personal communication, 9 January 2014). However, recent legal challenges may render this practice unsustainable in Europe.

[3] Individuals with similar names to the targets are also being unjustly sanctioned. In the Myanmar case, for instance, a British philosopher sharing the name of Myanmar's leading crony capitalist regularly has goods and financial transactions intercepted—a problem apparently suffered by everyone with this name (Trindle, 2014).

[4] The tendency of business elites to lobby for business concessions, not political change, is also observed in other cases, e.g. Iran (Fathollah-Nejad, 2014: 51).

resistance renders it politically unfeasible, as in South Africa. Moreover, even where strong collateral damage is absent, recent scholarship has begun to identify negative political consequences. Grauvogel and von Soest's (2014: 646) quantitative study suggests that 'not only comprehensive but also targeted sanctions may lead to "rally-round-the-flag" effects, which in turn contributes to the persistence of authoritarian regimes'. This clearly exposes as fanciful the notion that one can meaningfully target—and focus analysis exclusively upon—a small group of people and simply ignore their relationship to the rest of their society, as inverted liberalism proposes. This claim is also belied by the tendency of frustrated Western governments to escalate personally targeted sanctions into sector-wide measures that will inevitably have society-wide repercussions (Fathollah-Nejad, 2014: 53).

This discussion suggests that 'targeted' sanctions are more of a convenient myth than an effective policy. While their modest primary effects may avoid Iraq-style humanitarian catastrophes, their secondary effects remain uncontrollable and are by no means entirely benign. To broaden our understanding beyond these cases, rather than producing more technical evaluations or implementation guidelines, scholars should undertake research on the effects these instruments have on the ground, including through fieldwork.

Rethinking the Appeal of Sanctions

Given these various problems, it is reasonable to ask, as other scholars have, why sanctions continue to be used so frequently. This book has focused on the domestic effects of sanctions in target states, since it is a desire to change political outcomes there that invariably justifies their imposition, and the effects occur regardless of the actual intentions of sanctions senders. Nonetheless, as noted in the Introduction, senders' goals may not be limited to, or even include, a concern with the target state, but may instead reflect domestic or international political objectives (Jones and Portela, 2014). Accordingly, even if our cases underscore that sanctions carry frequently disastrous consequences for target populations, they are likely to persist for unrelated reasons.

The conduct of much contemporary sanctions policymaking is so shoddy as to call into serious question whether sanctions are even meant to have their supposedly intended effects. The very fact that the question of how sanctions are supposed to work has received so little attention itself suggests disinterest in how the ostensible goals of Western statecraft are going to be achieved. Eriksson's study of EU and UN policymaking, involving many interviews with officials, reveals a breathtaking 'lack of knowledge about how sanctions are meant to work' and a total absence of strategic thinking and evaluation. Accordingly, 'practice is piecemeal' and 'the playing out of sanctions is simply the result of rational, irrational and random procedures and practices' (Eriksson, 2011: 114, 241). The EU does not even have a mechanism to evaluate targeted sanctions: 'once [they] have been imposed, little political attention seems to be paid to the reactions and behaviours of the listed entities' (Eriksson, 2011: 187). This strongly suggests that EU policymakers, at least, do not actually care about their sanctions' impact on the ostensible targets.

Instead, the predominant appeal of sanctions—particularly targeted measures—for policymakers is seemingly that they offer a relatively cheap and easy way of appearing to 'do something' in response to short-term crises, with the real targets being international and domestic audiences. Accordingly, very little thought is devoted to their likely effect on target states, how sanctions are supposed to work to achieve their stated goals, or sometimes even what their goals are.[5] An obvious example is the EU sanctions imposed on fourteen Russian businessmen and banks in response to Russia's annexation of Crimea in March 2014. There was surely no plausible mechanism by which this could reverse the invasion or even constrain further Russian meddling in Ukraine. The sanctions can only be understood as responding to the need to react publicly to Russian malfeasance to appease international and domestic audiences, in a way that did not undermine more important interests like Russian gas supplies to Germany and the large Russian investments in the City of London (Unger, 2014; Watt, 2014).

My numerous interactions with European policymakers whilst researching this book further underscored the primacy of international and domestic audiences over any concern with domestic effects in the ostensible target states. One British official commented that the EU did not monitor the impact of its sanctions because member-state governments viewed the conclusion of tortuous European Council negotiations to impose restrictive measures as their real 'achievement'. In other cases, another official stated, sanctions are imposed to appease international partners like the US or even the African Union.[6] This would again render monitoring their effects on target states pointless. In the EU, at least, sanctions seem largely to serve expressive goals, to broadcast so-called 'European values', to inject content into an otherwise moribund Common Security and Foreign Policy, and to create an image of coherence and 'actorness' (Hellquist, 2012). As another official put it, the EU's approach is: 'I sanction, therefore I am.'[7] In this sense, EU sanctions policies are part of a much broader post-Cold War trend where foreign policy is not so

---

[5] FCO official, personal communication, 9 January 2014.
[6] Remark at a policy development workshop, convened by the author at the British FCO and held under Chatham House rules in April 2014.
[7] FCO official, personal communication, 9 January 2014.

much directed at securing clearly defined 'national interests' in a strategically coherent manner, but rather used to generate a sense of ethical meaning and political purpose where perhaps none previously existed (Laïdi, 1998; Chandler, 2009).

This attempt to produce moral and political kudos can also mean that the real target of sanctions may be domestic audiences. An official familiar with Zimbabwe commented that they were never consulted when EU sanctions there were up for renewal. Ministers were disinterested in their domestic impact in Zimbabwe because their main priority was to persuade their European counterparts to maintain sanctions in order to continue appeasing domestic liberals opposed to the Mugabe government. As the official commented: 'the ostensible target is not the real target'.[8] Other officials conceded that British-sponsored EU sanctions against Myanmar were largely driven by a need to appease campaign groups like Burma Campaign UK, expressing fear of a domestic backlash if they changed their policy.[9] The tendency of Western politicians to use sanctions for self-serving moral grandstanding is so extreme that the European Parliament has discussed imposing them on 40 per cent of the world's states (Hellquist, 2012). The US also has a long history of self-serving congressional activism on sanctions, often designed to appease particular ethnic constituencies (Preeg, 1999).

The use of sanctions therefore accords with patterns of contemporary intervention more generally, where the ostensible target can actually be the least important concern driving a policy. In humanitarian intervention, for example, a review of six key cases finds that 'soft security' concerns like relations with allies and regional stability were the primary motivating factors, followed by domestic politics, with humanitarian concern for the 'target' carrying the least explanatory weight (DiPrizio, 2002: 153).

Consequently, studying the domestic effects of sanctions in target states may not merely be irrelevant for policymakers' real interests; it may even be counterproductive. For instance, sanctions are demonstrably failing to transform Zimbabwean politics, despite inflicting severe damage on the economy and ordinary people (see Eriksson, 2011: ch. 9). Ruling ZANU-PF personnel have even privately remarked that the worst thing that could happen to them would be the lifting of sanctions, since they had been a useful scapegoat for their country's economic crisis.[10] Ironically, therefore, better knowledge about how sanctions were (not) 'working' domestically could only have hindered British ministers' attempts to have EU sanctions renewed. UN officials

---

[8] Remark at policy development workshop, April 2014.
[9] Remarks at a Wilton Park conference on Myanmar, held under Chatham House rules, 5–6 March 2012.
[10] Remark at policy development workshop, April 2014.

appear similarly reluctant to improve sanctions assessment, because 'politically sensitive evidence...could restrain the [UNSC] members' future use of sanctions' (Eriksson, 2011: 126). That is, fully exposing the disutility of sanctions in affecting the ostensible target states would delegitimize their use for powerful governments' real purposes—manipulating the international system or domestic opinion. As the Iraq case shows, these imperatives can be so overwhelming that they can even impede acknowledgement that sanctions have worked to secure their ostensible goals.

The normative connotations of this are typically ignored by sanctions scholars. That sanctions serve multiple goals is generally only recognized in order to defend sanctions against those arguing they 'do not work' because they effect little change in target states. Their advocates maintain that sanctions may still be 'successful' because they serve other international or domestic purposes (e.g. Giumelli, 2013b). That the profoundly unethical connotations of this argument are never explored is perhaps an indication of how deeply implicated many scholars have become in perpetuating sanctions as a practice. Put simply, if sanctions ostensibly intended to coerce a target government are instead being used for other international or domestic purposes, the state in question, and its population, are being instrumentalized for reasons that potentially have very little to do with them. This is a clear violation of Kant's categorical imperative to treat other people only as ends and never a means to some other end. It implies that, for the sake of broadcasting their supposed moral virtues, Western leaders are inflicting deeply unethical suffering on others.

This ethical violation is not excused by the shift to 'smart' sanctions. The advocates of smart sanctions suggest that focusing on a small number of those 'responsible' for objectionable policies vitiates ethical considerations. Building on an ethic imported, perhaps, from criminal law, they suggest that it is reasonable to inflict suffering on the guilty. Yet, as we have seen, targeted sanctions typically inflict direct or indirect collateral damage, undermining this defence. Moreover, if the targets are being punished merely to satisfy senders' domestic or international purposes, they are still being instrumentalized, and the categorical imperative applies regardless of their number. Furthermore, as we have seen, targeted sanctions artificially polarize between the good and bad, the responsible and innocent, in a way that disregards how states actually operate in practice. It is rarely, if ever, possible to single out individuals as wholly 'responsible' for something as socially contingent as a particular form of regime.

The studied ignorance of dynamics within target states further compounds the unethical nature of Western practices, implying a cavalier disregard for the lives of those affected. Paying attention to how sanctions (do not) work is thus not only a guide for more rational policymaking when target governments are the real targets; it is also an ethical imperative even—or perhaps especially—when they are not.

Recommendations for Sanctions Advocates and Policymakers

Despite yielding considerable analytical insight, the SCA may not significantly influence policymaking. Notwithstanding the potential benefits identified in the Introduction, the factors identified above, and the rather dismal consequences of sanctions in many cases, may dissuade policymakers from properly considering the domestic impacts of their economic statecraft. Nonetheless, I close with some basic arguments for those wanting to take SCA's insights seriously.

Abandon Analogical Reasoning

This study clearly demonstrates that any arguments that 'sanctions should be imposed upon or will work in country x because they worked in country y' have no valid foundation. The South Africa case, the most frequently invoked basis for such analogical reasoning, has very peculiar features that are simply not present elsewhere. This is of contemporary relevance for campaigners advocating for boycotts, disinvestment, and sanctions against Israel.

The key features that made sanctions work in South Africa as they did were: widespread popular politicization and mobilization stemming from decades of grass-roots organizing; the presence of a large working class predominantly in the opposition camp; the existence of a capitalist elite independent of state control or patronage; the immediate 1980s context of structural economic crisis; and the economy's dependency on transactions with the West. Furthermore, the peculiar nature of apartheid as a racialized system of minority domination made it harder for ruling elites to co-opt opponents and develop new strategies, and easier for resistance leaders to build broad-based support. These features are simply not present in many other contexts. Consequently imposing even identical sanctions would likely have dramatically different results. This underscores the importance of centring analysis on target societies, not on sanctions instruments themselves (cf. Crawford and Klotz, 1999b).

It also illustrates the need to analyse prospective or actual targets based on their socio-political and economic dynamics, not their moral attributes. For example, whether Israel is actually an 'apartheid state', as BDS campaigners maintain, is irrelevant for establishing how or whether sanctions could compel the Israeli government to stop brutalizing the Palestinians and grant them full political and civil rights. Weighing the moral equivalence of the two cases may be useful for determining whether the outside world has an imperative to act, but it does not tell us what action should be taken or would be effective. Whether sanctions can work can only be determined by close study of the target society and estimating the economic damage required to shift conflict dynamics in a progressive direction.

Undertaking such analysis for Israel/Palestine is beyond the scope of this book. However, a preliminary analysis suggests some stark differences from the South African context that may give BDS advocates pause for thought (Jones, forthcoming). Unlike the ANC/UDF-led South African opposition, Palestinians are deeply divided and politically defeated. The Palestinian leadership is split between Fatah—effectively co-opted, along with a sliver of Palestinian business elites, to run the 'Bantustan' Palestinian National Authority under Israeli tutelage—and Hamas, left governing a battered Gaza (and the target of Western sanctions). The 2005 call for BDS from Palestinian activists was an attempt to revive a defeated liberation struggle; sanctions never did this for South Africans. Moreover, the BDS movement has no strategy or united political platform beyond minimal commitments to human rights; unlike the ANC, there is no analysis of Israeli society, no articulated strategy for political transformation, and no sense of how BDS measures 'work' to advance their cause. So far, so-called BDS 'successes' have had no discernible effect on Israel's economy or politics. If an analogy is insisted upon, Palestine seems closer to South Africa in the 1960s than in the 1980s.

Planning and Evaluating Sanctions

The extraordinary vagueness in Western sanctions policy about goals, strategy, mechanisms, costs, and benefits ought to be challenged. Since even targeted sanctions can inflict considerable damage on targets, the current scattergun approach is morally unjustifiable, as well as frequently inefficacious. Unlike most existing scholarship, which neglects to explore how sanctions (do not) work, SCA provides a reasonable framework for policymakers to analyse prospective targets, estimate the potential impact of different sanctions on socio-political struggles in the target state, and evaluate and amend existing sanctions regimes. However, incorporating this approach into policymaking would require significant changes in the way that Western states operate.

Although SCA was developed to analyse past sanctions regimes, it could potentially be used to guide the planning of future ones. Once policymakers have identified a clear goal, SCA directs officials to study the conflict dynamics and political economy context of target states, providing an understanding of the forces supporting and opposing a particular regime and its policies, and of the scale and type of intervention required to shift them. This can then be compared to the policy options available to senders, to identify whether they are sufficient, or will simply lack traction in the target society. If there is a reasonable fit between the measures available and the scale of the senders' goals, the next step is to specify a clear and explicit causal pathway through which sanctions are expected to 'work' to deliver them. This would provide a baseline for an ongoing evaluation of the sanctions regime. The key test would be whether they trigger the mechanisms expected, and whether this leads to the political change envisaged. If they do not, policymakers must revise their analysis and adjust the sanctions regime accordingly, potentially incorporating unanticipated causal mechanisms. Where sanctions are lengthy and have significant socio-economic impacts, periodic reviews will also be required to take account of the shifting local dynamics.

This approach would impose stringent requirements on policymakers, which further diminishes the likelihood of its adoption, but this is entirely appropriate. The demand that senders propose concrete causal pathways through which sanctions should 'work' is essential to ensure that the policy has been properly thought through, and harm is not merely being inflicted indiscriminately for purposes other than changing outcomes in the target state. The only way to refute criticisms that target populations are being instrumentalized by sanctions senders for other purposes is to demonstrate clear planning and tell a plausible causal 'story' about how 'economic pain' is going to produce 'political gain'. If such a story cannot be told, policymakers simply ought not to impose sanctions; indeed, they should be prevented from doing so. Kant's categorical imperative aside, sanctions are a form of foreign intervention in the internal affairs of a sovereign state; this alone raises questions as to their legitimacy or even legality (Bickerton et al., 2007; Velásquez-Ruiz, 2012). Certainly, identifying the likely impact of sanctions and a plausible causal pathway for change is extremely complex. Although the SCA's emphasis on structural constraints helps limit the range of possible scenarios, establishing the likely strategic response of local forces will always be difficult. This reflects the fact that foreign intervention is a rather crude instrument whose primary effects are hard to foresee and whose secondary effects, once mediated through local responses, are even harder to predict and arguably impossible to control (Jones, 2010). SCA's merit is that it forces policymakers to confront this reality and its associated risks, rather than irresponsibly rushing to impose sanctions that harm target populations without adequate reflection. This reflection may convince many readers that the only responsible course is not to intervene at all. However, given the interests driving the imposition of sanctions, this outcome could only be generated by renewed social conflict within Western states themselves.

Bibliography

Note: CRRC denotes an archival document from the Conflict Records Research Centre, National Defense University, Washington D.C., followed by the record number.

Abdullah, Thabit A. J. 2006. *Dictatorship, Imperialism and Chaos: Iraq Since 1989*, London: Zed Books.

Abel, David. 2012. Former Minister of Finance and Planning, Myanmar. Interview with the author, Yangon, 6 July.

Abu Gulal, Saif. 2001. 'Sanctions: How Saddam Gained Upper Hand'. *Economic and Political Weekly* vol. 36(32), 3026–9.

Achen, Christopher H. and Snidal, Duncan. 1989. 'Rational Deterrence Theory and Comparative Case Studies'. *World Politics* vol. 41(2), 143–69.

Adam, Heribert and Moodley, Kogila. 1993. *The Opening of the Apartheid Mind: Options for the New South Africa*, Berkeley: University of California Press.

ADB [Asian Development Bank]. 2012. *Myanmar in Transition: Opportunities and Challenges*, Mandaluyong City: ADB.

Agnew, John. 2009. *Globalization and Sovereignty*, Lanham: Rowman and Littlefield.

Ahmad, Mahmood. 2002. 'Agricultural Policy Issues and Challenges in Iraq: Short- and Medium-Term Options'. In *Iraq's Economic Predicament*, edited by Kamil A. Mahdi, 169–99. Reading: Ithaca Press.

Al-Ali, Nadje. 2000. 'Sanctions and Women in Iraq'. In *Sanctions on Iraq: Background, Consequences, Strategies*, edited by Campaign Against Sanctions on Iraq, 73–84. Cambridge: CASI.

Al-Bayati, Hamid. 2011. *From Dictatorship to Democracy: An Insider's Account of the Iraqi Opposition to Saddam*, Philadelphia: University of Pennsylvania Press.

al-Hamdani, Ra'ad Majid. 2003. 'Memoir'. Baghdad, 25 November.

al-Jabbar, Faleh 'Abd. 1994. 'Why the Intifada Failed'. In *Iraq since the Gulf War: Prospects for Democracy*, edited by Fran Hazelton, 97–117. London: Zed Books.

Al-Khafaji, Isam. 1994. 'State Terror and the Degradation of Politics'. In *Iraq since the Gulf War: Prospects for Democracy*, edited by Fran Hazelton, 20–31. London: Zed Books.

Al-Kudayri, Tariq. 2002. 'Iraq's Manufacturing Sector: Status and Prospects for Rehabilitation and Reform'. In *Iraq's Economic Predicament*, edited by Kamil Mahdi, 201–29. Reading: Ithaca Press.

Alahmad, Nida. 2007. 'The Politics of Oil and State Survival in Iraq (1991–2003): Beyond the Rentier Thesis'. *Constellations* vol. 14(4), 586–612.

Alamgir, Jalal. 2008. 'Myanmar's Foreign Trade and its Political Consequences'. *Asian Survey* vol. 48(6), 977–96.

Alan Saw U. 2012. Executive Director, Karen Development Network, Myanmar. Interview with the author, Yangon, 23 July.

Alden, Chris. 1998. *Apartheid's Last Stand: The Rise and Fall of the South African Security State*, Basingstoke: Macmillan.

Alkadiri, Raad. 2001. 'The Iraqi Klondike: Oil and Regional Trade'. *Middle East Report* vol. 31 (220), 30–5.

Alkazaz, Aziz. 1993. 'The Distribution of National Income in Iraq, with Particular Reference to the Development of Policies Applied by the State'. In *Iraq: Power and Society*, edited by Derek Hopwood, Habib Ishow, and Thomas Koszinowski, 193–256. Reading: Ithaca Press.

Allen, Susan H. 2005. 'The Determinants of Economic Sanctions Success and Failure'. *International Interactions* vol. 31(2), 117–38.

Allen, Susan H. 2008a. 'The Domestic Political Costs of Economic Sanctions'. *Journal of Conflict Resolution* vol. 52(6), 916–44.

Allen, Susan H. 2008b. 'Political Institutions and Constrained Response to Economic Sanctions'. *Foreign Policy Analysis* vol. 4(3), 255–74.

Alnasrawi, Abbas. 1994. *The Economy of Iraq: Oil, Wars, Destruction of Development and Prospects, 1950–2010*, Westport: Greenwood Press.

Alnasrawi, Abbas. 2001. 'Iraq: Economic Sanctions and Consequences, 1990–2000'. *Third World Quarterly* vol. 22(2), 205–18.

ANC [African National Congress]. 1969. 'Strategy and Tactics of the ANC'. Morogoro Conference, Tanzania, 25 April–1 May; accessed at http://www.marxists.org/subject/africa/anc/1969/strategy-tactics.htm, 17 February 2014.

ANC [African National Congress]. 1985. 'The Nature of the South African Ruling Class'. Document of the National Preparatory Committee, ANC National Consultative Conference, Kabwe, Zambia, June; accessed at http://www.marxists.org/subject/africa/anc/1985/nature-ruling-class.htm, 17 February 2014.

Andreas, Peter. 2005. 'Criminalizing Consequences of Sanctions: Embargo Busting and Its Legacy'. *International Studies Quarterly* vol. 49(2), 335–60.

Anwar, Dewi Fortuna. 2002. 'The Fall of Suharto: Understanding the Politics of the Global'. In *Southeast Asian Responses to Globalization: Restructuring Governance and Deepening Democracy*, edited by Francis Loh Kok Wah and Joakim Öjendal, 191–229. Singapore: ISEAS.

Ardeth Maung Thawnghmung. 2011. 'The Politics of Everyday Life in Twenty-First Century Myanmar'. *Journal of Asian Studies* vol. 70(3), 641–56.

Arnove, Anthony. 2000. 'Introduction'. In *Iraq under Siege*, edited by Anthony Arnove, 9–20. London: Pluto Press.

ASEAN Secretariat. 2006. *Statistics of Foreign Direct Investment in ASEAN*, 8th edn, Jakarta: ASEAN.

Asiaweek. 1999. 'We Restored Order', 17 December.

Askari, Hossein G., Forrer, John, Teegen, Hildy, and Yang, Jiawen. 2003. *Economic Sanctions: Examining Their Philosophy and Efficacy*, London: Praeger.

Aung Than Oo. 2012. Vice-President, Myanmar Rice Industry Association. Interview with the author, Yangon, 24 July.

Avey, Paul C. and Desch, Michael C. 2014. 'What Do Policymakers Want From Us? Results of a Survey of Current and Former Senior National Security Decision Makers'. *International Studies Quarterly* vol. 58(2), 227–47.

Azam, Jean-Paul and Saadi-Sedik, Tahsin. 2004. 'Aid versus Sanctions for Taming Oppressors: Theory and Case Study of the Iraqi Kurds'. *Defence and Peace Economics* vol. 15(4), 343–64.

Babbage, Maria. 2004. 'White Elephants: Why South Africa Gave up the Bomb and the Implications for Nuclear Nonproliferation Policy'. *Journal of Public and International Affairs* vol. 15, 1–20.

Badgley, John. 1990. 'The Burmese Way to Capitalism'. *Southeast Asian Affairs 1990*, 229–39.

Badgley, John (ed.) 2004. *Reconciling Burma/Myanmar: Essays on US Relations with Burma*, Seattle: National Bureau of Asian Research.

Badiou, Alain. 2001. *Ethics: An Essay on the Understanding of Evil*, London: Verso.

Baldwin, David A. 1985. *Economic Statecraft*, Princeton: Princeton University Press.

Baldwin, David A. 1999–2000. 'The Sanctions Debate and the Logic of Choice'. *International Security* vol. 24(3), 80–107.

Baldwin, David A. and Pape, Robert A. 1998. 'Evaluating Economic Sanctions'. *International Security* vol. 23(2), 189–98.

Bangkok Post. 1989. 'Aung San Suu Kyi Calls for Trade Boycott', 4 June.

Baram, Amatzia. 1986. 'The Ruling Political Elite in Ba'thi Iraq, 1968–1986: The Changing Features of a Collective Profile'. *International Journal of Middle East Studies* vol. 21(4), 447–93.

Baram, Amatzia. 1997. 'Neo-Tribalism in Iraq: Saddam Hussein's Tribal Policies 1991–96'. *International Journal of Middle East Studies* vol. 29(1), 1–31.

Baram, Amatzia. 1998. 'Building towards Crisis: Saddam Husayn's Strategy for Survival'. Policy Paper No. 47, Washington Institute for Near East Policy, Washington, D.C.

Baram, Amatzia. 2000a. 'The Effect of Iraqi Sanctions: Statistical Pitfalls and Responsibility'. *Middle East Journal* vol. 54(2), 194–223.

Baram, Amatzia. 2000b. 'Saddam Husayn: Between His Power Base and the International Community'. *Middle East Review of International Affairs* vol. 4(4), 9–21.

Barber Cho. 2012. Joint General-Secretary, Myanmar Timber Merchants Association. Interview with the author, Yangon, 20 July.

Barber, James. 1979. 'Economic Sanctions as a Policy Instrument'. *International Affairs* vol. 55(3), 367–84.

Barghouti, Omar. 2011. *Boycott, Disinvestment, Sanctions: The Global Struggle for Palestinian Rights*, Chicago: Haymarket Books.

Barr, Michael. 2014. *The Ruling Elite of Singapore: Network of Power and Influence*, London: I. B. Tauris.

Batchelor, Peter. 1998. 'South Africa's Arms Industry: Prospects for Conversion'. In *From Defence to Development: Redirecting Military Resources in South Africa*, edited by Jacklyn Cock and Penny McKenzie, 97–121. Cape Town: David Philip.

Beasley-Murray, John, Cameron, Maxwell A., and Hershberg, Eric. 2009. 'Latin America's Left Turns: An Introduction'. *Third World Quarterly* vol. 30(2), 319–30.

Beinart, William. 1994. *Twentieth-Century South Africa*, Oxford: Oxford University Press.

Bellin, Eva. 2000. 'Contingent Democrats: Industrialists, Labor, and Democratization in Late-Developing Countries'. *World Politics* vol. 52(1), 175–205.

Bengio, Ofra. 2000. 'How Does Saddam Hold On?'. *Foreign Affairs* vol. 79(4), 90–103.

Bethlehem, Ronald W. 1988. *Economics in a Revolutionary Society: Sanctions and the Transformation of South Africa*, Craighall: AD Donker.

Bickerton, Christopher J., Cunliffe, Philip, and Gourevitch, Alexander (eds). 2007. *Politics without Sovereignty: A Critique of Contemporary International Relations* London: UCL Press.

Blair, Tony. 2010. *A Journey*, EPUB edn, London: Random House.

Blanchard, Jean-Marc F. and Ripsman, Norrin M. 1999. 'Asking the Right Question: When Do Economic Sanctions Work Best?'. *Security Studies* vol. 9(1), 219–53.

Blanchard, Jean-Marc F. and Ripsman, Norrin M. 2008. 'A Political Theory of Economic Statecraft'. *Foreign Policy Analysis* vol. 4(4), 371–98.

Blattman, Christopher and Miguel, Edward. 2010. 'Civil War'. *Journal of Economic Literature* vol. 48(1), 3–57.

Block, Fred. 1977. 'The Ruling Class Does Not Rule: Notes on the Marxist Theory of the State'. *Socialist Revolution* vol. 7(3), 6–28.

Boesak, Allan. 2011. Former Patron, United Democratic Front, South Africa. Interview with the author, by telephone, 12 September.

Bolks, Sean M. and Al-Sowayel, Dina. 2000. 'How Long Do Economic Sanctions Last? Examining the Sanctioning Process through Duration'. *Political Research Quarterly* vol. 53(2), 241–65.

Bonetti, Shane. 1997. 'A Test of the Public Choice Theory of Economic Sanctions'. *Applied Economic Letters* vol. 4(12), 729–32.

Boone, Peter, Gazdar, Haris, and Hussain, Athar. 1997. 'Sanctions against Iraq: Costs of Failure'. Center for Economic and Social Rights, Brooklyn, November; accessed at http://cesr.org/downloads/Sanctions%20Against%20Iraq%20Costs%20of%20Failure%201997.pdf, 12 June 2012.

Braude, Joseph. 2003. *The New Iraq: Rebuilding the Country for its People, the Middle East, and the World*, New York: Basic Books.

Brink, David. 2011. Former South African Business Leader. Interview with the author, Johannesburg, 7 September.

Brooks, Risa A. 2002. 'Sanctions and Regime Type: What Works, and When?'. *Security Studies* vol. 11(4), 1–50.

Bueno de Mesquita, Bruce and Smith, Alistair. 2011. *The Dictator's Handbook: Why Bad Behaviour is Almost Always Good Politics*, EPUB edn, New York: Public Affairs.

Bunge, Mario. 1997. 'Mechanism and Explanation'. *Philosophy of the Social Sciences* vol. 27(4), 410–65.

Bunton, Martin. 2008. 'From Developmental Nationalism to the End of Nation-state in Iraq?'. *Third World Quarterly* vol. 29(3), 631–46.

Bush, George W. 2010. *Decision Points*, EPUB edn, New York: Crown Publishers.

Byman, Daniel, Pollack, Kenneth, and Waxman, Matthew. 1998. 'Coercing Saddam Hussein: Lessons from the Past'. *Survival* vol. 40(3), 127–51.

Callahan, Mary. 2000. 'Cracks in the Edifice? Military–Society Relations in Burma since 1988'. In *Burma Myanmar: Strong Regime, Weak State?*, edited by Morten B. Pedersen, Emily Rudland, and Ronald J. May, 22–51. Adelaide: Crawford House Publishing.

Callahan, Mary. 2007a. *Making Enemies: War and State Building in Burma*, Ithaca: Cornell University Press.

Callahan, Mary. 2007b. *Political Authority in Burma's Ethnic Minority States: Devolution, Occupation and Coexistence*, Washington, D.C.: East-West Center.

Camroux, David and Egreteau, Renaud. 2010. 'Normative Europe Meets the Burmese Garrison State: Processes, Policies, Blockages and Future Possibilities'. In *Ruling Myanmar: From Cyclone Nargis to National Elections*, edited by Nick Cheesman, Monique Skidmore, and Trevor Wilson, 267–93. Singapore: ISEAS.

Carim, Xavier, Klotz, Audie, and Lebleu, Olivier. 1999. 'The Political Economy of Financial Sanctions'. In *How Sanctions Work: Lessons from South Africa*, edited by Neta C. Crawford and Audie Klotz, 159–77. London: Macmillan.

CBS. 1996. '60 Minutes', 12 May.

CCDP [Centre on Conflict Development and Peacebuilding]. 2011. 'Assessing the Impacts and Effectiveness of UN Targeted Sanctions'. Workshop Report, 2–4 June, Foreign and Commonwealth Office, London.

Centre for Peace and Conflict Studies. 2010. *Listening to Voices from Inside: Ethnic People Speak*, Phnom Penh: Centre for Peace and Conflict Studies.

Chalabi, Ahmed. 1994. 'The Rule of Law'. In *Iraq since the Gulf War: Prospects for Democracy*, edited by Fran Hazelton, 223–31. London: Zed Books.

Chan, Steve. 1997. 'In Search of Democratic Peace: Problems and Promise'. *Mershon International Studies Review* vol. 41(1), 59–91.

Chandler, David. 2009. *Hollow Hegemony: Rethinking Global Politics, Power and Resistance*, London: Verso.

Chandler, David. 2010. *International Statebuilding: The Rise of Post-Liberal Governance*, London: Routledge.

Chaudry, Kiren A. 1991. 'On the Way to Market: Economic Liberalization and Iraq's Invasion of Kuwait'. *Middle East Report* vol. 170, 14–23.

Chesterman, Simon and Pouligny, Beatrice. 2003. 'Are Sanctions Meant to Work? The Politics of Creating and Implementing Sanctions through the United Nations'. *Global Governance* vol. 9(4), 503–18.

Chong Wai Hoon, Koh Tse San, Seow Kok Boon, and Tio Guat Kuan. 1996. 'The Tourism Industry in Myanmar'. In *Business Opportunities in Myanmar*, edited by Tan Teck Meng, Low Aik Meng, John J. Williams, and Ivan P. Polunin, 275–84. Eaglewood Cliffs: Prentice Hall.

CIA [Central Intelligence Agency]. 1993. 'Prospects for Iraq: Saddam and Beyond', National Intelligence Estimate 93-42; December.

CIJ [Coalition for International Justice]. 2002. 'Sources of Revenue for Saddam and Sons: A Primer on the Financial Underpinnings of the Regime in Baghdad'. 18 September, Washington, D.C.

Clawson, Patrick. 1993. *How Has Saddam Survived? Economic Sanctions, 1990–1993*, Washington, D.C.: National Defense University.

Cockburn, Andrew and Cockburn, Patrick. 2000. *Out of the Ashes: The Resurrection of Saddam Hussein*, London: Verso.

Cohen, Robin. 1986. *Endgame in South Africa? The Changing Structures and Ideology of Apartheid*, London: James Currey.

Coleman, Colin. 2011. Executive Director of the Consultative Business Movement, 1989–94. Interview with the author, Johannesburg, 6 September.

Collier, Paul and Hoeffler, Anke. 2004. 'Greed and Grievance in Civil War'. *Oxford Economic Papers* vol. 56(4), 563–95.

Commonwealth Secretariat. 1989a. *Banking on Apartheid: The Financial Links Report*, London: James Currey.

Commonwealth Secretariat. 1989b. *South Africa: The Sanctions Report*, London: Penguin.

Cooper, J. H. 1989. 'On Income Distribution and Economic Sanctions'. *South African Journal of Economics* vol. 57(1), 10–14.

Cooper, Saths. 2011. Leading South African 'Black Consciousness' Activist; Deputy President and subsequently President, AZAPO, 1983–6. Interview with the author, Johannesburg, 29 August.

Coovadia, Cas. 2011. Head of the Johannesburg Area Committee of the United Democratic Front, South Africa. Interview with the author, Johannesburg, 30 August.

Cordesman, Anthony. 2000. *Iraqi Military Forces Ten Years after the Gulf War*, Washington, D.C.: CSIS.

Cordesman, Anthony and Hashim, Ahmed. 1997. *Iraq: Sanctions and Beyond*, Boulder: Westview.

Cortright, David and Lopez, George A. 2000. *The Sanctions Decade: Assessing UN Strategies in the 1990s*, Boulder: Lynne Rienner.

Cortright, David and Lopez, George A. 2002a. 'Introduction: Assessing Smart Sanctions: Lessons from the 1990s'. In *Smart Sanctions: Targeting Economic Statecraft*, edited by David Cortright and George A. Lopez, 1–22. Plymouth: Rowman and Littlefield.

Cortright, David and Lopez, George A. (eds). 2002b. *Smart Sanctions: Targeting Economic Statecraft*, Plymouth: Rowman and Littlefield.

Cox, Robert W. 1987. *Production, Power, and World Order: Social Forces in the Making of History*, New York: Columbia University Press.

Crawford, Neta C. 1999a. 'How Arms Embargoes Work'. In *How Sanctions Work: Lessons from South Africa*, edited by Neta C. Crawford and Audie Klotz, 45–74. London: Macmillan.

Crawford, Neta C. 1999b. 'Trump Card or Theatre? An Introduction to Two Sanctions Debates'. In *How Sanctions Work: Lessons from South Africa*, edited by Neta C. Crawford and Audie Klotz, 3–24. London: Macmillan.

Crawford, Neta C. and Klotz, Audie. 1999a. 'How Sanctions Work: A Framework for Analysis'. In *How Sanctions Work: Lessons from South Africa*, edited by Neta C. Crawford and Audie Klotz, 25–42. London: Macmillan.

Crawford, Neta C. and Klotz, Audie (eds). 1999b. *How Sanctions Work: Lessons from South Africa*, London: Macmillan.

Crawford-Browne, Terry. 2011. Advisor on Sanctions to Archbishop Desmond Tutu, 1986–94. Interview with the author, Cape Town, 9 September.

CRRC. 1977–8. 'Two Speeches by Saddam Hussein When he was the Vice-President of the Revolutionary Command Council', SH-RVCC-D-000-805; April 1977 and March 1978.

CRRC. 1987–95. 'Miscellaneous Memos Concerning Activities Dealing with Warheads and Chemical Materials', SH-MICN-D-000-743; October 1987–December 1995.

CRRC. 1991a. 'Meeting between Saddam Hussein and High Ranking Officials after the 1st Gulf War', SH-SHTP-A-001-458; 16 December.

CRRC. 1991b. 'Saddam Speaks about Sanctions on Iraq and the Situation of the Ba'th Party after the Invasion by the Coalition Forces', SH-SHTP-A-001-461; 21 December.

CRRC. 1991–2. 'General Security Directorate Recommendations on Roles, Relations, and Traditions of Iraqi Tribes after the 1991 Rebellion', SH-IDGS-D-000-370.

CRRC. 1992a. 'Meeting between Saddam Hussein and Military Commanders Regarding Expectations of Post-Gulf War Attacks and Uprisings', SH-RVCC-D-000-610; February.

CRRC. 1992b. 'Meeting with Saddam Hussein, Tariq Aziz, and Other Senior Officials Discussing the Black Market, Asceticism Policy under the Sanction and the Increase of US Dollar Exchange Rate in Relation to the Iraqi Dinar', SH-SHTP-A-001-465; 17 August.

CRRC. 1992c. 'Message to the President Regarding the Tribal Conflict between al-Yazidiah and al-Hadidyin', SH-MISC-D-000-098; 1 March.

CRRC. 1992–4. 'Iraqi Intelligence Service Investigative Reports about Failed Bombings Intended to Destroy the Residence of the US Ambassador in Jakarta, Japanese Embassy and American Airlines in Philippines', SH-IISX-D-000-475; January 1992–May 1994.

CRRC. 1993a. 'Meeting between Saddam Hussein and his Cabinet Regarding the Iraqi Economy and Progress with Jordan', SH-SHTP-A-001-464; 30 April.

CRRC. 1993b. 'Meeting between Saddam Hussein and the Revolutionary Command Council Regarding the Rules of the United Nations Security Council', SH-SHTP-A-001-198.

CRRC. 1993c. 'Saddam Hussein Meeting with Military Officials', SH-SHTP-D-000-757.

CRRC. 1994a. 'A Meeting between Saddam Hussein and the Council of Ministers Discussing the Iraqi Economy', SH-SHTP-A-001-478.

CRRC. 1994b. 'Saddam Hussein and his Political Advisors Discuss International Interest in Iraqi Oil, Iraqi Army Deserters, and an Initiative to Settle Disputes with Saudi Arabia', SH-SHTP-A-001-238; 3 September.

CRRC. 1994c. 'Saddam Hussein Meeting with Members of Al-'Ubur Conference, National Command, Iraqi Regional Command and Revolutionary Command Council', SH-SHTP-D-000-759.

CRRC. 1994d. 'Saddam Hussein Meeting with the Revolutionary Command and the State Command', SH-SHTP-D-000-712; probably October.

CRRC. 1994e. 'Saddam Hussein Meeting with the Revolutionary Command Council Regarding Sanctions and Kuwait', SH-SHTP-A-001-294; 3 September.

CRRC. 1994f. 'Saddam Hussein Meeting with the Revolutionary Council', SH-SHTP-A-000-734; 26 November.

CRRC. 1994g. 'Saddam Meeting with Ba'ath Party Members Discussing the Economic Situation of the Iraqi Population While under Economic Sanctions', SH-SHTP-A-001-459.

CRRC. 1994–8. 'Correspondence between Russian Export Company and Iraqi Defense Minister Regarding Offer to Assist Iraq with Developing Cruise Missiles', SH-MODX-D-000-478.

CRRC. 1995a. 'Meeting between Saddam Hussein and High Ranking Technical Officers Regarding Iraqi Army Weapons Development', SH-SHTP-A-001-481.

CRRC. 1995b. 'Meeting between Saddam Hussein and Iraqi Ministers Regarding the Treason of Hussein Kamil', SH-SHTP-A-000-762; August.

CRRC. 1995c. 'Meeting between Saddam Hussein and the Security Council Regarding Iraqi Biological and Nuclear Weapons Programs', SH-SHTP-A-001-011; 5 February.

CRRC. 1995d. 'Meeting between the Former Iraqi President Saddam Hussein and his Members of Command', SH-SHTP-A-000-990.

CRRC. 1995e. 'Meeting Headed by Saddam Hussein on the Details of Husayn Kamil's Escape', SH-SHTP-A-001-260.

CRRC. 1995f. 'Minutes of a Meeting between Tariq Aziz and Rolf Ekeus Regarding Iraqi Chemical and Nuclear Programs', SH-MISC-D-000-772; September.

CRRC. 1995g. 'Report by the Director of Iraq's Intelligence Service Regarding the Defection of Hussein Kamil', SH-IISX-D-000-407; 29 August.

CRRC. 1995h. 'Saddam Hussein Meeting with Council of Ministers', SH-SHTP-A-000-989; 15 April.

CRRC. 1995i. 'Saddam Hussein Meeting with Senior Ba'ath Party Officials to Discuss UN Weapons Inspections and the Absence of WMD in Iraq', SH-SHTP-A-001-295; after August.

CRRC. 1995j. 'Saddam Hussein Meeting with the Military Office to Discuss Sanctions, Jordan, and Iraqi Elections', SH-SHTP-A-001-463; 9 September.

CRRC. 1996a. 'Letters of Apology from Hussein Kamil al-Majid to Saddam Hussein Requesting Forgiveness and Permission to Return to Iraq', SH-SPPC-D-000-915; February.

CRRC. 1996b. 'Saddam Hussein meeting with Revolutionary Command Council', SH-SHTP-D-000-799, 28 September.

CRRC. 1998a. 'Interrogation Reports on Fedayeen Saddam Organization Affiliates Accused of Being Arms Dealers', SH-FSDM-D-000-351; May–November.

CRRC. 1998b. 'Iraqi Air Force Meeting with Chief of Staff Regarding the UN Inspection and How to Move Documents Related to Chemical Agents and Weapons', SH-AADF-D-000-209; 19 November.

CRRC. 1998c. 'Iraqi Minister of Defense Request for an Investigation Regarding Documents Pertaining to WMDs Being Found by a United Nations Inspection Team', SH-GMID-D-000-890; July.

CRRC. 1999a. 'Correspondence within the Chief of Staff of the Fedayeen Saddam Office Regarding Opposition Groups and Newspapers Issued by Opposition Groups', SH-FSDM-D-001-093; January–May.

CRRC. 1999b. 'Study of Ba'ath Party Division Command Members Regarding the Economic Sanctions and Their Effects on the Social Values of Iraqi Society', SH-BATH-D-000-492.

CRRC. 2001a. 'A Meeting between Saddam Hussein and High Ranking Iraqi Officials Discussing Kurdish Parties and Organizations', SH-SHTP-A-001-441; 4 November.

CRRC. 2001b. 'Reports about the United States Seeks to Recruit Iraqi Opposition against the Saddam Hussein Regime', SH-IISX-D-000-488; April.

CRRC. 2001c. 'Republican Guard Emergency Action Plan for Attempted Overthrow of the Iraqi Regime and Analysis of Geographical and Population Considerations', SH-RPGD-D-000-684.

CRRC. 2001d. 'Study Issued by the Institute of Preparing and Training, Senior Leaders Course, titled "Method of Defeating the Opposition Parties Inside and Outside Iraq"', SH-IISX-D-000-360.

CRRC. 2002. 'Meeting between Saddam Hussein and Nijirfan [Nechirvan] al-Barzani Regarding the Situation in Iraq and Possibility of US Attack', SH-SPPC-D-000-304; 14 March.

CRRC. 2003. 'Ba'ath Party Files on al-Diwaniyyah Emergency and Maneuver Plans during the War', SH-BATH-D-000-778; 18 February–23 April.

CRRC. nd-a. 'Discussions between Iraqi Ministers Regarding Continued Support for the Conflict between the Kurdish Factions led by Mas'ud Barzani and Jalal Talabani', SH-SHTP-A-000-905.

CRRC. nd-b. 'Meeting between President Saddam Hussein and his Cabinet Talking about the 706 Decision to Pumping the Oil in Exchange for Medicine and Foodstuffs and the UN Stance for the Kurdish and Shia Case', SH-SHTP-A-000-774; probably 1995/1996.

CRRC. nd-c. 'Meeting between Saddam Hussein and His Senior Advisors Discussing the Continuation of the International Sanctions against Iraq', SH-SHTP-A-001-488; after March 1994.

CRRC. nd-d. 'Meeting between Saddam Hussein and Iraqi Ministers Regarding Iraq under Sanctions', SH-SHTP-A-001-298; probably after 1996.

CRRC. nd-e. 'Meeting between Saddam Hussein and Officials Regarding the Treason of Hussein Kamil and Other Developments in Iraq', SH-SHTP-A-000-833; after 7 August 1995.

CRRC. nd-f. 'Meeting between Saddam Hussein and the Revolutionary Council Regarding Relations with the United Nations Security Council', SH-SHTP-A-001-143; after April 1995.

CRRC. nd-g. 'Meeting between Saddam Hussein and Unidentified High Ranking Officials Regarding US Plans to Attack Iraq, Irrigation Projects, and Other Military Issues', SH-SHTP-A-000-565; after August 1995.

CRRC. nd-h. 'Saddam and his Cabinet Contemplate the Results of Their Efforts Concerning the Lifting of Sanctions and Resolution 715', SH-SHTP-A-000-873; between October 1991 and November 1993.

CRRC. nd-i. 'Saddam and Political Advisors Discussing the Production of Biological Materials in Iraq, the Iran–Iraq War, UN Inspections, and the Arab-Israeli Conflict', SH-SHTP-D-000-760; likely mid-1990s.

CRRC. nd-j. 'Saddam and Top Political Advisers Discussing Relations with Saudi Arabia and other Neighbours', SH-SHTP-A-001-253; circa 9–10 October 1994.

CRRC. nd-k. 'Saddam Hussein's Speech with the Revolutionary Members and National Command', SH-RVCC-V-001-402; circa 1991–2.

CRRC. nd-l. 'Saddam Hussein and Iraqi Commanders Discussing Weapons Inspections and how the United States Intends to Continue the Sanctions on Iraq', SH-SHTP-D-000-797; probably early 1996.

CRRC. nd-m. 'Saddam Hussein and Senior Political Advisors Discussing the Treason of Hussein Kamil', SH-SHTP-A-000-837; after 7 August 1995.

CRRC. nd-n. 'Saddam Hussein Meets his Top Officials, Including Tariq 'Aziz and Ali Hasan al-Majid, Announces the Execution of 50 Iraqi Traders, Talks Also about UN Team for Weapons of Mass Destruction (WMD), the Economy and Governorate, and Ministry Performances', SH-SHTP-A-001-012; probably mid-1992.

Dahl, Robert. 1985. *A Preface to Economic Democracy*, Cambridge: Polity.

Dashti-Gibson, Jaleh, Davis, Patricia, and Radcliff, Benjamin. 1997. 'On the Determinants of the Success of Economic Sanctions: An Empirical Analysis'. *American Journal of Political Science* vol. 41(2), 606–18.

Davidson, James and Shambaugh, George. 2000. 'Who's Afraid of Economic Incentives? The Efficacy–Externality Tradeoff'. In *Sanctions as Economic Statecraft: Theory and Practice*, edited by Steve Chan and A. Cooper Drury, 37–64. London: Macmillan.

Davies, Robert. 1989. 'After Cuito Cuanavale: The New Regional Conjuncture and the Sanctions Question'. In *Sanctions against Apartheid*, edited by Mark Orkin, 198–206. New York: St Martin's Press.

Davis, Eric. 2005. *Memories of State*, 1st edn, Berkeley: University of California Press.

Davis, Jennifer. 1995. 'Sanctions and Apartheid: The Economic Challenge to Discrimination'. In *Economic Sanctions: Panacea or Peacebuilding in a Post-Cold War World?*, edited by David Cortright and George A. Lopez, 173–84. Boulder: Westview Press.

Davis, Stephen P. 1991. 'Economic Pressure on South Africa: Does it Work?'. In *Effective Sanctions on South Africa: The Cutting Edge of Economic Intervention*, edited by George W. Shepherd, 65–80. New York: Praeger.

Dawisha, Adeed. 1999. '"Identity" and Political Survival in Saddam's Iraq'. *Middle East Journal* vol. 53(4), 553–67.

De Klerk, F. W. 2004. 'The Effect of Sanctions on Constitutional Change in South Africa'. Speech at the Institut Choiseul, Paris, 14 June.

De Villiers, Les. 1995. *In Sight of Surrender: The US Sanctions Campaign against South Africa*, Westport: Praeger.

Delport, Tertius. 1991. South African National Party legislator, 1987–94; Deputy Minister for Provincial Affairs and Constitutional Development, 1990–1; Minister for Local Government, 1991–4; National Party negotiator, CODESA. Interview with Padraig O'Malley, 2 September; accessed at http://www.nelsonmandela.org/omalley/index.php/site/q/03lv00017/04lv00344/05lv00511/06lv00594.htm, 7 November 2011.

Delport, Tertius. 2011. Interview with the author, by telephone, 13 September.

Deyo, Frederic. 2006. 'South-East Asian Industrial Labour: Structural Demobilisation and Political Transformation'. In *The Political Economy of Southeast Asia: Markets,*

Power and Contestation, edited by Garry Rodan, Kevin Hewison, and Richard Robison, 283–304. 3rd edn, Oxford: Oxford University Press.

DiPrizio, Robert C. 2002. *Armed Humanitarians: US Interventions from Northern Iraq to Kosovo*, Baltimore: Johns Hopkins University Press.

Dodge, Toby. 2006. 'The Sardinian, the Texan and the Tikriti: Gramsci, the Comparative Autonomy of the Middle Eastern State and Regime Change in Iraq'. *International Politics* vol. 43(4), 453–73.

Dodge, Toby. 2009. 'Coming Face to Face with Bloody Reality: Liberal Common Sense and the Ideological Failure of the Bush Doctrine in Iraq'. *International Politics* vol. 46 (2–3), 253–75.

Dodge, Toby. 2010. 'The Failure of Sanctions and the Evolution of International Policy Towards Iraq, 1990–2003'. *Contemporary Arab Affairs* vol. 3(1), 83–91.

Dorussen, Han and Mo, Jongryn. 2001. 'Ending Economic Sanctions: Audience Costs and Rent-Seeking as Commitment Strategies'. *Journal of Conflict Resolution* vol. 45(4), 395–426.

Doxey, Margaret P. 1980. *Economic Sanctions and International Enforcement*, 2nd edn, London: Macmillan.

Doxey, Margaret. 1999. *United Nations Sanctions: Current Policy Issues*, Halifax: Centre for Foreign Policy Studies.

Doyle, Chris. 2000. 'Sanctions and the Middle East'. In *Sanctions on Iraq: Background, Consequences, Strategies*, edited by Campaign Against Sanctions on Iraq, 167–82. Cambridge: CASI.

Drezner, Daniel W. 1999. *The Sanctions Paradox: Economic Statecraft and International Relations*, Cambridge: Cambridge University Press.

Drezner, Daniel W. 2000. 'The Complex Causation of Sanction Outcomes'. In *Sanctions as Economic Statecraft: Theory and Practice*, edited by Steve Chan and A. Cooper Drury, 212–33. London: Macmillan.

Drezner, Daniel W. 2012. 'An Analytically Eclectic Approach to Sanctions and Nonproliferation'. In *Sanctions, Statecraft and Nuclear Proliferation*, edited by Etel Solingen, 154–73. Cambridge: Cambridge University Press.

Drury, A. Cooper. 1998. 'Revisiting *Economic Sanctions Reconsidered*'. *Journal of Peace Research* vol. 35(4), 497–509.

Drury, A. Cooper. 2000. 'How and Whom the US President Sanctions: A Time-Series Cross-Section Analysis of US Sanction Decisions and Characteristics'. In *Sanctions as Economic Statecraft: Theory and Practice*, edited by Steve Chan and A. Cooper Drury, 17–36. London: Macmillan.

Du Plessis, Barend. 1991. South African National Party legislator, 1974–92; Minister of Finance, 1984–92. Interview with Padraig O'Malley, 20 August; accessed at http://www.nelsonmandela.org/omalley/index.php/site/q/03lv00017/04lv00344/05lv00511/06lv00562.htm, 7 November 2011.

Du Plessis, Barend. 2011. Interview with the author, by telephone, 5 September.

Duelfer, Charles. 2004. *Comprehensive Report of the Special Advisor to the DCI on Iraq's WMD*, Washington, D.C.: CIA.

Durr, Kent. 2011. South African National Party legislator, 1977–91; Deputy Minister of Finance, 1983–8; Chair of the Cabinet Subcommittee on Sanctions, 1986–90;

Cabinet Minister for Trade and Industry, 1989–91; Ambassador to United Kingdom, 1991–5. Interview with the author, Cape Town, 9 September.

Economy Watch. 2013. 'South Africa Economic Statistics and Indicators', 6 May 2013; accessed at http://www.economywatch.com/economic-statistics/country/South-Africa/, 26 May 2014.

Eglin, Colin. 2011. South African Progressive Federal Party/Democratic Party legislator, 1974–2004; Leader of the Opposition, 1977–9, 1986–7. Interview with the author, Cape Town, 14 September.

Egreteau, Renaud. 2011. 'Jade or JADE? Debating International Sanctions on Burma's Gem Industry'. *Asia Pacific Bulletin* vol. 132, 1–2.

Eley, Geoff. 2002. *Forging Democracy: The History of the Left in Europe, 1850–2000*, Oxford: Oxford University Press.

Elliott, Kimberly A. 1997. 'Evidence on the Costs and Benefits of Economic Sanctions'. Testimony to the US Congress, 23 October; accessed at http://www.iie.com/publications/testimony/testimony.cfm?ResearchID=294, 11 January 2010.

Elliott, Kimberly A. 1998. 'The Sanctions Glass: Half Full or Completely Empty?'. *International Security* vol. 23(1), 50–65.

Elliott, Kimberly A. 2002. 'Analyzing the Effects of Targeted Sanctions'. In *Smart Sanctions: Targeting Economic Statecraft*, edited by David Cortright and George A. Lopez, 171–82. New York: Rowman and Littlefield.

Elliott, Kimberly A. 2005. 'Trends in Economic Sanctions Policy: Challenges to Conventional Wisdom'. In *International Sanctions: Between War and Words in the Global System*, edited by Peter Wallensteen and Carina Staibano, 3–14. Abingdon: Frank Cass.

Elliott, Kimberly A. and Uimonen, Peter P. 1993. 'The Effectiveness of Economic Sanctions with Application to the Case of Iraq'. *Japan and the World Economy* vol. 5(4), 403–9.

Englehart, Neil A. 2005. 'Is Regime Change Enough for Burma? The Problem of State Capacity'. *Asian Survey* vol. 45(4), 622–44.

Eriksson, Mikael. 2011. *Targeting Peace: Understanding UN and EU Targeted Sanctions*, Farnham: Ashgate.

Erwin, Alec. 2011. General-Secretary of the Federation of South African Trade Unions (FOSATU), 1979–83; Education Secretary, FOSATU, 1983–5, and Confederation of South African Trade Unions, 1986–8; National Executive Officer, National Union of Metalworkers of South Africa, 1988–93; negotiator, CODESA, 1990–3; ANC minister, 1993–2004. Interview with the author, Cape Town, 12 September.

Escribà-Folch, Abel. 2012. 'Authoritarian Responses to Foreign Pressure: Spending, Repression, and Sanctions'. *Comparative Political Studies* vol. 45(6), 683–713.

Escribà-Folch, Abel and Wright, Joseph. 2010. 'Dealing with Tyranny: International Sanctions and Survival of Authoritarian Rulers'. *International Studies Quarterly* vol. 54(2), 335–59.

European Commission. 2007. *The EC–Burma/Myanmar Strategy Paper, 2007–2013*, Brussels: European Commission.

Evans, Gavin. 2011. South African End Conscription Campaign activist; ANC member, 1980–91. Interview with the author, by telephone, 19 September.

Evans, Peter B. 1995. *Embedded Autonomy: States and Industrial Transformation*, Princeton: Princeton University Press.

Evans, Michael and Phillips, Mark. 1988. 'Intensifying the Civil War: The Role of the South African Defence Force'. In *State, Resistance and Change in South Africa*, edited by Philip Frankel, Noam Pines, and Mark Swilling, 117–45. London: Croom Helm.

Evans, Peter B., Rueschemeyer, Dietrich, and Skocpol, Theda (eds). 1985. *Bringing the State Back In*, Cambridge: Cambridge University Press.

Falleti, Tulia G. and Lynch, Julia F. 2009. 'Context and Causal Mechanisms in Political Analysis'. *Comparative Political Studies* vol. 42(9), 1143–66.

Fathollah-Nejad, Ali. 2014. 'Why Sanctions against Iran Are Counterproductive: Conflict Resolution and State–Society Relations'. *International Journal* vol. 69(1), 48–65.

FBI [Federal Bureau of Investigation]. 2004. Report of Conversation between Supervisory Special Agent George L. Shapiro and Saddam Hussein, Baghdad, 11 June.

Findlay, Ronald and Lundahl, Mats. 1987. 'Racial Discrimination, Dualistic Labor Markets and Foreign Investment'. *Journal of Development Economics* vol. 27(1–2), 139–48.

Fine, Ben and Rustomjee, Zavareh. 1996. *The Political Economy of South Africa: From Minerals-Energy Complex to Industrialisation*, London: Zed Books.

Finer, S. E. 1985. 'The Retreat to the Barracks: Notes on the Practice and the Theory of Military Withdrawal from the Seats of Power'. *Third World Quarterly* vol. 7(1), 16–30.

Fink, Christina. 2007. *Living Silence in Burma: Surviving under Military Rule*, 2nd edn, London: Zed Books.

Fourie, Andre. 2011. South African National Party legislator, 1981–99; Minister for Land and Regional Affairs, 1989–94. Interview with the author, Cape Town, 13 September.

Francke, Rahim. 1994. 'The Opposition'. In *Iraq Since the Gulf War: Prospects for Democracy*, edited by Fran Hazelton, 153–77. London: Zed Books.

Francke, Rahim. 1995. 'The Iraqi Opposition and the Sanctions Debate'. *Middle East Report* vol. 193, 14–17.

Free Burma Coalition. 1997. *The Free Burma Coalition Manual: How You Can Help Burma's Struggle for Freedom*, Madison: FBC.

Freedom House. 2014. 'Iraq'. *Freedom in the World* reports, various years; accessed at http://www.freedomhouse.org/report/freedom-world/1998/iraq#.UtfT4LRo44c, 16 January.

Galtung, Johan. 1967. 'On the Effects of International Economic Sanctions: With Examples from the Case of Rhodesia'. *World Politics* vol. 19(3), 378–416.

Garfield, Richard. 2000. 'Changes in Health and Well-being in Iraq during the 1990s'. In *Sanctions on Iraq: Background, Consequences, Strategies*, edited by Campaign Against Sanctions on Iraq, 32–51. Cambridge: CASI.

Gazdar, Haris and Hussain, Athar. 2002. 'Crisis and Response: A Study of the Impact of Economic Sanctions in Iraq'. In *Iraq's Economic Predicament*, edited by Kamil Mahdi, 31–83. Reading: Ithaca Press.

Geddes, Barbara. 1999. 'What Do We Know about Democratization after Twenty Years?'. *Annual Review of Political Science* vol. 2, 115–44.

Geddes, Barbara. 2004. 'Authoritarian Breakdown'. Unpublished MS.

Geddes, Barbara. 2006. 'Stages of Development in Authoritarian Regimes'. In *World Order after Leninism*, edited by Vladimir Tismaneanu, Marc Morjé Howard, and Rudra Sil, 149–70. Seattle: University of Washington Press.

Geddes, Barbara. 2009. 'Changes in the Causes of Democratization through Time'. In *The SAGE Handbook of Comparative Politics*, edited by Todd Landman and Neil Robinson, 278–98. London: Sage.

Gelb, Stephen. 1988. 'Moving Forward on Sanctions'. *Transformation* vol. 7, 70–9.

Gelb, Stephen. 1991. 'South Africa's Economic Crisis: An Overview'. In *South Africa's Economic Crisis*, edited by Stephen Gelb, 1–32. London: Zed Books.

Geldenhuys, Jannie. 2009. *At the Front: A General's Account of South Africa's Border War*, Johannesburg: Jonathan Ball.

George, Alexander L. and Bennett, Andrew. 2005. *Case Studies and Theory Development in the Social Sciences*, London: MIT Press.

Gerring, John. 2007. 'The Mechanismic Worldview: Thinking inside the Box'. *British Journal of Political Science* vol. 38(1), 161–79.

Giumelli, Francesco. 2013a. *The Success of Sanctions: Lessons Learned from the EU Experience*, Farnham: Ashgate.

Giumelli, Francesco. 2013b. 'How EU Sanctions Work: A New Narrative'. European Union Institute for Security Studies Chaillot Paper 129, May.

Giumelli, Francesco and Ivan, Paul. 2013. 'The Effectiveness of EU Sanctions: An Analysis of Iran, Belarus, Syrian and Myanmar (Burma)'. European Policy Centre Issue Paper 76, November.

Gleditsch, Kristian S. and Choung, Jinhee Lee. 2004. 'Autocratic Transitions and Democratization'. Paper presented at the International Studies Association convention, Montreal, 17 March.

Gordon, Joy. 2010. *Invisible War: The United States and the Iraq Sanctions*, Cambridge, MA: Harvard University Press.

Gould, Chandré and Folb, Peter. 2002. *Project Coast: Apartheid's Chemical and Biological Warfare Programme*, Geneva: UN Institute for Disarmament Research.

GPAAWC [Grassroots Palestinian Anti-Apartheid Wall Campaign]. 2007. 'Towards a Global Movement: A Framework for Today's Anti-Apartheid Activism'. June.

Graham-Brown, Sarah. 1999. *Sanctioning Saddam: The Politics of Intervention in Iraq*, New York: I. B. Tauris.

Gramsci, Antonio. 1971. *Selections from the Prison Notebooks*, London: Lawrence and Wishart.

Grauvogel, Julia and von Soest, Christian. 2014. 'Claims to Legitimacy Count: Why Sanctions Fail to Instigate Democratisation in Authoritarian Regimes'. *European Journal of Political Research* vol. 53(4), 635–53.

Greenberg, Stanley. 1987. 'Ideological Struggles within the South African State'. In *The Politics of Race, Class and Nationalism in Twentieth-Century South Africa*, edited by Shula Marks and Stanley Trapido, 389–418. London: Longman.

Griffin, Harriet. 2000. 'The Iraqi Exodus'. In *Sanctions on Iraq: Background, Consequences, Strategies*, edited by Campaign Against Sanctions on Iraq, 66–72. Cambridge: CASI.

Gurr, Ted. 1970. *Why Men Rebel*, Princeton: Princeton University Press.

Haas, Richard N. 1997. 'Sanctioning Madness'. *Foreign Affairs* vol. 76(6), 74–85.

Hackland, Brian. 1987. 'Incorporationist Ideology as a Response to Political Struggle: The Progressive Party of South Africa, 1960–1980'. In *The Politics of Race, Class and Nationalism in Twentieth-Century South Africa*, edited by Shula Marks and Stanley Trapido, 366–88. London: Longman.

Haggard, Stephan and Noland, Marcus. 2012. 'Engaging North Korea: The Efficacy of Sanctions and Inducements'. In *Sanctions, Statecraft and Nuclear Proliferation*, edited by Etel Solingen, 232–60. Cambridge: Cambridge University Press.

Hall, Stuart. 1986. 'Gramsci's Relevance for the Study of Race and Ethnicity'. *Journal of Communication Inquiry* vol. 10(2), 5–27.

Halliday, Denis. 1999. 'The Impact of the UN Sanctions on the People of Iraq'. *Journal of Palestine Studies* vol. 28(2), 29–37.

Halliday, Fred. 1994. *Rethinking International Relations*, London: Macmillan.

Hameiri, Shahar. 2010. *Regulating Statehood: State Building and the Transformation of the Global Order*, Basingstoke: Palgrave.

Han Tha Myint. 2012. Central Executive Committee Member, National League for Democracy, Myanmar. Interview with the author, Yangon, 25 July.

Hanlon, Joseph and Omond, Roger. 1987. *The Sanctions Handbook*, Harmondsworth: Penguin.

Harn Yanghwe. 2000. 'EU–ASEAN Relations: A Burmese/Myanmar Perspective'. *Panorama* vol. 2(2), 71–82.

Harris, Laurence. 1986. 'South Africa's External Debt Crisis'. *Third World Quarterly* vol. 8(3), 793–817.

Harvey, Robert. 2001. *The Fall of Apartheid: The Inside Story from Smuts to Mbeki*, Basingstoke: Palgrave Macmillan.

Hayes, J. P. 1987. *Economic Effects of Sanctions on Southern Africa*, Aldershot: Gower.

Hellquist, Elin. 2012. 'Creating "The Self" by Outlawing "The Other"? EU Foreign Policy Sanctions and the Quest for Credibility', PhD thesis, European University Institute.

Hengeveld, Richard and Rodenburg, Jaap. 1995a. 'Marc Rich: Fuel for Apartheid'. In *Embargo: Apartheid's Oil Secrets Revealed*, edited by Richard Hengeveld and Jaap Rodenburg, 138–59. Amsterdam: Amsterdam University Press.

Hengeveld, Richard and Rodenburg, Jaap. 1995b. '"The Last Peaceful Weapon"'. In *Embargo: Apartheid's Oil Secrets Revealed*, edited by Richard Hengeveld and Jaap Rodenburg, 9–24. Amsterdam: Amsterdam University Press.

Hengeveld, Richard and Rodenburg, Jaap. 1995c. 'The Spear of the Nation'. In *Embargo: Apartheid's Oil Secrets Revealed*, edited by Richard Hengeveld and Jaap Rodenburg, 25–55. Amsterdam: Amsterdam University Press.

Hengeveld, Richard and Rodenburg, Jaap. 1995d. 'The Impact of the Oil Embargo'. In *Embargo: Apartheid's Oil Secrets Revealed*, edited by Richard Hengeveld and Jaap Rodenburg, 194–205. Amsterdam: Amsterdam University Press.

Herring, Eric. 2002. 'Between Iraq and a Hard Place: A Critique of the British Government's Case for UN Economic Sanctions'. *Review of International Studies* vol. 28(1), 39–56.

Hewison, Kevin, Robison, Richard, and Rodan, Garry. 1993. 'Introduction: Changing Forms of State Power in Southeast Asia'. In *Southeast Asia in the 1990s: Authoritarianism,*

Democracy and Capitalism, edited by Kevin Hewison, Richard Robison, and Garry Rodan, 2–8. St Leonards, Australia: Allen and Unwin.

Hiro, Dilip. 2002. *Iraq in the Eye of the Storm*, New York: Thunders Mouth Press.

Hirsch, Alan. 1989. 'Sanctions, Loans and the South African Economy'. In *Sanctions against Apartheid*, edited by Mark Orkin, 270–84. New York: St Martin's Press.

Hla Saw. 2012. General Secretary, Rakhine Nationalities Development Party, Myanmar. Interview with the author, Yangon, 11 July.

Holiday, Ian. 2005. 'Doing Business with Rights Violating Regimes: Corporate Social Responsibility and Myanmar's Military Junta'. *Journal of Business Ethics* vol. 61(4), 329–42.

Houtman, Gustaaf. 2005. 'Sacralizing or Demonizing Democracy? Aung San Suu Kyi's "Personality Cult"'. In *Burma at the Turn of the Twenty-First Century*, edited by Monique Skidmore, 133–53. Honolulu: University of Hawaii Press.

Hovi, Jon, Huseby, Robert, and Spring, Detlef. 2005. 'When Do (Imposed) Economic Sanctions Work?'. *World Politics* vol. 57(4), 479–99.

Hufbauer, Gary C., Schott, Jeffrey C., and Elliott, Kimberly A. 1985. *Economic Sanctions Reconsidered*, 1st edn, Washington, D.C.: Petersen Institute for International Economics.

Hufbauer, Gary C., Schott, Jeffrey C., and Elliott, Kimberly A. 1990. *Economic Sanctions Reconsidered*, 2nd edn, Washington, D.C.: Petersen Institute for International Economics.

Hufbauer, Gary C., Schott, Jeffrey C., Elliott, Kimberly A., and Oegg, Barbara. 2007. *Economic Sanctions Reconsidered*, 3rd edn, Washington, D.C.: Petersen Institute for International Economics.

Hughes, Caroline. 2003. *The Political Economy of Cambodia's Transition, 1991–2001*, London: RoutledgeCurzon.

Hughes, Caroline. 2007. 'Transnational Networks, International Organizations and Political Participation in Cambodia: Human Rights, Labour Rights and Common Rights'. *Democratization* vol. 14(5), 834–52.

IMF [International Monetary Fund]. 1999. *Myanmar: Recent Economic Developments*, Washington, D.C.: IMF.

IMF. 2011. 'World Economic and Financial Surveys'. http://www.imf.org/external/pubs/ft/weo/2011/02/weodata/index.aspx, accessed 5 March 2012.

INFID. 2007. 'Profile of Indonesia's Foreign Debt'. Working Paper, August.

Innes, Duncan. 1989. 'Multinational Companies and Disinvestment'. In *Sanctions against Apartheid*, edited by Mark Orkin, 226–39. New York: St Martin's Press.

INSCR [Integrated Network for Societal Conflict Research]. 2012. 'Polity IV: Regime Authority Characteristics and Transitions Datasets'. http://www.systemicpeace.org/inscr/p4v2012.xls, accessed 27 July 2013.

Irrawaddy. 2008. 'Tracking the Tycoons', September.

IRRC [Investor Responsibility Research Centre]. 1990. *The Impact of Sanctions on South Africa: Part I, The Economy*, Washington, D.C.: IRRC.

ISG [Iraq Survey Group]. 2004. 'Key Findings'. Central Intelligence Agency, Washington, D.C; accessed at https://www.cia.gov/library/reports/general-reports-1/iraq_wmd_2004/Comp_Report_Key_Findings.pdf, 29 January 2013.

Ishow, Habib. 1993. 'The Development of Agricultural Policies since 1958'. In *Iraq: Power and Society*, edited by Derek Hopwood, Habib Ishow, and Thomas Koszinowski, 172–91. Reading: Ithaca Press.

ITTO [International Tropical Timber Organization]. 2012. 'Annual Review Statistics Database', accessed at http://www.itto.int/annual_review_output/, 27 September 2012.

Jabar, Faleh. 1997. 'The State, Society, Clan, Party and Army in Iraq: A Totalitarian State in the Twilight of Totalitarianism'. In *From Storm to Thunder: Unfinished Showdown between Iraq and US*, edited by Faleh A. Jabar, Ahmad Shikara, and Keiko Sakai, 1–28. Tokyo: Institute of Developing Economies.

Jabar, Faleh. 2000. 'Shaykhs and Ideologues: Detribalization and Retribalization in Iraq, 1968–1998'. *Middle East Report* vol. (215), 28–31, 48.

Jabar, Faleh. 2003a. *The Shi'ite Movement in Iraq*, London: Saqi.

Jabar, Faleh. 2003b. 'Clerics, Tribes, Ideologues and Urban Dwellers in the South of Iraq: The Potential for Rebellion'. In *Iraq at the Crossroads: State and Society in the Shadow of Regime Change*, edited by Toby Dodge and Steven Simon, 161–77. Oxford: Oxford University Press.

Jabar, Faleh. 2003c. 'The Iraqi Army and Anti-Army: Some Reflections on the Role of the Military'. In *Iraq at the Crossroads: State and Society in the Shadow of Regime Change*, edited by Toby Dodge and Steven Simon, 115–29. Oxford: Oxford University Press.

James, Helen. 2005. *Governance and Civil Society in Myanmar: Education, Health and Environment*, London: Routledge.

Jayasuriya, Kanishka. 2005. 'Beyond Institutional Fetishism: From the Developmental to the Regulatory State'. *New Political Economy* vol. 10(3), 381–7.

Jayasuriya, Kanishka and Rodan, Garry. 2007. 'Beyond Hybrid Regimes'. *Democratization* Special Issue, vol. 14(5).

Jessop, Bob. 1990. *State Theory: Putting the Capitalist State in its Place*, Cambridge: Polity.

Jessop, Bob. 1992. 'From Social Democracy to Thatcherism: Twenty-Five Years of British Politics'. In *Social Change in Contemporary Britain*, edited by Nicholas Abercrombie and Alan Warde, 45–68. Cambridge: Polity Press.

Jessop, Bob. 2008. *State Power: A Strategic-Relational Approach*, Cambridge: Polity.

Joffe, Hilary. 1989. 'The Policy of South Africa's Trade Unions towards Sanctions and Disinvestment'. In *Sanctions against Apartheid*, edited by Mark Orkin, 57–67. New York: St Martin's Press.

Johansson, Anne E. 2000. 'A Silent Emergency Persists: The Limited Efficacy of U.S. Investment Sanctions on Burma'. *Pacific Rim Law & Policy Journal* vol. 9(2), 317–51.

Jones, David M. 1998. 'Democratization, Civil Society, and Illiberal Middle Class Culture in Pacific Asia'. *Comparative Politics* vol. 30(2), 147–69.

Jones, Lee. 2008. 'ASEAN's Albatross: ASEAN's Burma Policy, from Constructive Engagement to Critical Disengagement'. *Asian Security* vol. 4(3), 271–93.

Jones, Lee. 2010. '(Post-)Colonial Statebuilding and State Failure in East Timor: Bringing Social Conflict back in'. *Conflict, Security and Development* vol. 19(3), 547–75.

Jones, Lee. 2012. *ASEAN, Sovereignty and Intervention in Southeast Asia*, Basingstoke: Palgrave Macmillan.

Jones, Lee. 2013. 'Sovereignty, Intervention, and Social Order in Revolutionary Times'. *Review of International Studies* vol. 39(5), 1149–67.

Jones, Lee. 2014a. 'Explaining Myanmar's Transition: The Periphery is Central', *Democratization* vol. 21(5), 780–802.

Jones, Lee. 2014b. 'The Political Economy of Myanmar's Transition'. *Journal of Contemporary Asia* vol. 44(1), 144–70.

Jones, Lee. forthcoming. 'Sanctioning Apartheid: Comparing the South African and Palestinian Campaigns for Boycotts, Disinvestment and Sanctions'. In *Boycotts: Past and Present*, edited by David Feldman, Basingstoke: Palgrave Macmillan.

Jones, Lee and Portela, Clara. 2014. 'Evaluating the "Success" of International Economic Sanctions: Multiple Goals, Interpretive Methods and Critique'. Centre for the Study of Global Security and Development Working Paper 3.

Kaempfner, William H. and Lowenberg, Anton D. 1988. 'The Theory of International Economic Sanctions: A Public Choice Approach'. *American Economic Review* vol. 78(3), 786–93.

Kaempfner, William H. and Lowenberg, Anton D. 1991. 'Economic Sanctions and Interest Group Analysis: A Reply'. *South African Journal of Economics* vol. 59(1), 53–6.

Kaempfner, William H. and Lowenberg, Anton D. 1992. *International Economic Sanctions: A Public Choice Approach*, Oxford: Westview Press.

Kasrils, Ronnie. 2013. 'Boycott, Bricks and the Four Pillars of the South African Struggle'. In *Generation Palestine: Voices from the Boycott, Disinvestment and Sanctions Movement*, edited by Rich Wiles, 18–33. London: Pluto.

Katzman, Kenneth. 2003. 'Iraq: Weapons Threat, Compliance, Sanctions and US Policy'. United States Congressional Research Service, Washington, D.C.

Katzman, Kenneth and Blanchard, Christopher M. 2005. 'Iraq: Oil-For-Food Program, Illicit Trade, and Investigations'. United States Congressional Research Service, Washington, D.C.

Kaufman, Stuart J. 2012. 'The End of Apartheid: Rethinking South Africa's "Peaceful" Transition', unpublished MS, University of Delaware, October; accessed at https://www.sas.upenn.edu/polisci/sites/www.sas.upenn.edu.polisci/files/kaufman.pdf, 18 March 2014.

Khin Maung Swe. 2012. Chairman, National Democratic Force, Myanmar. Interview with the author, Yangon, 4 July.

Khin Zaw Win. 2007. 'Reality Check on the Sanctions Policy against Myanmar'. In *Myanmar: State, Society and Ethnicity*, edited by N. Ganesan and Kyaw Yin Hlaing, 278–87. Singapore: ISEAS.

Khong, Yuen Foong. 1992. *Analogies at War: Korea, Munich, Dien Bien Phu, and the Vietnam Decisions of 1965*, Princeton: Princeton University Press.

Kiik, Laur. 2012. 'Environmentalism and the Ethno-National Struggle in Kachin Land, Northern Burma'. Paper presented at the Southeast Asian Symposium, University of Oxford, 10–11 March.

Kirshner, Jonathan. 1997. 'The Microfoundations of Economic Sanctions'. *Security Studies* vol. 6(3), 32–64.

Kirshner, Jonathan. 2002. 'Economic Sanctions: The State of the Art'. *Security Studies* vol. 11(4), 160–79.

Ko Ko Gyi. 2012. Leading Activist, '88 Generation of Students. Interview with the author, Yangon, 9 July.

Koh Kim Seng. 2011. *Misunderstood Myanmar: An Introspective Study of a Southeast Asian State in Transition*, Singapore: Humanities Press.

Kreps, Sarah and Pasha, Zain. 2012. 'Threats for Peace? The Domestic Distributional Effects of Military Threats'. In *Sanctions, Statecraft and Nuclear Proliferation*, edited by Etel Solingen, 174–207. Cambridge: Cambridge University Press.

Krogh, Desmond. 2011. Governor of the Reserve Bank of Rhodesia/Zimbabwe, 1973–83; Anti-Sanctions Coordinator and Advisor Extraordinary to the South African Minister of Finance, 1986–90. Interview with the author, Pretoria, 31 August.

Kubba, Laith. 1994. 'Human Rights, Sanctions and Sovereignty'. In *Iraq since the Gulf War: Prospects for Democracy*, edited by Fran Hazelton, 147–52. London: Zed Books.

Kudo, Toshihiro. 2008. 'The Impact of US Sanctions on the Myanmar Garment Industry'. *Asian Survey* vol. 48(6), 997–1017.

Kyaw Yin Hlaing. 2004. 'Will Western Sanctions Bring Down the House?'. In *Reconciling Burma/Myanmar: Essays on US Relations with Burma*, edited by John Badgley, 73–85. Seattle: National Bureau for Asian Research.

Kyaw Yin Hlaing. 2007. 'Burma: Civil Society Skirting Regime Rules'. In *Civil Society and Political Change in Asia: Expanding and Contracting Political Space*, edited by Muthiah Alagappa, 389–418. Stanford: Stanford University Press.

Kyaw Yin Hlaing. 2012. 'Understanding Recent Political Changes in Myanmar'. *Contemporary Southeast Asia* vol. 34(2), 197–216.

Laïdi, Zaki. 1998. *A World without Meaning: Crisis of Meaning in International Politics*, London: Routledge.

Lake, Anthony. 1994. 'Confronting Backlash States'. *Foreign Affairs* vol. 73(2), 45–55.

Larkin, Stuart. 2012. 'Myanmar at the Crossroads: Rapid Industrial Development or Deindustrialization', accessed at http://www.burmalibrary.org/docs12/Stuart_Larkin-Myanmar_at_the_Crossroads.pdf, 5 August 2012.

Leading South African Businessman. 2011. Interview with the author, Johannesburg, 2 September.

Lekota, Mosiuoa. 2011. Secretary, United Democratic Front, South Africa, 1983–5; ANC National Executive Committee member, 1990–2007. Interview with the author, Johannesburg, 6 September.

Lektzian, David and Souva, Mark. 2007. 'An Institutional Theory of Sanctions Onset and Success'. *Journal of Conflict Resolution* vol. 51(6), 848–71.

Levy, Philip I. 1999. 'Sanctions on South Africa: What Did They Do?'. *American Economic Review* vol. 89(2), 415–20.

Lewis, Paul. 1991. 'After the War', *New York Times*, 22 March.

Liddell, Zunetta. 2001. 'International Policies towards Burma: Western Governments, NGOs and Multilateral Organisations'. In *Challenges to Democratization in Burma: Perspectives on Multilateral and Bilateral Responses*, 131–82. Stockholm: International IDEA.

Liddington, David. 2012. 'What Has Been the Effect of EU Sanctions on Burma?', accessed at http://blogs.fco.gov.uk/davidlidington/2012/04/25/what-has-been-the-effect-of-eu-sanctions-on-burma, 28 September 2012.

Lim Chong Yah. 2014. *Singapore's National Wages Council: An Insider's View*, Singapore: World Scientific.

Lindsay, James M. 1986. 'Trade Sanctions as Policy Instruments: A Re-Examination'. *International Studies Quarterly* vol. 30(2), 153–73.

Lintner, Bertil. 1998. 'Drugs and Economic Growth: Ethnicity and Exports'. In *Burma: Prospects for a Democratic Future*, edited by Robert I. Rotberg, 165–83. Washington: Brooking Institution Press.

Lipton, Merle. 1986. *Capitalism and Apartheid: South Africa, 1910–1986*, Aldershot: Wildwood House.

Lipton, Merle. 1990. 'The Challenge of Sanctions'. Discussion Paper 1, Centre for the Study of the South African Economy and International Finance, London School of Economics.

Lodge, Tom. 1988. 'State of Exile: The African National Congress of South Africa, 1976–86'. In *State, Resistance and Change in South Africa*, edited by Philip Frankel, Noam Pines, and Mark Swilling, 229–58. London: Croom Helm.

Lodge, Tom. 1989. 'Sanctions and Black Political Organisations'. In *Sanctions against Apartheid*, edited by Mark Orkin, 34–51. New York: St Martin's Press.

Lopez, George A. and Cortright, David. 2004. 'Containing Iraq: Sanctions Worked'. *Foreign Affairs* vol. 83(4), 90–103.

Lowenberg, Anton D. 1997. 'Why South Africa's Apartheid Economy Failed'. *Contemporary Economic Policy* vol. 15(3), 62–72.

Lundahl, Mats. 1984. 'Economic Effects of a Trade and Investment Boycott against South Africa'. *Scandinavian Journal of Economics* vol. 86(1), 68–83.

McEachern, Patrick. 2008. 'Interest Groups in North Korean Politics'. *Journal of East Asian Studies* vol. 8(3), 235–58.

McGillivray, Fiona and Stam, Allan C. 2004. 'Political Institutions, Coercive Diplomacy, and the Duration of Economic Sanctions'. *Journal of Conflict Resolution* vol. 48(2), 154–72.

Mack, Andrew and Kahn, Asif. 2000. 'The Efficacy of UN Sanctions'. *Security Dialogue* vol. 31(3), 279–92.

Maharaj, Mac. 2011. Member of ANC's Revolutionary Council since 1978; Member of ANC National Executive Committee, 1985–99; Secretary, CODESA, 1991–4. Interview with the author, Pretoria, 8 September.

Mahdi, Kamil. 1998. 'Rehabilitation Prospects for the Iraqi Economy'. *The International Spectator* vol. 33(3), 41–67.

Mahoney, James and Rueschemeyer, Dietrich (eds). 2003. *Comparative Historical Analysis in the Social Sciences*, Cambridge: Cambridge University Press.

Major, Solomon and McGann, Anthony J. 2005. 'Caught in the Crossfire: "Innocent Bystanders" as Optimal Targets of Economic Sanctions'. *Journal of Conflict Resolution* vol. 49(3), 337–59.

Makiya, Kanan. 1998. *The Republic of Fear: The Politics of Modern Iraq*, 2nd edn, Berkeley: University of California Press.

Malan, Magnus. 2006. *My Life with the SA Defence Force*, Pretoria: Protea Book House.

Maloka, Tshidiso. 1999. '"Sanctions Hurt but Apartheid Kills!": The Sanctions Campaign and Black Workers'. In *How Sanctions Work: Lessons from South Africa*, edited by Neta C. Crawford and Audie Klotz, 178–92. London: Macmillan.

Manby, Bronwen. 1992. 'South Africa: The Impact of Sanctions'. *Journal of International Affairs* vol. 46(1), 193–217.

Mann, Michael. 1988. 'The Giant Stirs: South African Business in the Age of Reform'. In *State, Resistance and Change in South Africa*, edited by Philip Frankel, Noam Pines, and Mark Swilling, 52–86. London: Croom Helm.

Manzo, Kate and McGowan, Pat. 1992. 'Afrikaner Fears and the Politics of Despair: Understanding Change in South Africa'. *International Studies Quarterly* vol. 36(1), 1–24.

Marinov, Nikolay. 2005. 'Do Economic Sanctions Destabilize Country Leaders?'. *American Journal of Political Science* vol. 49(3), 564–76.

Marks, Shula and Trapido, Stanley. 1987. 'The Politics of Race, Class and Nationalism'. In *The Politics of Race, Class and Nationalism in Twentieth-Century South Africa*, edited by Shula Marks and Stanley Trapido, 1–70. London: Longman.

Marr, Phebe. 2004. *The Modern History of Iraq*, 2nd edn, Boulder: Westview Press.

Marshall, Andrew R. C. and Min Zayar Oo. 2013. 'Myanmar Old Guard Clings to $8-billion Jade Empire', *Globe and Mail*, 4 October.

Martin, Isaac W., Mehrota, Ajay K., and Prasad, Monica (eds). 2009. *The New Fiscal Sociology: Taxation in Comparative and Historical Perspective*, Cambridge: Cambridge University Press.

Martin, James. 1998. *Gramsci's Political Analysis: A Critical Introduction*, Houndmills: Macmillan.

Marx, Anthony W. 1997. 'Apartheid's End: South Africa's Transition from Racial Domination'. *Ethnic and Racial Studies* vol. 20(3), 474–96.

Marx, Karl. 1852. 'The Eighteenth Brumaire of Louis Bonaparte', accessed at http://www.marxists.org/archive/marx/works/1852/18th-brumaire/ch01.htm, 15 June 2013.

May, R. J., Lawson, Stephanie, and Selochan, Viberto. 2004. 'Introduction: Democracy and the Military in Comparative Perspective'. In *The Military and Democracy in Asia and the Pacific*, edited by R. J. May, Stephanie Lawson, and Viberto Selochan, 1–28. Canberra: ANU E-Press.

Mayall, James. 1984. 'The Sanctions Problem in International Economic Relations: Reflections in the Light of Recent Experience'. *International Affairs* vol. 60(4), 631–42.

Mayntz, Renate. 2004. 'Mechanisms in the Analysis of Social Macro-Phenomena'. *Philosophy of the Social Sciences* vol. 34(2), 237–59.

Mazaheri, Nimah. 2010. 'Iraq and the Domestic Political Effects of Economic Sanctions'. *Middle East Report* vol. 64(2), 253–68.

Meth, Charles. 1989. 'Sanctions and Unemployment'. In *Sanctions against Apartheid*, edited by Mark Orkin, 240–52. New York: St Martin's Press.

Meyer, Roelf. 2011. South African National Party legislator, 1979–96; Deputy Minister of Law and Order and subsequently Constitutional Development, 1986–91; Cabinet Minister for Defence and subsequently Constitutional Affairs, 1991–6; lead National

Party negotiator, CODESA, 1990–3. Interview with the author, Johannesburg, 5 September.

Migdal, Joel S. 1988. *Strong Societies and Weak States: State–Society Relations and State Capabilities in the Third World*, Princeton: Princeton University Press.

Milieudefensie. 2009. *Sanctioned But Not Stopped*, Amsterdam: Milieudefensie.

Mills, Greg and Williams, David. 2006. *Seven Battles That Shaped South Africa*, Cape Town: Tafelberg.

Ministry of Hotels and Tourism. 2011. *Myanmar Tourism Statistics 2011*, Yangon: Ministry of Hotels and Tourism.

Mitchell, Timothy. 2009. *Carbon Democracy: Political Power in the Age of Oil*, London: Verso.

Mkhize, Herbert. 2011. Vice-President, Commercial, Catering and Allied Workers' Union, 1983–6; National Executive Committee member, COSATU, 1985–94. Interview with the author, Johannesburg, 1 September.

Moe Kyaw. 2012. Joint General-Secretary, Union of Myanmar Federated Chamber of Commerce and Industry. Interview with the author, Yangon, 7 July.

Moe Myint. 2012. Chief Executive Officer, MPRL E&P Ltd, Myanmar. Interview with the author, Yangon, 18 July.

Moore, Barrington. 1966. *Social Origins of Dictatorship and Democracy: Lord and Peasant in the Making of the Modern World*, New York: Beacon Press.

Moore, Peter and Parker, Christopher. 2007. 'The War Economy of Iraq'. *Middle East Report* vol. 37(243) accessed at http://www.merip.org/mer/mer243/war-economy-iraq, 1 January 2013.

Moravcsik, Andrew. 1997. 'Taking Preferences Seriously: A Liberal Theory of International Politics'. *International Organization* vol. 51(4), 513–53.

Morgan, T. Clifton. 1995. 'Clinton's Chinese Puzzle: Domestic Politics and the Effectiveness of Economic Sanctions'. *Issues and Studies (Taipei)* vol. 31(8), 19–45.

Morgan, T. Clifton and Schwebach, Valerie. 1995. 'Economic Sanctions as an Instrument of Foreign Policy: The Role of Domestic Politics'. *International Interactions* vol. 36(3), 25–52.

Morgan, T. Clifton and Schwebach, Valerie. 1997. 'Fools Suffer Gladly: The Use of Economic Sanctions in International Crises'. *International Studies Quarterly* vol. 41(1), 27–50.

Morris, Mike. 1986. 'State, Capital and Growth: The Political Economy of the National Question'. In *South Africa's Economic Crisis*, edited by Stephen Gelb, 33–58. London: Zed Books.

Morton, Adam D. 2007. *Unravelling Gramsci: Hegemony and Passive Revolution in the Global Economy*, London: Pluto.

Morton, Adam D. 2011. *Revolution and State in Modern Mexico: The Political Economy of Uneven Development*, Boulder: Rowman and Littlefield.

Mufamadi, Sydney. 2011. General Secretary, General and Allied Workers' Union, 1984–7; Transvaal Publicity Secretary, UDF, 1984–90; Assistant Secretary-General, COSATU, 1985–7; Member, ANC National Executive Committee, 1991–2008; Member, SACP Central Committee; SACP and ANC delegate, CODESA, 1990–3. Interview with the author, by telephone, 15 September.

Mullins, Dawie. 2011. Head of Economic Research, Department of the Economic Advisor to the South African President, 1974–89. Interview with the author, Pretoria, 31 August.

Murray, Hugh. 1986. 'Seizing the Moment'. In *Sanctions: A Leadership Publication*, edited by Hugh Murray, 24–7. 2nd edn, Cape Town: Argus Leadership Publications.

Myat Thein. 2004. *Economic Development of Myanmar*, Singapore: ISEAS.

Myo Nyunt. 2012. General-Secretary, Peace and Democracy Party, Myanmar. Interview with the author, Yangon, 11 July.

Nader, Alizera. 2012. 'Influencing Iran's Decisions on the Nuclear Program'. In *Sanctions, Statecraft and Nuclear Proliferation*, edited by Etel Solingen, 211–31. Cambridge: Cambridge University Press.

Natali, Denise. 2010. *The Kurdish Quasi-State: Development and Dependency in Post-Gulf War Iraq*, Syracuse: Syracuse University Press.

Naw Angelene. 1996. 'Tourism Development and Visit Myanmar Year'. In *Business Opportunities in Myanmar*, edited by Tan Teck Meng, Low Aik Meng, John J. Williams, and Ivan P. Polunin, 265–74. Englewood Cliffs: Prentice Hall.

New York Times. 2012. 'A Conversation with Aung San Suu Kyi', 30 September.

NLD [National League for Democracy]. 2011. 'Sanctions on Burma' 8 February; http://www.nldburma.org/media-press-release/press-release.html?start=20, accessed 26 September 2012.

North, Douglass C., Wallis, John J., Webb, Steven, and Weingast, Barry R. 2007. *Limited Access Orders in the Developing World: A New Approach to the Problems of Development*, Washington, D.C.: World Bank.

Nossal, Kim Richard. 1989. 'International Sanctions as International Punishment'. *International Organization* vol. 43(2), 301–22.

O'Donnell, Guillermo and Schmitter, Philippe C. 1986. *Transitions from Authoritarian Rule: Tentative Conclusions about Uncertain Democracies*, Baltimore: Johns Hopkins University Press.

Oeschlin, Manuel. 2014. 'Targeting Autocrats: Economic Sanctions and Regime Change'. *European Journal of Political Economy* vol. 36, 24–40.

Ollman, Bertell. 2003. *Dance of the Dialectic: Steps in Marx's Method*, Champaign: University of Illinois Press.

O'Meara, Dan. 1983. *Volkscapitalisme*, Johannesburg: Ravan Press.

O'Meara, Dan. 1996. 'Politics in the Apartheid State: Analysing the Materiality of the Political'. *Social Dynamics: A Journal of African Studies* vol. 22(2), 37–73.

Orkin, Mark. 1989a. 'Introduction: The Case for Sanctions against Apartheid'. In *Sanctions against Apartheid*, edited by Mark Orkin, 1–33. New York: St Martin's Press.

Orkin, Mark. 1989b. 'Politics, Social Change, and Black Attitudes to Sanctions'. In *Sanctions against Apartheid*, edited by Mark Orkin, 81–102. New York: St Martin's Press.

Palan, Ronen, Murphy, Richard, and Chavagneux, Christian. 2010. *Tax Havens: How Globalization Really Works*, Ithaca: Cornell University Press.

Palkki, David and Smith, Shane. 2012. 'Contrasting Causal Mechanisms: Iraq and Libya'. In *Sanctions, Statecraft and Nuclear Proliferation*, edited by Etel Solingen, 261–94. Cambridge: Cambridge University Press.

Pallister, David, Stewart, Sarah, and Lepper, Ian. 1987. *South Africa Inc.: The Oppenheimer Empire*, Sandton: Media House.

Pape, Robert A. 1997. 'Why Economic Sanctions Do Not Work'. *International Security* vol. 22(2), 90–136.

Pape, Robert A. 1998. 'Why Economic Sanctions *Still* Do Not Work'. *International Security* vol. 23(1), 66–77.

Paul, T. V. 2010. 'State Capacity and South Asia's Perennial Insecurity Problems'. In *South Asia's Weak States: Understanding the Regional Insecurity Predicament*, edited by T. V. Paul, 3–27. Stanford: Stanford University Press.

Pawson, Ray. 2000. 'Middle-Range Realism'. *Archives Européennes de Sociologie* vol. 41(2), 283–325.

Pedersen, Morten B. 2006. 'A Comprehensive International Approach to Political and Economic Development in Burma/Myanmar'. In *Myanmar's Long Road to National Reconciliation*, edited by Trevor Wilson, 276–90. Singapore: ISEAS.

Pedersen, Morten B. 2008. *Promoting Human Rights in Burma: A Critique of Western Sanctions Policy*, Lanham: Rowman and Littlefield.

Phone Win. 2012. Executive Director, Mingalar Myanmar NGO. Interview with the author, Yangon, 14 July.

Posel, Deborah. 1987. 'The Language of Domination, 1978–1983'. In *The Politics of Race, Class and Nationalism in Twentieth-Century South Africa*, edited by Shula Marks and Stanley Trapido, 419–43. London: Longman.

Post, Jerrold M. and Baram, Amatzia. 2002. 'Saddam is Iraq: Iraq is Saddam'. Future Warfare Series no. 17, USAF Counterproliferation Center, Air University, Maxwell Air Force Base, Alabama.

Poulantzas, Nicos. 1976. *State, Power, Socialism*, London: New Left Books.

Preeg, Ernest H. 1999. *Feeling Good or Doing Good with Sanctions: Unilateral Economic Sanctions and the U.S. National Interest*, Washington, D.C.: CSIS Press.

Pridham, Geoffrey. 1991. 'International Influences and Democratic Transition: Problems of Theory and Practice in Linkage Politics'. In *Encouraging Democracy: The International Context of Regime Transition in Southern Europe*, edited by Geoffrey Pridham, 1–30. Leicester: Leicester University Press.

Prominent Myanmar Pro-Democracy Activist. 2012. Interview with the author, Yangon, 9 July.

Przeworski, Adam and Wallerstein, Michael. 1988. 'Structural Dependence of the State on Capital'. *American Political Science Review* vol. 82(1), 11–29.

Purkayastha, Prabir and Kidwai, Ayesha. 2013. 'India's Freedom Struggle and Today's BDS Movement'. In *Generation Palestine: Voices from the Boycott, Disinvestment and Sanctions Movement*, edited by Rich Wiles, 47–56. London: Pluto.

Rahim, Ayad. 1994. 'Attitudes to the West, Arabs and Fellow Iraqis'. In *Iraq since the Gulf War: Prospects for Democracy*, edited by Fran Hazelton, 178–93. London: Zed Books.

Rai, Milan. 2000. 'Popular Anti-Sanctions Groups in the UK'. In *Sanctions on Iraq: Background, Consequences, Strategies*, edited by Campaign Against Sanctions on Iraq, 160–6. Cambridge: CASI.

Remmer, Karen L. 1995. 'New Theoretical Perspectives on Democratization'. *Comparative Politics* vol. 28(1), 103–22.

Ritter, Scott. 2005. *Iraq Confidential: The Untold Story of America's Intelligence Conspiracy*, London: I. B. Tauris.

Roberts, Christopher. 2006. *Myanmar and the Argument for Engagement: A Clash of Contending Moralities?*, IDSS Working Paper series no. 108, Singapore: IDSS.

Robinson, William I. 1996. *Promoting Polyarchy: Globalization, US Intervention, and Hegemony*, Cambridge: Cambridge University Press.

Robinson, William I. 2003. *Transnational Conflicts: Central America, Social Change and Globalization*, London: Verso.

Robison, Richard. 1986. *Indonesia: The Rise of Capital*, Sydney: Allen and Unwin.

Robison, Richard and Hadiz, Vedi R. 2004. *Reorganising Power in Indonesia: The Politics of Oligarchy in an Age of Markets*, New York: RoutledgeCurzon.

Robison, Richard and Hadiz, Vedi R. 2006. 'Indonesia: Crisis, Oligarchy, and Reform'. In *The Political Economy of Southeast Asia: Markets, Power and Contestation*, edited by Garry Rodan, Kevin Hewison, and Richard Robison, 109–36. 3rd edn, Oxford: Oxford University Press.

Rodan, Garry. 2006. 'Singapore: Globalisation, the State, and Politics'. In *The Political Economy of Southeast Asia: Markets, Power and Contestation*, edited by Garry Rodan, Kevin Hewison, and Richard Robison, 137–69. 3rd edn, Oxford: Oxford University Press.

Rodan, Garry, Hewison, Kevin, and Robison, Richard (eds). 2006. *The Political Economy of Southeast Asia: Markets, Power and Contestation*. 3rd edn, Oxford: Oxford University Press.

Rodman, Kenneth A. 1994. 'Public and Private Sanctions against South Africa'. *Political Science Quarterly* vol. 109(2), 313–34.

Rohde, Achim. 2010. *State–Society Relations in Ba'thist Iraq*, New York: Routledge.

Rosenberg, Justin. 1994. *The Empire of Civil Society: A Critique of the Realist Theory of International Relations*, London: Verso.

Rowe, David M. 2001. *Manipulating the Market: Understanding Economic Sanctions, Institutional Change, and the Political Unity of White Rhodesia*, Ann Arbor: University of Michigan Press.

Rueschemeyer, Dietrich, Stephens, Evelyne H., and Stephens, John D. 1992. *Capitalist Development and Democracy*, Cambridge: Polity Press.

Saboi Jum. 2012. Director, Shalom Foundation, Myanmar. Interview with the author, 18 July.

Sadan, Mandy. 2009. 'Minorities and Political Governance: The Myanmar Situation'. In *Political Governance and Minority Rights: The South and South-east Asian Scenario*, edited by Lipi Ghosh, 151–79. London: Routledge.

Sai Sam Kham. 2012. Executive Director, Metta Foundation, Myanmar. Interview with the author, Yangon, 12 July.

Sakai, Keiko. 2001. 'Ten Years with Sanctions: Transformation of Iraqi Economic Policy, 1999–2000'. In *Politics, Economy and Sanctions in the Persian Gulf States in a Changing Environment*, edited by Sadashi Fukuda, 26–36. Tokyo: Institute of Developing Economies.

Sakai, Keiko. 2003. 'Tribalization as a Tool of State Control in Iraq: Observations on the Army, the Cabinets and the National Assembly'. In *Tribes and Power*, edited by Faleh Abdul-Jabar and Hosham Dawod, 136–61. London: Saqi.

Salman, Emad. 2000. 'Sanctions from an Iraqi Perspective'. In *Sanctions on Iraq: Background, Consequences, Strategies*, edited by Campaign Against Sanctions on Iraq, 85–91. Cambridge: CASI.

Sassoon, Joseph. 2012. *Saddam Hussein's Ba'th Party*, Cambridge: Cambridge University Press.

Saul, John S. and Gelb, Stephen. 1986. *The Crisis in South Africa*, London: Zed Books.

Schenker, David. 2003. *Dancing with Saddam: The Strategic Tango of Jordanian–Iraqi Relations*, Lanham: Lexington Books.

Schieber, Michael T. 1976. 'South Africa's Military Strength in a Changing Political Context'. *Africa Today* vol. 23(1), 27–45.

Scholtz, Clive. 1995. 'Drive Now and Pay Forever: The Apartheid Way'. In *Embargo: Apartheid's Oil Secrets Revealed*, edited by Richard Hengeveld and Jaap Rodenburg, 254–68. Amsterdam: Amsterdam University Press.

Seng Raw. 2001. 'Views from Myanmar: An Ethnic Minority Perspective'. In *Burma: Political Economy under Military Rule*, edited by Robert H. Taylor, 159–63. London: Hurst & Company.

Senior Anglo-American Executive. 2011. Interview with the author, Johannesburg, 8 September.

Shambaugh, George. 1999. *States, Firms, and Power: Successful Sanctions in United States Foreign Policy*, Albany: State University of New York Press.

Shaxson, Nicholas. 2012. *Treasure Islands: Tax Havens and the Men Who Stole the World*, London: Vintage.

Shin, Doh Chull. 1994. 'On the Third Wave of Democratization: A Synthesis and Evaluation of Recent Theory and Research'. *World Politics* vol. 47(1), 135–70.

Simpson, Adam. 2013. 'Challenging Hydropower Development in Myanmar (Burma): Cross-border Activism under a Regime in Transition'. *Pacific Review* vol. 26(2), 129–52.

Singh, Harjinder. 1992–3. 'Impact of Sanctions and Armed Struggle on South African Economy'. *Africa Quarterly* vol. 32(1–4), 127–47.

Skidmore, Monique. 2004. *Karaoke Fascism: Burma and the Politics of Fear*, Philadelphia: University of Pennsylvania Press.

Sluglett, Peter and Farouk-Sluglett, Marion. 2001. *Iraq since 1958: From Revolution to Dictatorship*, 3rd edn, New York: I. B. Tauris.

Solingen, Etel. 1998. *Regional Orders at Century's Dawn: Global and Domestic Influences on Grand Strategy*, Princeton: Princeton University Press.

Solingen, Etel. 2004. 'Southeast Asia in a New Era: Domestic Coalitions from Crisis to Recovery'. *Asian Survey* vol. 44(2), 189–212.

Solingen, Etel. 2005. 'ASEAN Cooperation: The Legacy of the Economic Crisis'. *International Relations of the Asia-Pacific* vol. 5(1), 1–29.

Solingen, Etel. 2012a. 'Introduction: The Domestic Distributional Effects of Sanctions and Positive Inducements'. In *Sanctions, Statecraft and Nuclear Proliferation*, edited by Etel Solingen, 3–28. Cambridge: Cambridge University Press.

Solingen, Etel (ed.). 2012b. *Sanctions, Statecraft, and Nuclear Proliferation*, Cambridge: Cambridge University Press.

Staibano, Carina. 2005. 'Trends in UN Sanctions: From Ad Hoc Practice to Institutional Capacity-Building'. In *International Sanctions: Between War and Words in the Global System*, edited by Peter Wallensteen and Carina Staibano, 31–54. Abingdon: Frank Cass.

Stansfield, Gareth. 2003. 'The Kurdish Dilemma: The Golden Era Threatened'. In *Iraq at the Crossroads: State and Society in the Shadow of Regime Change*, edited by Toby Dodge and Steven Simon, 131–47. Oxford: Oxford University Press.

Starnberger Institute. 1989. *The Impact of Economic Sanctions against South Africa*, Harare: Nehanda.

Steenkamp, Willem. 1989. *South Africa's Border War*, Gibraltar: Ashanti.

Steinberg, David I. 2001. *Burma: The State of Myanmar*, Washington, D.C.: Georgetown University Press.

Steinberg, David I. 2004. 'Burma/Myanmar: A Guide for the Perplexed?'. In *Reconciling Burma/Myanmar: Essays on US Relations with Burma*, edited by John Badgley, 41–54. Seattle: National Bureau of Asian Research.

Steinberg, David I. 2007. 'The United States and its Allies: The Problem of Burma/Myanmar Policy'. *Contemporary Southeast Asia* vol. 29(2), 219–37.

Stoneman, Colin. 1990. 'Destroying its Own Economy'. In *South Africa: The Sanctions Report: Documents and Statistics*, edited by Joseph Hanlon, 180–94. London: James Currey.

Stoner, Kathryn, Diamond, Larry, Girod, Desha, and McFaul, Michael. 2013. 'Transitional Successes and Failures: The International–Domestic Nexus'. In *Transitions to Democracy: A Comparative Perspective*, edited by Kathryn Stoner and Michael McFaul. EPUB edn, Baltimore: Johns Hopkins University Press.

Stoner, Kathryn and McFaul, Michael (eds). 2013. *Transitions to Democracy: A Comparative Perspective*, Baltimore: Johns Hopkins University Press.

Sunter, Clem. 1987. *The World and South Africa in the 1980s*, Cape Town: Human and Rousseau.

Svolik, Milan. 2012. *The Politics of Authoritarian Rule*, New York: Cambridge University Press.

Sylvan, David J. 1983. 'Ideology and the Concept of Economic Security'. In *Dilemmas of Economic Coercion: Sanctions in World Politics*, edited by Miroslav Nincic and Peter Wallensteen, 211–41. London: Praeger.

Taylor, Robert H. 2004. 'Myanmar's Political Future: Is Waiting for the Perfect the Enemy of Doing the Possible?'. In *Reconciling Burma/Myanmar: Essays on US Relations with Burma*, edited by John Badgley, 29–40. Seattle: National Bureau for Asian Research.

Taylor, Robert H. 2009. *The State in Myanmar*, London: Hurst.

Tha Thun Oo. 2012. Executive Committee member, Union of Myanmar Federated Chambers of Commerce and Industry; Chief Executive Officer, Today Media Group. Interview with the author, Yangon, 20 July.

Than Nyein. 2012. Party leader, National Democratic Force, Myanmar. Interview with the author, Yangon, 5 July.

Than Than Nu and Thu Wei. 2012. General Secretary and Chairman, Democratic Party of Myanmar. Interview with the author, Yangon, 7 July.

Thiha Saw. 2012. Editor, *Myanmar Dana*. Interview with the author, Yangon, 24 July.

Thinan Myo Nyun. 2008. 'Feeling Good or Doing Good: Inefficacy of the US Unilateral Sanctions against the Military Government of Burma/Myanmar'. *Washington University Global Studies Law Review* vol. 7(3), 455–518.

Tierney, Dominic. 2005. 'Irrelevant or Malevolent? UN Arms Embargoes in Civil Wars'. *Review of International Studies* vol. 31(4), 645–64.

Tilly, Charles. 2001. 'Mechanisms in Political Processes'. *Annual Review of Political Science* vol. 4(1), 21–41.

Tin Maung Maung Than. 2005. *State Dominance in Myanmar: The Political Economy of Industrialization*, Singapore: ISEAS.

TNI [Transnational Institute]. 2011. *Financing Dispossession: China's Opium Substitution Programme in Northern Burma*, Amsterdam: TNI.

Tonkin, Derek. 2007. 'The 1990 Elections in Myanmar: Broken Promises or a Failure of Communication?' *Contemporary Southeast Asia* vol. 29(1), 33–54.

TRC. 1998. *Truth and Reconciliation Commission of South Africa Report*, vol. 2, Cape Town: TRC.

Trindle, Jamila. 2014. 'Help! I'm a British Philosophy Professor With the Same Name as a Burmese Heroin Kingpin!' Foreign Policy, 10 February; accessed at http://www.foreignpolicy.com/articles/2014/02/10/help_im_a_british_philosophy_professor_with_the_same_name_as_a_burmese_heroin_ki, 13 March 2014.

Tripp, Charles. 2007. *A History of Iraq*, 3rd edn, Cambridge: Cambridge University Press.

Tripp, Charles. 2013. *The Power and the People: Paths of Resistance in the Middle East*, Cambridge: Cambridge University Press.

Turnell, Sean. 2009. *Fiery Dragons: Banks, Moneylenders and Microfinance in Burma*, Copenhagen: NIAS Press.

U Myint. 2010. *Myanmar Economy: A Comparative View*, Stockholm: Institute for Security and Development Policy.

Udehn, Lars. 1996. *The Limits of Public Choice: A Sociological Critique of the Economic Theory of Politics* London: Routledge.

UNCTAD [United Nations Conference on Trade and Development]. 2012. 'UNCTAD-Stat', accessed at http://unctadstat.unctad.org, 5 March 2012.

Unger, David J. 2014. 'Why Europe Can't Hit Russia with its Biggest Club: Energy Sanctions', *Christian Science Monitor*, 18 March.

UNOIPOFF [United Nations Office of the Iraq Programme Oil-for-Food]. 2002. 'Humanitarian Imports'. 31 December, accessed at http://www.un.org/depts/oip/background/basicfigures2.html, 14 November 2013.

UNSCOM/IAEA [United Nations Special Commission and the International Atomic Energy Agency]. 1995. 'Note for the File', minutes of discussion between General Hussein Kamal, Prof. M. Zifferero (IAEA), N. Smidovich (CIA), and R. Ekeus (UNSCOM); Aman, 22 August.

US Embassy. 2003a. 'Burma Sanctions: The Government Stumbles Forward', Yangon, 16 August, accessed at http://wikileaks.org/cable/2003/08/03RANGOON994.html, 28 September 2012.

US Embassy. 2003b. 'Insiders' Views on How to Influence Burma's Ruling Generals', Yangon, 3 June, accessed at http://wikileaks.org/cable/2003/06/03RANGOON646.html, 23 August 2012.

US Embassy. 2006a. 'Mandalay: Diplomatic Views', Yangon, 3 March, accessed at http://wikileaks.org/cable/2006/03/06RANGOON290.html, 23 August 2012.

US Embassy. 2006b. 'Workers Strike for Higher Pay', Yangon, 5 July accessed at http://wikileaks.org/cable/2006/07/06RANGOON924.html, 23 August 2012.

US Embassy. 2007a. 'Burma: How the Well Connected Make Money', Yangon, 2 February, accessed at http://wikileaks.org/cable/2007/02/07RANGOON114.html, 23 August 2012.

US Embassy. 2007b. 'Burmese Workers Demand Higher Wages', Yangon, 17 September, accessed at http://wikileaks.org/cable/2007/09/07RANGOON893.html, 23 August 2012.

US Embassy. 2007c. 'Eden Group Prospering Due to Regime Connections', Yangon, 16 November, accessed at http://wikileaks.org/cable/2007/11/07RANGOON1113.html, 23 August 2012.

US Embassy. 2008a. 'Burmese Gem and Jade Exports on the Rise', Yangon, 23 September, accessed at http://wikileaks.org/cable/2008/09/08RANGOON750.html, 27 September 2012.

US Embassy. 2008b. 'Regime Cronies Continue Wheeling and Dealing', Yangon, 3 March, accessed at http://wikileaks.org/cable/2008/03/08RANGOON162.html, 23 August 2012.

US Embassy. 2008c. 'Top Cronies Feeling the Pinch of US Sanctions', Yangon, 25 March, accessed at http://wikileaks.org/cable/2008/03/08RANGOON222.html, 23 August 2012.

US Embassy. 2009a. 'Burma's Generals: Starting the Conversation', Yangon, 2 April, accessed at http://wikileaks.org/cable/2009/04/09RANGOON205.html, 23 August 2012.

US Embassy. 2009b. 'Burma: Gem Dealers Complain about Financial Crisis, Sanctions', Yangon, 9 June, accessed at http://wikileaks.org/cable/2009/06/09RANGOON340.html, 23 August 2012.

US Embassy. 2009c. 'Burma: Meeting with Aung San Suu Kyi on Sanctions', Yangon, 9 October, accessed at http://wikileaks.org/cable/2009/10/09RANGOON688.html, 23 August 2012.

US Embassy. 2009d. 'Burma: Removal of U Moe Myint from the Visa Ban', Yangon, 18 March, accessed at http://wikileaks.org/cable/2009/03/09RANGOON174.html, 23 August 2012.

US Embassy. 2009e. 'US Economic Sanctions on Burma: Some Reflections', Yangon, 16 July, accessed at http://wikileaks.org/cable/2009/07/09RANGOON446.html, 23 August 2012.

US Embassy. 2012b. 'How EU Sanctions Affect Burma's Timber Industry', Yangon, 12 September, accessed at http://wikileaks.org/cable/2008/09/08RANGOON721.html, 27 September 2012.

Valverde, Mariana and Mopas, Michael. 2004. 'Insecurity and the Dream of Targeted Governance'. In *Global Governmentality: Governing International Spaces*, edited by Wendy Larner and William Walters, 233–50. London: Routledge.

van der Gaag, Nikki and Arbuthnot, Felicity. 2000. 'Experiencing Iraq Today'. In *Sanctions on Iraq: Background, Consequences, Strategies*, edited by Campaign Against Sanctions on Iraq, 144–59. Cambridge: CASI.

Van Heerden, Auret. 1990a. 'Business Fights Sanctions'. In *South Africa: The Sanctions Report: Documents and Statistics*, edited by Joseph Hanlon, 195–205. London: James Currey.

Van Heerden, Auret. 1990b. 'Trade Union Gains from Sanctions'. In *South Africa: The Sanctions Report: Documents and Statistics*, edited by Joseph Hanlon, 206–9. London: James Currey.

Van Heerden, Neil. 2011. Director-General of Ministry of Foreign Affairs, South Africa, 1987–92. Interview with the author, by telephone, 16 September.

van Wyck, Koos. 1988. 'State Elites and South Africa's International Isolation: A Longitudinal Comparison of Perception'. *Politikon* vol. 15(1), 63–89.

Velásquez-Ruiz, Marco A. 2012. 'International Law and Economic Sanctions Imposed by the United Nations Security Council'. *International Law: Revista Colombiana de Derecho International* vol. 21, 223–54.

Viljoen, Piet. 2011. South African diplomat; Consul-General, New York, 1988–92. Interview with the author, by telephone, 20 September.

Volcker, Paul A., Goldstone, Richard J., and Pieth, Mark. 2005. 'Manipulation of the Oil-for-Food Programme by the Iraqi Regime'. Independent Inquiry Committee into the United Nations Oil-For-Food Programme; 27 October.

von Soest, Christian and Wahman, Michael. 2014. 'Are Democratic Sanctions Really Counterproductive?'. *Democratization* vol. DOI: 10.1080/13510347.2014.888418.

Wah Wah Tun. 2012. President, Myanmar Women's Entrepreneurial Association. Interview with the author, Yangon, 26 July.

Waldmeir, Patti. 1998. *Anatomy of a Miracle: The End of Apartheid and the Birth of a New South Africa*, New Brunswick: Rutgers University Press.

Wallensteen, Peter. 1983. 'Economic Sanctions: Ten Modern Cases and Three Important Lessons'. In *Dilemmas of Economic Coercion: Sanctions in World Politics*, edited by Miroslav Nincic and Peter Wallensteen, 87–129. London: Praeger.

Wallensteen, Peter, Eriksson, Mikael, and Staibano, Carina (eds). 2003. *Making Targeted Sanctions Effective: Guidelines for the Implementation of UN Policy Options*, Uppsala: Uppsala University.

Wallensteen, Peter and Staibano, Carina (eds). 2005. *International Sanctions: Between War and Words in the Global System*, Abingdon: Frank Cass.

Wassenaar, Andreas D. 1977. *The Assault on Private Enterprise*, Cape Town: Tafelberg.

Watt, Nicholas. 2014. 'UK Seeking to Ensure Russia Sanctions Do Not Harm City of London', *The Guardian*, 3 March.

Weber, Max. 1946. *From Max Weber: Essays in Sociology*, 1st edn, New York: Oxford University Press.

Weiss, Linda. 1998. *The Myth of the Powerless State: Governing the Economy in a Global Era*, Ithaca: Cornell University Press.

Weiss, Thomas G., Cortright, David, Lopez, George A., and Minear, Larry. 1997a. 'Political Gain and Civilian Pain'. In *Political Gain and Civilian Pain: Humanitarian Impacts of Economic Sanctions*, edited by Thomas G. Weiss, David Cortright, George A. Lopez, and Larry Minear, 215–46. Oxford: Rowman and Littlefield.

Weiss, Thomas G., Cortright, David, Lopez, George A., and Minear, Larry (eds). 1997b. *Political Gain and Civilian Pain: Humanitarian Impacts of Economic Sanctions*, Oxford: Rowman and Littlefield.

Wessels, Leon. 2011. South African National Party legislator, 1977–96; Deputy Minister for Law and Order and Foreign Affairs, 1988–91; Cabinet Minister for Manpower, 1991–4. Interview with the author, Johannesburg, 7 September.

Wilks, Stephen. 2013. *The Political Power of the Business Corporation*, Cheltenham: Edward Elgar.

Wimmer, Andreas and Glick Schiller, Nina. 2002. 'Methodological Nationalism and Beyond: Nation-State Building, Migration and the Social Sciences'. *Global Networks* vol. 2(4), 301–34.

Woods, Kevin. 2011. 'Ceasefire Capitalism: Military–Private Partnerships, Resource Concessions and Military-State Building in the Burma–China Borderlands'. *Journal of Peasant Studies* vol. 38(4), 747–70.

Woods, Kevin. 2013. 'Timber Trade Flows and Actors in Myanmar: The Political Economy of Myanmar's Timber Trade'. Forest Trends, November.

Woods, Kevin M., Palkki, David, and Stout, Mark E. 2011. *The Saddam Tapes: The Inner Workings of a Tyrant's Regime, 1978–2001*, Cambridge: Cambridge University Press.

World Bank. 2012. 'Arms Imports (Constant 1990 US$)', accessed at http://data.worldbank.org/indicator/MS.MIL.MPRT.KD, 5 March 2012.

Yaphe, Judith. 2003. 'America's War on Iraq: Myths and Opportunities'. In *Iraq at the Crossroads: State and Society in the Shadow of Regime Change*, edited by Toby Dodge and Steven Simon, 23–44. Oxford: Oxford University Press.

Yousif, Bassam. 2010. 'The Political Economy of Sectarianism in Iraq'. *International Journal of Contemporary Iraqi Studies* vol. 4(3), 357–67.

Zaw Nay Aung, Gibson, Dave, Bhula, Shabana, and Christensen, Jacob. 2011. *Burma Sanctions Regime: The Half-full Glass and a Humanitarian Myth*, London: Burma Independence Advocates.

Zaw Win Min and Khine Khine Nwe. 2012. Vice-President and Joint General-Secretary of the Union of Myanmar Federated Chambers of Commerce and Industry. Interview with the author, Yangon, 13 July.

Ziliak, Stephen T. and McCloskey, Deirdre N. 2011. *The Cult of Statistical Significance: How the Standard Error Cost Us Jobs, Justice, and Lives*, Ann Arbor: University of Michigan Press.

Zöllner, Hans-Bernd. 2009. 'Neither Saffron Nor Revolution: A Commentated and Documented Chronology of the Monks' Demonstrations in Myanmar in 2007 and their Background'. Südostasien Working Paper 36.

Zondi, Musa. 2011. Member, National Council, Inkatha, South Africa, since 1979; Chair, Inkatha Youth Brigade, 1984–97. Interview with the author, Cape Town, 14 September.

Zurbrigg, Sheila. 2007. 'Economic Sanctions on Iraq: Tool for Peace, or Travesty?'. *Muslim World Journal of Human Rights* vol. 4(2), 1–63.

Index

Page numbers in **bold** indicate tables and in *italic* indicate figures, footnotes are indicated by a letter n between page number and note number.